COLLECTION MANAGEMENT

5/4/12	5- 2	9/24/10

Understanding
PERENNIALS

A Frances Tenenbaum Book

Houghton Mifflin Harcourt

BOSTON   NEW YORK

2009

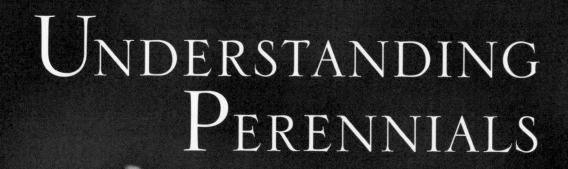

UNDERSTANDING
PERENNIALS

A NEW LOOK AT

AN OLD FAVORITE

William Cullina

Copyright © 2009 by William Cullina

For information about permission to reproduce selections from this book,
write to Permissions, Houghton Mifflin Harcourt Publishing Company,
215 Park Avenue South, New York, New York 10003.

www.hmhbooks.com

Library of Congress Cataloging-in-Publication Data
Cullina, William.
    Understanding perennials : a new look at an old favorite / William Cullina.
        p. cm.
"A Frances Tenenbaum book."
Includes bibliographical references and index.
ISBN 978-0-618-88346-2
1. Perennials. I. Title.
SB434.C795 2009
635.9'32 — dc22   2008/36760   *635.932*

Book design by Anne Chalmers
Layout: Eugenie S. Delaney
Typefaces: Minion, The Sans, Serlio, Hoeffler Titling

Printed in the United States of America
DOW 10 9 8 7 6 5 4 3 2 1

ACKNOWLEDGMENTS

As with all my books, this project would have never been possible without the guidance, support, and enthusiasm of my editor, Frances Tenenbaum. A writer simply could not hope for a more sincere, astute, and knowledgeable editor. In her nearly four decades as a garden book editor, she has shepherded a plethora of wonderful horticultural references to completion, and I am pleased to add this, my fifth book with her, to the list. Thank you, Frances! I am also deeply grateful to my wife, Melissa, for the support she has given me during this project. The birth of our twins halfway through threatened to sideline the project under a flood of diapers and baby bottles, but together we made it to the other side. Melissa has also brought her considerable botanical talent and knowledge of the science of plants to bear in this work, helping me clarify the ideas and concepts she has more familiarity with than I.

From the start I felt that images would be especially important in a book like this, and I have done my best to include photographs that illuminate as well as inspire. I want to thank all the gardeners and institutions that have opened up their gardens for me to capture with my camera. The list includes the New England Wild Flower Society's Garden in the Woods and Nasami Farm, Arnold Arboretum, Cox Arboretum, Denver Botanic Gardens, Birmingham Botanical Gardens, North Hill (the garden of Joe Eck and Wayne Winterrowd), Joe Pye Weed's Garden, Winterthur, Mt. Cuba Center, New York Botanical Garden, Kanapaha Botanical Gardens, Coastal Maine Botanical Gardens (where I have now begun to work), John Bartram's Garden, Chanticleer, Morris Arboretum, Scott Arboretum, North Carolina Botanical Garden, Juniper Level Botanic Garden, Steven M. Still Garden at Ohio State University, and, last but not least, Duke Gardens.

CONTENTS

Understanding
PERENNIALS

PREFACE

People garden for many reasons. For some, it is merely to apply exterior decoration meant to impress the neighbors or suppress their criticisms. Others garden for food, or out of a sense of responsibility for the environment and the connections it fosters with other forms of life. For me, the true joy of gardening is the time spent lost in the intricate islands of my own backyard, where the worries of life are shuffled and shrunk by the overwhelming buzzing, digesting, swaying majesty of life. I can leave the house feeling angry about some small transgression, or obsessing about an overdue bill I forgot to pay, but after a few minutes marveling over the color of a leaf or the size of the laurel I planted five years ago, the problems are diffused like drops of ink in a pool of cool water.

When I travel for speaking engagements or classes, I am often introduced as an expert in this or that, but, false modesty aside, I still view myself as merely a student thrilled daily by some small new discovery in the garden or woods. Just yesterday I was photographing a trillium flower when I noticed a mosquito plunged deep and quivering inside the bloom. Aha, I thought to myself; this mosquito must be a pollinator I have

ABOVE: Tulips mixed with pansies grace the entrance to the Birmingham Botanical Gardens in Birmingham, Alabama.

RIGHT: *Darmera peltata.* Seen up close, flowers reveal themselves in a whole new way. The flowers of this umbrella leaf look like pink sea anemones poised to capture prey.

never considered. As I turned the flower for a better angle out fell the mosquito—dead and shrunken—along with a tiny, irritated crab spider with an intricate ivory body and fierce looking legs. The spider had waited patiently on this bloom, chosen to match its own skin, until the hapless male mosquito alighted on it. Whether the mosquito was indeed intent on pollination or just needed a place to rest I will never know, but it was an interesting little interlude nonetheless. When I give talks, it is small anecdotes like these that resonate with the listeners, in part because they hint at the marvelous and mystifying world that is all around us. What I strive for in my work is to connect these stories to weave tales that in small ways help us see the interconnectedness of everything—spiders, mosquitoes, trilliums, me, and you. For many years I wished to write a book that carried this idea forward like a string of aha! moments woven into a web; for perennials, at least, this dream is now a reality.

It is hard to take yourself too seriously when you are digging in the dirt, but it is more difficult to preserve your humility when *writing* about gardening. Pompous phrases and unequivocal explanations blend with exaggerated rhetoric all too often in the pages of garden books—especially when

the author has given up the trowel completely. If I start writing like that, please unplug my computer! Seriously, when I conceived of this project, I saw it as an opportunity to both fill a real need for what amounts to an owner's manual for plants and to challenge myself to grow and learn, for as any teacher knows, the best way to truly understand something is to try to explain it to others. You will have to be the judge as to whether I have succeeded. What I hope is that as you read these pages you will discover one aha! moment after another hidden like crab spiders in the plants you thought you knew so well.

LEFT: *Salvia* × *superba* 'May Night' with *Iris pallida* 'Aureovariegata'.

INTRODUCTION

Whether we live in the forest or the desert, the windswept coast or the landlocked heartland, we are surrounded by plants. We eat them, we build things from them, burn them, mow them, admire them; but do we understand them? After a lifetime of living with and studying plants, after decades learning to grow them and write about them, I have to say they are still surprisingly alien to me. To delve into horticulture as I have has been much like setting off to a distant country where the language and customs are foreign and difficult to understand. You see life going on around you, but there is the unsettling sense that you are always an outsider looking in on some great ball complete with parquet floors and full-length curtains. The locals are in there dancing, but you cannot even hear the music or smell the shrimp and pork loin simmering on the heaped and feasted table.

Like it or not, if we choose to garden, we become willing immigrants to the kingdom of plants. Some of us never do learn the language, preferring to fumble around with lambskin gloves and sharpened spade while developing a rude sort of horticultural sign language that depends heavily on conjec-

ABOVE: *Hosta* 'Krossa Regal' with *Astilbe chinensis* at the Coastal Maine Botanical Gardens, in Boothbay.

TOP: I learn about perennials through trial and error as well as observation. When I see a challenging plant like *Hakonechloa macra* 'Aureola' (Japanese mountain grass) growing luxuriantly, my first thought is "Why is this plant doing so well here?" It is also helpful to see the same plant doing poorly, so I can develop a frame of reference to divine its wants and needs.

BOTTOM: I have learned a great deal from propagating and growing perennials in a nursery, where the conditions are more controlled and problems are often a bit easier to diagnose. What I have gained by growing coralbells and foam-flowers in the nursery has made me a better gardener.

Lychnis viscaria. I feel almost a palpable sense of joy from plants that are doing their best.

ture and leaves more than a fair share of casualties jutting root first from the compost pile. Others of us try to assimilate, and we do a fair job learning some of the basic customs and phrases from gardening books and university night classes—enough to feel comfortable talking Latin with other immigrants at the garden center or strolling around the garden path on a sunny summer day, nodding pleasantly at the passing trees. Rare are the individuals that can ever fully immerse themselves in this alien culture of plants. I am not talking about someone in the throes of some tree-hugging, wigged-out, "*be* the roots, *be* the tree" pseudophotosynthetic mysticism. I refer only to the lucky few among us who really understand plants. Just as some folks are more adept at learning a

new language, some are just better at understanding the mysterious idiom of plants, a subtle vernacular involving action and reaction, growth and retraction, cycles and seasons, adaptation and evolution, life and death; like all knowledge, this understanding is a blend of science, intuition, and some puddle-jumping leaps of faith.

We all know someone like this, and it is easy to envy his or her way with plants and the ability to help them thrive with such apparent effortlessness and grace. Is this something you are born with, or can it be learned? As one who writes about and teaches gardening, I am heartily invested in the second supposition, and I do believe that it can be taught, though admittedly some students will have an easier time than others.

LEFT: *Hibiscus moscheutos.* I study perennials in their natural habitats as often as I can, because in the more challenging wild environment, most species will grow only in conditions they are ideally suited for. Swamp mallow grows wild on marsh and river banks; its lack of drought tolerance limits its placement in the garden.

ABOVE: Nature is simply miraculous. I am constantly amazed by the endless variations on a theme in the plant kingdom. *Paris quadrifolia* (paris, above) is closely related to *Trillium grandiflorum* (showy trillium, below), though you would never know it from their flowers. Though they look different in bloom and hail from separate continents, their needs and wants are really quite similar.

Sanguisorba canadensis (Canadian burnet) with *Muhlenbergia capillaris* (hair-awn muhly).

The problem, from an educator's point of view, is that one immigrant teaching another can never convey the true subtleties of language and culture that come naturally to the native-born. This fact is reflected in the gardening texts we turn to for guidance. Most are really compendiums of an oral history and mythology passed down from one generation of writers to the next. As the *Odyssey* or the *Bhagavad-Gita* do with human experience, they frame and anthropomorphize horticulture in a way that makes plants somewhat understandable but still leaves them largely *unknowable*. There is comfort as well as frustration in our horticultural mythology—comfort when it answers our questions, and frustration when it raises many new ones for which it has no answers.

I have internalized our horticultural traditions, and I know that my writing is shaped by them, but I have always felt that the best teachers are the plants themselves, and often their own instruction contradicts that of my human teachers. Though gardening myths, like all myths, have a built-in sort of self-preservation that makes them hard to dispel, at least science seeks to constantly challenge its own assumptions about the world, and it is because of this that science provides us the best tool in our quest for true horticultural understanding. Unfortunately though, the language of science is often even more complex and unintelligible to the uninitiated than the language of plants. Mostly this stems from a need for linguistic precision to match the mathematical precision of the scientific method, but there is always the danger that we adopt scientific lingo to seem smarter or more informed than the next gardener. Precise technical language is useful when you are researching the intricacies of a particular physiological process, but it becomes cumbersome and unnecessary when attempting to describe the larger processes of life. Scientific language also strives for an objective clarity that is cold and nonintuitive. To quote completely at random from McFadden and Keeton's *Biology: An Exploration of Life,*

OPPOSITE: *Narcissus* at Winterthur, in Delaware.

ABOVE: *Iris cristata*.

RIGHT: *Iris* 'Belle of Amherst'.

When a monohybrid cross is made between two contrasting homozygous individuals (C/C and c/c in our example above), regardless of the character involved, the second generation, F2, is 1:2:1. And whenever there is dominance, the expected phenotypic ratio is 3:1. If these ratios are not obtained in large samples, it can be assumed that some complicating condition is present, which must be identified.

What?? To be fair, I have excerpted this from a longer narrative, but I think you get my point. (What they are saying is that if you cross-pollinate two plants that each carry one copy of the recessive gene for, say, white flowers, you would expect that one-fourth of their offspring would have white flowers. If not, then more than one gene is involved.) Some scientific language is very poetic and expressive. Words such as *embryogenesis* or *totipotent* roll off the tongue like *lugubrious* or *prophylactic,* but they are still meaningless without a glossary of terms. In general, though, scientific writing has about as much majesty as a glass of brake fluid, and for this reason, science has had a hard time winning over hearts and minds ever since the days of the Enlightenment.

While thinking about all of these questions and problems one day on my drive to the nursery (it was a long drive!), I had the idea to write a book that was more fundamental even than my *Understanding Orchids.* Originally, I had the notion to call it *Understanding Plants,* but on reflection the subject proved too imposing for a reasonable tome, so I have focused on herbaceous perennials, plants that are at a human scale and that gardeners and naturalists know, love, and can relate to more easily than giant trees or minuscule mosses. What I have aimed for is a work that translates the language and culture of plants and the language of science into words and concepts we can understand, and to do it with as much clarity, poetry, and purpose as I can muster. This not only makes the reading easier and more fun and the concepts more accessible, it more fluidly conveys some of the majesty and wonder that I feel every time I stop to smell the wild roses. While we will always be spectators at the great Chlorophyll Ball, if we try hard enough, I think we can still smell the fragrances, hear the music, and even sway to the magnificent dance of soil, sun, leaf, flower, and bee.

CHAPTER 1

WHAT IS A PERENNIAL?

We toss the name *perennial* around quite a bit in gardening circles, and I think most folks understand the term as it is commonly used. However, since perennials are the subject of this book, I want to be clear about things. As used in this book, the word is shorthand for *hardy herbaceous perennial*, in other words *a plant that survives from year to year in a temperate climate but dies back to just above or below the ground at the onset of the dormant season*. Some very important ramifications of all this inform everything the plant does and everything that we do to it. Surviving from year to year requires a certain conservatism and thriftiness that annual species (those that complete their life cycle in one growing season) do not have to worry about.

Annual versus Perennial

The sun is the engine that drives the botanical economy, and carbohydrates are the currency. Annuals have little need for

ABOVE: *Pulmonaria saccharata.* Lungwort is a spring blooming perennial that stores up energy in its roots during the growing season, allowing a surge of growth and flowering as soon as the ground thaws the following spring.

savings, instead squandering their resources on reproduction because their time on the earth is short, and in their seeds lie their only path to immortality. Since we like flowers and grow many plants primarily for this reason, free-flowering annuals have a ready appeal. On the other hand, perennials must be more conservative with their savings, using the bulk of it to build strong, resilient roots and stems, and stockpiling a good portion as insurance against times of scarcity. Temperate perennials have to be even more careful than tropical ones, as they must spend a large part of the calendar year in cold- or drought-induced dormancy, where photosynthesis has either stopped or is at least severely diminished. Added to this burden are the resources it takes to both survive the cold and have some energy left for a new surge of growth once warm and wet weather returns. Though stems and leaves die back to the ground each year in preparation for dormancy, roots, rhizomes, bulbs, tubers, and corms remain alive and safely underground. We grow perennials for their leaves and flowers, but it is these less glamorous things hidden in the soil that truly define the group. I often take it for granted that my perennials will come back from one year to the next. Every spring when I find those inevitable plastic labels marking not the location of a thriving, unfurling plant but rather the grave of another unfortunate that did not survive the winter, I feel shock, surprise, and remorse. How could it not have lived—it is supposed to be a perennial? Trees and shrubs can live for

RIGHT: *Sanguinaria canadensis.* This is a piece of the bloodroot from my grandmother's garden. I'd like to think that perhaps she got a division of the plant from her mother just as my mother got one from her.

BELOW: *Geranium phaeum.* Geraniums are easy, reliable garden perennials. This evocatively colored species blooms for several weeks in spring, though others bloom in summer and even on into fall.

Glaucidium palmatum. Japanese wood poppy is a long-lived, undeniably elegant relative of peonies that bewitches all who see it in bloom. I grew this individual from seed about ten years ago, and it just gets better each season.

centuries, but the story of their lives is captured for all to see in their trunks and limbs—a lightning strike here, a collision with a car there, a battle with a hurricane, attack by a woodpecker—all leave signs and marks in the wood that read like a sort of written history of its struggle for survival. Herbaceous perennials possess nothing as permanent as woody limbs. In essence they are in a near-constant state of renewal. Roots or rhizomes may live for five years or merely one before they are replaced by brand new copies. This continual rebirth is the essence of herbaceous perennials. It sets them apart from both annual and woody plants, yet it is a difficult concept for us humans to understand.

Reinventing Oneself

Perennials are immortal. That geranium or iris out in your perennial border can (theoretically, at least) live forever.

Herbaceous perennials do not age the way animals do because their bodies are being constantly renewed and reborn. Animals have a predetermined body shape that begins forming at conception and is complete by adulthood. We may replace some of the cells in our bones and arteries as we age, but the structures themselves remain. The liver cells that beget other liver cells become more forgetful and lethargic as the years go by, and like those bootleg Grateful Dead cassette tapes I used to listen to in college (the ones that were copies of copies of copies of copies), much of the original information becomes lost or garbled with time. Stem cells—those muchheralded miracle cells obtained from human embryos—are so remarkable because they can potentially become any type of cell in the human body. A stem cell can beget a liver cell or a blood cell or a brain cell, and these are not just copies of copies of copies, but new originals with all the nuance and none of the noise that accumulates in the telephone game of time.

Alas, with the exception of stem cells in bone marrow, we lose these progenitors, along with all their potential for renewal, even before we are born. In a very real way, our developmental fate is sealed within a few weeks of conception.

Perennials have their own version of stem sells, called *meristematic cells* (from the Greek *meristos,* meaning "to divide"), but unlike animals, they retain them all their lives. This allows the plant to completely re-create itself over time: to live in a constant state of becoming, so to speak. It is amazing to think that the green and gold (*Chrysogonum virginianum*) growing in my woodland garden retains not a single root, leaf, or even cell from the plant I set there five years ago, but genetically it is the same exact individual. While woody plants retain some of their past in the nonliving skeleton of trunk and branch, many herbaceous perennials grow entirely new bodies every year. Tired of the old body, well, grow a new one. Don't I wish! It comes as little surprise, therefore, that the current title of oldest living thing on earth goes not to a tree or even a suckering shrub, but to a five-mile-wide clonal mat of a Mediterranean sea grass, *Posidonia australis,* estimated to be over 100,000 years old!

What is remarkable is that every growing root tip, shoot, or bud has a meristem that can develop into new leaves, stems, roots, or flowers. All it takes is exposure to the right hormone and roots will grow instead of leaves. Just think—if we had this ability, instead of just idly wishing we had eyes in the back of our head, an extra set of arms, a new heart, or more hair, we could just grow them.

Meristematic cells in growing tips allow the plant to grow taller or longer, but what if it needs to *swell?* Woody plants as well as some perennials also have what are called *lateral meristems* in stems, roots, and crowns that allow these parts to thicken and increase in diameter. Think of these as bands of embryonic tissue that layer on new cells like coats of paint. In this way roots or stems far removed from growing tips can increase in girth as needed.

Beyond the theoretical implications of floral immortality are some practical ones, chief among them the simple fact that if you have a perennial that you like, you can make more and more and more of it. You can't do that with the pet hermit crab your son wants desperately to share with his friend. We may take for granted how ridiculously easy it is to divide a daylily, but just imagine how different gardening would be if you could not share a special plant with your friends. I have

some bloodroot in my garden that my mother was given by her mother—a pass-along plant that has crossed generations and links me with someone who is no longer with us. Every spring when it blooms it takes me right back to Grandma Blasig's garden and the patch under the big catalpa tree that she brought with her from the family farm when she and my grandfather retired and moved to town. I do buy some plants anonymously from nurseries, but more often than not, the plants I treasure most are the ones given to me by friends or loved ones, and a walk around my garden brings back a flood of memories about the people and the places that link these flowers to me. There is no greater thrill than to share a special plant with a friend and know that one day that friend may do

Mimulus cardinalis. Scarlet monkey flower hails from the Pacific coast of the United States. Though grown as an annual in colder parts of the country, it is a true perennial, which grows from a spreading rhizome.

the same. Pictures may fade and memories may blur, but I know that the cheery white flowers of the bloodroot down in my woods will be as sharp and vibrant as they were 75 years ago in the woodlot of the family farm now long gone. Plants are immortal, and sometimes a bit of their immortality rubs off on us.

The part of the bloodroot that lives on from one season to the next is its rhizome, a special kind of stem that grows along or under the ground rather than away from it. Many of the perennials we cultivate grow from rhizomes each year, though others survive the winter with specialized stems called corms, tubers, and bulbs, or with the aid of thick, swollen roots. Whether a particular plant grows from a rhizome or a bulb is more than an academic question, for this fundamental choice influences everything from its very shape to the conditions it prefers and the way we must cultivate and propagate it. So what exactly is a bulb and how does it differ from a rhizome or tuber?

Bulbs

True bulbs are found chiefly in four families: lily, iris, onion, and amaryllis. Though they may represent only a small fraction of all the plants on earth, they are on the whole showy and easily grown perennials, and I doubt there is any garden that does not contain at least a few. Bulbs have a certain similarity to seeds. Like seeds, they do not look anything like a growing plant, yet they can be bagged and stored for a time, then planted, watered, and presto—there is a plant again. If you cut a tulip bulb in half from top to bottom, the interior is revealed as a series of overlapping layers attached to a sort of flattened disk at the bottom. At the center of all the layers is a small greenish bud that grows from a flattened area called the

ABOVE: *Camassia leichtlinii* ssp. *suksdorfii.* Though many bulbs are laced with toxins to discourage consumption, camas lilies are quite edible if prepared correctly and were one of the staple foods of Native Americans in the Pacific Northwest. This is a particularly dark form that has been in the collections of Garden in the Woods for many years.

BELOW: *Allium carinatum* ssp. *pulchellum.* I grew this onion from seed 12 years ago and planted some of the small bulbs in a well-drained, sunny spot. It has since taken charge of its own reproduction and I have to pull out many of the pungent bulbs to keep it in check.

Dicentra culcullaria. **Dutchman's breeches** grow from loose little bulbs that shatter very easily when handled. This is no accident; the individual scales are designed to break off when dug up by a hungry rodent. Mice and voles are as forgetful as squirrels, so even those scales carried off and cached may survive and produce a new plant colony.

Erythronium albidum. Mature **white trout lily** bulbs will produce offsets or daughters that can be teased apart and replanted separately as the plants yellow and go dormant for the year.

ABOVE: *Narcissus* sp. **Daffodil** bulbs multiply rapidly, and after five years or so they benefit from division, as the individual bulbs tend to crowd each other for space and nutrients. Fall is the ideal time to do this, but you can also split them up in spring just as they emerge from the ground.

LEFT: *Lilium superbum*. **Turk's Cap Lily.** In this image you can clearly see how a new daughter bulb is growing out from the older mother bulb on the right. Because the stem is somewhat stretched, it is easier to see that the scales are really modified leaves compressed to make the bulb.

bulb plate, which is simply a stem that has been squished down to the size of a nickel. The layers (scales) are modified leaves that never turn green and remain underground, swollen with food reserves to feed the rapid growth of the small central bud. When winter has passed or the rains return, the scales shunt huge amounts of food and nutrients to the expanding bud, facilitating the astoundingly quick growth you have witnessed if you have ever forced an amaryllis or daffodil indoors. With very few exceptions, bulbs are the type A personalities of the plant world, sprouting fast, blooming quickly and luxuriantly, then quickly fading again. After this magnificent albeit brief show, seeds are set and any remaining food stores left in the bulb become absorbed by the new daughter bulb or bulbs that begin growing from it before the leaves yellow. Thus, the

Tulipa batalinii. Though smaller than familiar garden tulips, wild or species tulips like *Tulipa batalinii* are elegant and refined. For some reason they also seem to be more reliably perennial than the hybrid tulips if planted in well-drained soil.

A cross section through a dormant tulip bulb reveals its structure. Swollen white **storage leaves (scales)** enfold the **small yellowish bud** at the center. The flower is at the center of the bud, wrapped by the immature leaves. Both bud and scales are attached to a **disklike bulb plate at the bottom** from which roots will also emerge. It is clear from this picture that when you buy tulips in the fall, the blooms are already fully formed and waiting for spring, so it pays to purchase top-quality bulbs and to plant them quickly so they do not dry out. Though the papery brown "skin" (really dried scales) will protect the bulb for a short while, if left out of the ground too long the outer scales will dry and die, weakening the bulb and compromising growth and flowering the following spring.

daffodil bulb you planted last fall will have been completely used up, absorbed, and replaced with new bulbs by next fall. Under good growing conditions, most mother bulbs will form multiple daughters each season. As one begets two beget four, a single bulb will develop into a healthy clump after a few years. Since each bulb is a self-contained copy of its brethren, the clumps are very easily divided once they are fully formed.

This process of growth and reabsorption of the mother continues on after the plant has gone dormant during the summer, so most bulbs are dug, divided, and sold in autumn. Fall planting also allows the bulbs to form roots while the ground still retains some warmth and, most importantly, gets them in the ground in time to receive the proper winter chilling necessary to bloom properly in spring. If you have ever tried to force tulip bulbs indoors without first potting them and placing them in the refrigerator for a few months, you know what happens if they do not receive the proper chilling—absolutely nothing! (For more on chilling and its effects see p. 88.) Remember, too, that unlike most seeds, bulbs are not really designed to stay out of the soil for months at a time. Whether you are digging them yourself or purchasing them from a nursery, get them replanted as soon as you can so they do not dry out severely. Many bulbs, especially sensitive species such as trout lilies (*Erythroniums*), will dry out and die within a week or two if not handled properly.

Like acorns or walnuts, a big, juicy bulb is an irresistible treat for a squirrel, chipmunk, or vole. A few types such as daffodils are naturally laced with poisons to keep the munchers at bay, but most bulbs are easy prey. Ironically, bulb planters—those little cylinders that you twist into the earth to remove a core of soil so you can plant the bulb—make it very easy for squirrels to find and eat all your carefully planted tulip bulbs. Squirrels find buried food by sniffing and feeling out small pockets of disturbed soil where they or you have recently buried goodies. Bulb planters are also a problem because they do not loosen the underlying soil where the roots have to penetrate. It is far better to dig the entire area to a depth of 12 inches and plant the bulbs properly. The squirrels will have a much harder time zeroing in on the bulbs.

Bulb-eating rodents have a more difficult time smelling and excavating deep bulbs, so most wild bulbs grow surprisingly deep in the earth. Even tiny trout lily or crocus bulbs are often six to eight inches below the surface, and large lilies may settle a foot or more down. If your bulbs are dormant and your soil is not heavy, wet clay (which most bulbs resent anyway), do not be afraid to set them at least six inches deep. I have even planted larger lily bulbs 12 inches deep in an area frequently ravaged by voles, and these have survived beautifully because the critters give up when they get only half that deep. Deep planting also shelters tender bulbs from the worst of the cold. As a rule, temperatures a foot deep in the ground are 10 to even 20 degrees F warmer than they are just below the surface.

Many bulbs have one other trick up their sleeve to survive herbivory (bulbivory?). Should rodents discover the bulbs, any of the scalelike storage leaves that may be dislodged and left behind can sprout roots and leaves and eventually regenerate the plant. Rodents like to cache food in larders, but if said animal dies before all the food is consumed, these small bulb scales will grow into a new colony. When you are digging lilies, try partially crumbling up one of the bulbs as you replant it, and you should find a good crop of small lilies growing up with the large ones within a year or two.

A number of other perennials produce starchy under-

Lilium canadense 'Apple Red', a lovely form of Canada lily that I grew from seed. It takes about four years for seedling bulbs to grow large enough to produce flowers. However, you can dig up the bulbs in the fall and pull off and replant a few of the scales, which will mature in just two years. It is a good idea to propagate a few backup plants in this way and share them with a friend just in case a hungry rodent dispatches the original.

ground structures to survive the dormant period, and though not technically bulbs, they are often sold and referred to as bulbs. I am referring specifically to corms and tubers (you may hear bulbs, corms, and tubers referred to collectively as *geophytes* by the cognoscente). Anatomically the three types are very different, however, and as a consequence they need to be handled a bit differently in the garden.

Corms and tubers function much like bulbs, fueling rapid growth and permitting long dormancy when conditions are too shady, cold, or dry. Accordingly, corms, tubers, and

bulbs are all primarily found in Mediterranean climates (regions with wet, mild winters and warm, dry summers), alpine regions, woodlands, and deserts.

Corms

Whereas a bulb is composed mostly of modified leaves, a corm is a short, squat stem full of starchy food reserves. Corms can be dug and shipped fairly easily when dormant, just like bulbs, but they are more delicate and prone to mechanical damage or desiccation for the following reason. I am sure you have noticed that as an onion bulb dries out, it does so one layer at a time. The dead outer layers act as a jacket to shield the moist, living ones closer to the center. One scale may get bruised and infected, but because of the bulb's layered structure, it usually will not spread to the rest of the bulb. Because it is a stem, the corm has no ability to compartmentalize damage like a bulb can. If any part becomes bruised or cut, rot can easily enter and spread throughout the whole corm. If you have ever grown a cyclamen in a pot only to have the entire thing rot and die within a few days, you will understand what I mean. Corms are packed with food and irresistible to fungi and bac-

TOP LEFT: *Claytonia caroliniana.* The knobby corm of **Carolina spring beauty** photographed as it resumes growth in early spring.

TOP RIGHT: *Claytonia virginica.* Like fumeworts, **spring beauties** are active for only a few months in spring, so the food-rich corms are essential for the plants to weather their long dormancy. A large corm will produce dozens of these cheery little flowers and still stock up enough food for the next long slumber.

BOTTOM FAR LEFT: *Arisaema triphyllum.* **Jack-in-the-pulpit** corms slough off their outer skin and entire root system in autumn. This one is about halfway into this curious yearly molt.

BOTTOM LEFT: *Arisaema sikokianum.* **Japanese cobra lily** is one of the most remarkable perennials I have ever grown. It used to be quite rare in cultivation here, but in the last ten years both seeds and plants have become fairly easily available.

RIGHT: *Corydalis solida.* **Fumewort** corms are about the size of a marble. In earliest spring the plant grows a mound of fine leaves and short spikes of lovely pink, violet-red, or blue flowers. Soon after flowering, the plant goes dormant and rests for ten months underground.

teria should they gain entry through the skin. Handle bare root corms carefully and beware of any that are bruised, soft, or discolored, indicating disease has already set in.

Just like any stem, a corm has small dormant buds scattered along it, and these will often sprout and grow into new daughter corms. It is quite easy to dig corms as the leaves yellow and divide the mothers and daughters apart to increase your stock. It is harder to come up with a general rule regarding the proper depth to plant corms. Some jack-in-the-pulpits thrive when planted up to two feet deep, whereas cyclamens will quickly rot unless the top half of the corm protrudes from the ground. Some corms have secondary meristems that allow them to grow quite large after a few years. Cyclamen corms start out the size of peas but can grow as large as grapefruits after 10 years or so.

Tubers

Whereas thickened or swollen vertical stems are considered corms, horizontal rhizomes modified for the same purpose are considered tubers (the potato is the classic example). Like a corm, each node on a tuber has a dormant eye or bud, and these can all grow a new rhizome and eventually new tubers, as anyone who has ever left a potato too long in the cupboard has plainly seen. Since tubers are formed from creeping rhizomes, tuberous plants spread more quickly than corm-bearing ones do. Just to confuse things further, a few species produce swollen, tuberous roots instead of tuberous stems. From an anatomical point of view these two have some basic differences, but from the practical side you can handle them the same. Tubers and tuberous roots, like corms, are more delicate than bulbs for the same reasons. Generally they should be planted three to six inches deep.

TOP RIGHT: *Rhexia virginica* tuberous root. **Meadow beauties** produce swollen tuberous roots complete with stem and leaf buds. This not only ensures that the plant will return the following year, it gives the species more mobility. After a few years meadow beauties can spread several yards from their original location in search of greener pastures.

BOTTOM RIGHT: *Rhexia virginica* with **hoverfly.** For one so small, the large, pollen-covered yellow anthers must seem an impossible feast. Hoverfly larvae are voracious predators and consume quantities of aphids and other pests.

Other Types of Rhizomes

The majority of perennials grow from a rhizome that is much more clearly stemlike than a corm or tuber, albeit a stem that creeps along or under the ground rather than growing upward. Sheltered in the soil or leaf litter, these horizontal stems are far less vulnerable to cold or fire than aboveground parts. Though they do not resemble corms or tubers, conventional rhizomes do function in much the same way. They store food and nutrients necessary for dormancy and growth, and they harbor the meristems from which new shoots or leaves arise and new roots descend. Perennial rhizomes take on a variety of forms from thin and wiry to fat and stiff. Some grow

long and meandering, while others remain very short and congested. A large individual plant may consist of hundreds of separate but interconnected rhizomes. Although they start out life connected, individual rhizomes eventually detach from their neighbors as the connecting sections die. In this way, should part of the system be eaten or attacked by disease, the rest may go on unimpeded. Rhizomes, like any stem, consist of nodes where leaves, sheaths, or aerial stems attach, and internodes (the sections of stem in between nodes). Roots grow

TOP LEFT: *Iris cristata* rhizome. Each fibrous scale on this crested iris rhizome harbors a bud that has grown into a new stem.

TOP RIGHT: *Monarda russeliana.* Wild bergamot rhizomes spread quickly just under the surface. Eventually each tip makes a 90-degree turn and begins growing upward as an aboveground stem.

MIDDLE LEFT: *Polygonatum odoratum* var. *pluriflorum* 'Variegatum'. Variegated Solomon's seal forms a mat of interlaced rhizomes and roots.

MIDDLE RIGHT: *Trillium cuneatum* rhizome. Notice how small daughter rhizomes have begun to grow from the mature rhizome of a whippoorwill trillium.

BOTTOM LEFT: *Dodecatheon clevelandii* ssp. *insulare.* Padre's shooting star grows from a short, vertical rhizome or stem ringed with fat, fleshy roots. The small bud atop each root will grow into a new plant.

Why Divide Perennials?

Digging up perennials, ripping apart the roots, and replanting the pieces with a handful of fertilizer, a wink, and a prayer is a chore to some and a welcome right of spring to others. But why do we do it? Plants certainly don't get divided in the wild unless caught in a landslide or in the jaws of a hungry herbivore. It is possible to plant a perennial garden and never touch the plants again for 10 or even 20 years (assuming you chose the plants very carefully and are good about annual weeding, mulching, and fertilization). However, in reality, most perennial gardens I have planted get a bit tired after five to seven years and benefit from minor or even major surgery. Gardening is a process of constant experimentation—trying new plants or new configurations, discarding those that lack vigor, winter-hardiness, or aesthetic appeal, and filling in the holes thus created. In many ways, those plants that do eventually get large enough to warrant division are the true survivors—the true perennials. Division, though it seems like lots of work, is really a sign of success. Try to remember that as you strain your lower back hacking apart a large ornamental grass with a woefully inadequate and impossibly dull little shovel.

There are three principal reasons to divide perennials:

- For the purposes of propagation
- To reinvigorate a clump that has died out in the middle or lost vigor
- To reposition wandering plants straying from their original location

When you plant a new garden, having lovingly turned the soil and incorporated wheelbarrow after wheelbarrow of good compost, the perennials will send out roots lustily into the loose and unoccupied soil. A large and healthy root system translates into lots of leaves and flowers, so the few years after establishment are the glory days for a perennial garden. After 5 or 10 years, though, the effect of the compost has worn off, and the roots of the perennials (along with every tree within 50 feet) will have fully occupied the space. If you spread a one- to two-inch layer of compost before you mulch each spring, you can greatly prolong the life of a particular garden by simply keeping the soil invigorated. Without this annual replenishment, as it reaches middle age, the garden will not grow as luxuriantly as it did in youth, and it becomes evident that a major renovation is in order. This may come as a welcome chance to undo some unfortunate combinations or remove unsatisfactory selections while dividing and spreading favored plants around. Division for the purpose of increase is one of the most satisfactory, though slightly intimidating, chores in horticulture—especially if the plant in hand is particularly rare and choice. (For tips on dividing various perennials, see the propagation section, p. 211.) I for one am always optimistic (some would say cheap) when buying plants, figuring I can get away with one for now and divide it in a few years. In the nursery and gardens we divide lady's slippers (*Cypripedium* spp.) and trilliums not because they need it but because we always need more!

Cypripedium 'Gisela'. Lady's slipper orchids really benefit from division every five years or so as the rhizomes become very congested over time, choking each other off and weakening the plant. This lovely specimen in my front yard is still two years away from surgery but when I do split it up, I'll have some to share with friends.

Since all rhizomatous perennials, even those that are tightly clumping, crawl slowly out in an ever-expanding circle, it is common for older specimens to develop a bald spot in the center so choked with old roots and rhizomes that new shoots no longer grow there. Shasta daisies are notorious for this, but, given enough time, many clumping species will go bald and thus need dividing for aesthetic reasons.

As we all know, some aggressively rhizomatous perennials need dividing every few years to simply keep them in check. Running bamboos, Gooseneck loosestrife (*Lysimachia clethroides*), chameleon plant (*Houttuynia cordata* 'Chameleon'), goutweed (*Aegopodium podagraria*), and most species in the knotweed family (Polygonaceae) are so aggressive that I wonder why anyone plants them. Others, for example, bee balms (*Monarda* spp.), obedient plant (*Physostegia virginiana*), and some asters, will more than double in spread each year and thus need a figurative haircut every two to four years unless you intend to let them run wild.

Given all this, some perennials rarely, if ever, require dividing. Certainly taprooted species (p. 31) fall into this category, as do some corms, bulbs, and others with abbreviated rhizomes. If division is not your cup of tea, see my list of species that rarely need it (p. 217).

Miscanthus sinensis. This old clump of maiden grass is long overdue for division. The center has died out as the creeping rhizomes have moved ever outward. This is the ideal time to divide this plant as spring growth has only just begun.

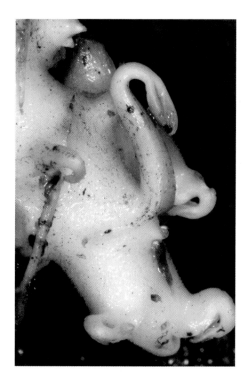

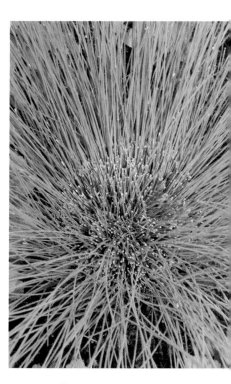

Cardamine diphylla rhizome. Even though it is blanched white from its life underground, the rhizome of a toothwort is clearly just a horizontal stem lined with developing leaves.

Hydrastis canadensis. Goldenseal is a legendary medicinal plant with beautiful golden roots and a vertical rhizome. Notice the purplish sheathing bracts that enfold the expanding leaves. Where each of these bracts attaches to the rhizome there is a visible ring much like a leaf scar on a twig.

Juncus effusus. Soft rush grows from a dense branching rhizome with very short internodes, giving a tufted or mounded shape to the plant as a whole.

from the rhizome either at the nodes or internodes, depending on the species. If the internodes are very short, the resulting plant will be densely clumping (caespitose); picture a tussock-forming clump of bunchgrass. If the internodes are moderate in length, as with border phlox, the plant becomes a spreading clump. If the internodes are very long, the plant will quickly spread, as do many mints. Mints and other perennials with long, wandering rhizomes can become weedy or aggressive but are useful where a groundcover or large colony is desired. When rhizomes grow above the surface of ground, as with strawberries, they are considered stolons, but structurally and functionally these are the same as rhizomes, and stolons often plunge belowground to become rhizomes or vice versa, so the two terms are used interchangeably in many references. Stolons typically have extremely long internodes, and since they grow aboveground, and so don't need to tunnel through

Physostegia angustifolia. With its long, wandering rhizomes, this slender, obedient plant is anything but obedient!

OPPOSITE: *Astilbe chinensis* var. *taquetii* 'Superba' has a dense woody rhizome (often called a crown) that is difficult to divide without a knife or pruners. The procedure is very similar to the one pictured for *Actaea racemosa* on page 214.

RIGHT: *Polemonium reptans.* Unlike the goldenseal rhizome pictured on page 23, which sits vertically underground, spreading **Jacob's ladder** springs from a very short aboveground stem with remarkably short internodes between leaves, roots, and branches.

soil and around rock, they are very fast growing. Stoloniferous plants are considered very aggressive and fast spreading—at least in popular usage.

Quite a few rhizomatous species retain some leaves at the tips of the rhizomes during the dormant season. These begin growing as soon as the weather is favorable, bloom, and sprout new rhizomes and roots at the base to perpetuate the plant. Rhizomatous perennials are generally easy to dig and divide, especially in the spring or fall, when they are not in active growth. The exceptions are slow-growing woodlanders such as trillium, whose short, fat rhizomes are often reluctant to branch unless the plant is mature and conditions are ideal.

Vertical Rhizomes

Coralbells, columbines, and a fair number of other perennials including hostas and astilbes grow from a short, congested vertical stem or stems all connected together at the base. This leads to a tidy, clumping habit that has obvious appeal to the gardener. Though in some cases the stems all fuse into one common root system, making division difficult, these are by and large similar to rhizomatous species with very short internodes.

The next time you are in the garden, notice the difference between a clumping species and a highly stoloniferous one. More than anything else, how it grows belowground will predict not only the plant's mature shape and appearance, but how we use it in the garden. I will even go so far as to say that these patterns of growth influence the way we see and value the species itself. Bulbs, corms, and tubers are ephemeral yet precious, as if their little stores of energy resonate with our instinct to horde and save. Clumping species are neat, reliable, and cautious—their knuckled core the perennial equivalent of a wizened old oak's trunk. Wildly rhizomatous species are inquisitive, carefree, but perhaps a bit higher maintenance, like that happy-go-lucky younger brother you are always bailing out of jail. These characteristics certainly set the tone for a garden, and we can use different plants and different patterns to set the mood. In a very real sense, a bulb garden's fleeting show encourages us to appreciate the moment. A garden full of rhizomatous perennials has a sort of carefree, nature-gone-wild exuberance, while one filled with clumping species is more formal and rhythmic.

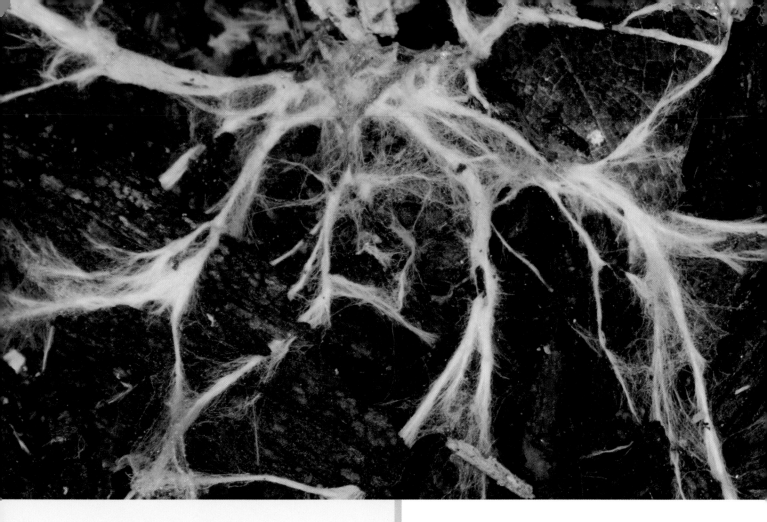

CHAPTER 2

At the Roots

Just as we have a bias toward things that move, we have a bias for things above the ground. Life under the soil is as mysterious to me as life in the ocean, and in many ways just as far out of reach. I can turn over the earth and peer into the teaming clod my shovel has dislodged, but it tells me only slightly more about life underground than the contents of a fishing net tell me about life underwater. At least I can don scuba gear and visit the watery realm for an hour or so, but I would need a wizard to shrink me to the size of the period at the end of this sentence before I could hope to dive in to the duff just under my feet. The world under the soil is a kingdom in miniature filled with tiny creatures deftly navigating the microscopic caves, channels, and crevices between tiny particles, roots, and stones. It is a tremendously complex, three-dimensional environment akin to a limitless castle with countless rooms and myriad floors on which life's subterranean microdramas progress unseen by all of us stomping around on the roof.

Not including vertebrates such as snakes and moles, the soil in your woods or prairie is home to an incredibly diverse

ABOVE: **Fungal hyphae.** The "roots" of various fungi knit the rotting leaves and bark of the forest floor together like fairy's yarn.

TOP: *Polygonatum macranthum* rhizome. The amazing, somewhat sinister-looking roots and rhizome of this Japanese Solomon's seal seem almost animated. The brown circle at the center of the photograph is the scar where last year's stem attached.

BOTTOM: The thick nest of roots and rhizomes fuels the rapid growth of this giant Japanese Solomon's seal. Large specimens attain heights of five feet in the rich woodland garden.

community of organisms, including invertebrates such as ants, termites, centipedes, earthworms, snails, spiders, tiny springtails, and mites, and a vast collection of microflora (algae, fungi, yeasts, and bacteria) and microfauna (protozoa, nematodes, rotifers, tardigrades, and turbellarians). A square yard of healthy forest soil might contain as many as 1,000 species of invertebrates, roots from 50 species of plants, 5,000 species of bacteria, 25 species of mites, 100 different insects, 40 different nematodes, and 300 species of fungi—and the list goes on (in contrast, the soil from a chemically addicted suburban lawn probably has only about one-tenth this diversity). That is perhaps a 10-fold increase in biodiversity over the square yard just above the soil surface. You would have to go to a rich, tropical rainforest to find life in this abundance and density aboveground. The main reason for this amazing diversity is that life is more stable in the soil than it is aboveground because temperatures underground vary much less than air temperatures, and water is much more plentiful and reliably available. Furthermore, all those little bits of rock and organic debris provide a highly varied landscape for species to colonize.

Fungi may flower aboveground and ants might forage, but plants are truly the only members of this subterranean community that also live permanently in the land above. They can do this because they have evolved a unique, two-parted anatomy that allows them to gain sustenance and support from the earth and light from the sky. Though they share some basic structural similarities to stems, roots are different in many ways. They are supremely well adapted both to anchor the plant and to obtain the water and nutrients that it needs to grow. However, since they have evolved in a fairly stable environment, they are on the whole less tolerant of extremes in temperature and moisture than stems and leaves.

Root Structure

Roots serve three main functions for the perennial: they anchor it to terra firma, absorb and transport water and

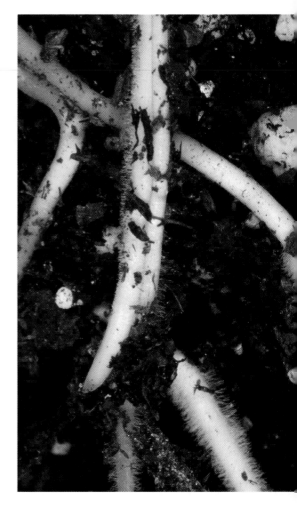

ABOVE: *Phlox stolonifera* rhizome/root. The root caps on these emerging **creeping phlox** rhizomes are bright green. Their hardened, lubricated points allow the roots to tunnel through soil and rock in search of moisture and nutrients. The shell of the root cap is quickly shed as the root expands to make way for the delicate root hairs that follow.

RIGHT: *Polygonatum biflorum* var. *commutatum.* Each of these **giant Solomon's seal** roots has a zone of root hairs just after the growing tip. Most of the water and nutrient absorption takes place among these fine hairs, which penetrate soil and organic particles and give the root enormous surface area to slurp up what it needs.

nutrients essential for its survival, and store food and nutrients. These last sustain the plant during dormancy, fuel a surge of new growth in spring, and allow it to recover if browsed, chewed, cut, or otherwise damaged. To bully its way through the soil, every actively growing root tip is jacketed by an amazing structure called the root cap, which functions as both soldier and diplomat. Its helmetlike shape protects the delicate growing point as the root pushes aggressively through soil and rock, applying pressures as high as 100 to 200 pounds per square inch concentrated in a very small point. If you imagine this as the pressure an average man balanced on a toothpick could exert on the ground beneath, it is no wonder that roots can tunnel though rock and soil with such relentlessness and precision. You may be wondering why roots have so much trouble in compacted soil if they can tunnel with such force. As I talk about below, it is a lack of oxygen rather than the physical state of compacted soil that gives roots so much trouble.

To survive under the enormous pressures demanded of it, the root cap is continually being sloughed off and renewed as the root proceeds, and as it grows it exudes a slippery goop that lubricates the tip so it can more easily slip between soil particles.

Feeder Roots

If you look carefully just behind the cap and growing point (root meristem) of an actively growing root tip, you can see a fuzzy collar of root hairs. Root tips are the primary place where absorption of water and nutrients takes place, and these root hairs exponentially increase the surface area available for that. (Incredibly, it has been estimated that root hairs represent as much as 60 percent of the surface area of the entire root system in an actively growing young plant!) Much of a perennial's yearly root system is composed of thin feeder roots (often thinner than the period at the end of this sentence) that constantly grow and die in response to warmth, cold, dampness, and drought. Many perennials shed 50 percent or more of their small roots during dormancy, and many other such roots are killed during periods of drought. It is amazing to me that so much of the root system is sacrificed like this every year, and it is one of the reasons that perennials can recover from transplanting so quickly with a modicum of care. These fine roots can quickly invade and take advantage of pockets of water or fertility in the soil. Within a few weeks of applying organic mulch, it is already full of these hunter-gatherers of the subterranean world. They are understandably delicate, however, and improper planting methods will also retard their development.

It is important to remember when transplanting perennials that the process of digging out the plant inevitably damages or severs many of the fine root tips and greatly reduces the ability of newly transplanted plants to take up water and nutrients for a few weeks (the same is true after drought damage). When the plant is dormant or the weather is cool or the rains are plentiful, and so water stress is low, this is not such a problem, but during hot summer weather, it is a good idea to prune back the top of the plant by half to lessen water loss and water stress until the compromised root system can regrow. Just as emphysema victims require increased oxygen for their damaged lungs to function, such transplants require frequent irrigation for the first several weeks as the root system recovers. Fertilizer will also help the roots recover, but it should be applied in moderation, as high soluble-salt levels can further impede water uptake (see p. 35).

Container-grown perennials have their root system intact, but modern container mixes are very different from garden soil, and roots may go through a difficult transition period after planting. Basically, container mixes are much looser and more freely draining than garden soil. This is necessary because pots hold a lot of water for their size, and if you try to use garden soil in a container you will end up with a little swamp. The problem, though, is that when you plant the perennial in garden soil, the latter actually pulls moisture from the root ball. I will not bore you with the details of soil physics; suffice to say that finer soils have a much greater water-holding capacity than coarse ones and as such will pull moisture into them. You can imagine that is disastrous for fine roots trying to get started at the edge of the root ball. There is a simple remedy, though: simply shake or wiggle off about one-third of the container mix before setting the roots into the soil. In this way, some of the roots will be in direct contact with garden soil once you have backfilled the whole and tamped it down.

Bare-root perennials used to be much more common in the industry, but they have been largely superseded by container-grown plants. Regardless, at times bare-rooting is necessary, for example, to transport plants across state or national borders, to store plants under refrigeration, or simply to make dividing and replanting easier. Bare-root perennials—especially if out of the ground for more than a few days—will

Matteuccia struthiopteris transplanted using sodium polyacrylate crystals. This bareroot ostrich fern is soaking in a bucket of water-soaked crystals (not visible in the first image) that cling to the roots when the plant is removed (center). I did not even water the plant after setting it into the soil, and six weeks later it is thriving (third image).

Maianthemum hybridum. **Broad-leaved bunch-flower** is outfitted with contractile roots that retract like springs, pulling the plant deeper into the soil. After contracting, the roots retain their folded appearance.

Let the bucket sit 15 minutes to absorb the water before dipping the roots. You can just dip and swirl the roots or let them soak for 15 minutes or so while you attend to other plants. After dipping several plants the crystals should be replenished.

Though it seems extreme, I prefer bare-root transplanting early in the growing season because it reduces incompatibility problems between soil types. Just make sure when you tamp the soil down around the roots, you try to preserve some of the three-dimensional structure they had previously. I do this by dribbling or working soil in between the roots with my fingers.

Mechanics

Older sections of each root function to transport and store the raw materials and products of photosynthesis and to anchor the plant in the soil. The main body of the root is called the cortex. It is a cylinder of cells that transports water into the central plumbing of the root, stores food reserves (starch), and provides mechanical (tensile) strength to cable the plant in place. Some species—especially woodland perennials with juicy rhizomes or corms that are preyed upon by mammals or others and are prone to frost heaving—have contractile roots in which the inner part of the cortex contracts like a recoiling spring. The root contracts only once it has grown deep enough to be firmly anchored in the soil, and as it contracts it pulls the rhizome, corm, or bulb deeper into the earth so as to avoid discovery by a vole or mouse. Contracted roots have a folded appearance like the bellows of an accordion, and successive ones can work the plant six inches deeper into the ground over several seasons. At the center of the root lie the xylem tubes that transport water to the leaves and the phloem that transports nutrients upward and sugars downward from the canopy.

In the Beginning

The first or primary root is ready to begin growing once the seed has matured. It is telling that the root, not the shoot, is the first part of the seedling to emerge, as it must burrow into the soil and begin slurping up water and nutrients before the leaves can expand. This first root is called the taproot or seminal root, and it may tunnel deep into the soil and swell to the size of a parsnip, or it may quickly branch and be supplanted by a network of smaller secondary roots. Species with large taproots are more common in dry soils, as they can grow very

have lost all of their fine roots and some of their large roots. Fortunately, they are usually dormant so they should survive transplanting. A technique that has become very popular lately to facilitate reestablishment is to dip the root mass in a slurry of water and sodium polyacrylate crystals. These are the crystals in baby diapers, and they are sold in garden centers to help hold moisture in containers. The crystals can absorb up to 600 times their own weight in water and cling to roots like jelly. They act like a supplemental fine root system until the real one gets going. Different folks have their own recipes, but I find 1 teaspoon of sodium polyacrylate added to half a gallon of warm water is about right for fine-rooted species. (This is about how much you can scrape out of the cottony batting in one baby diaper!) For perennials with roots thicker than one-sixteenth of an inch in diameter, add 2 teaspoons to give the mixture a more jellylike consistency for better adhesion.

Asclepias tuberosa taproot. **Butterfly weed** retains its primary root, which swells markedly into a food- and water-storing taproot fringed with finer, more transitory feeder roots.

OPPOSITE; TOP LEFT: *Baptisia australis.* **False indigos** are difficult to divide and transplant because their large taproots resent being disturbed.

OPPOSITE; TOP RIGHT: *Gentiana clausa.* Though **bottle gentian** does not have a true taproot, its fleshy root system does not recover easily after transplanting, and plants are often lost in this way. Bees learn to pry the closed blooms open.

OPPOSITE; BOTTOM: *Silphium laciniatum.* **Compass plant** has been known to grow a taproot 40 feet long in deep prairie soils.

deep in search of water. The taproot of prairie dock (*Silphium terebinthinaceum*) has been excavated and measured at over 40 feet, though in New England roots do not usually grow that deep as our bedrock (and thus the water table) is closer to the surface.

Species that produce large taproots are notoriously difficult to divide and transplant, simply because not only does the enormous root provide access to deep water, it also functions as a larder, storing food supplies that other plants store in bulbs or rhizomes. Unless you include a backhoe in your arsenal of gardening tools, it is inevitable that when you dig out a plant with a 10-foot taproot, you will come away with only, perhaps, the top 12 inches of root: 80 percent of the plant's root system and food reserves remain behind in the

ground. It is especially important to move these perennials when they are dormant and preferably in early spring. The excavated stub will eventually sprout one or more new tips, and with time the plant will reestablish a new taproot. It may take a year or two for the root system to recover, and until then do not expect exuberant aboveground growth. Of course, that 80 percent of the root system that stayed behind will likely resprout as well, as anyone who has tried to remove dandelions from their lawn can attest. Dandelions aside, taprooted perennials are by nature thrifty and slow growing, spending their youth banking away food reserves in an ever-growing root, while aboveground growth proceeds at a much slower pace. Though they may take years to mature, this conservative strategy serves them well in times of drought, fire, or herbivory and allows them to quickly recover from traumas that might kill faster-growing, less-thrifty neighbors. Putting all its eggs in one taproot basket is certainly risky for the plant, as the juicy tubers are tempting targets for both foraging mammals and fungi, but it makes sense in dry areas as well as grazing-prone or fire-prone areas. A large, deep taproot is truly a subterranean water tank that can store up to 10 percent of the rain that falls on the plant during the year, allowing it to continue to grow and photosynthesize during drought, when shallower-rooted neighbors become quickly stressed. Impressive food reserves also allow the plant to rebound quickly after browsing or fire—also something anyone who has tried to kill a dandelion with repetitive mowing quickly learns. Many biennials also produce taproots because they are a quick and efficient way of storing food reserves necessary for quick growth, flowering, and seed set the second year.

The Achilles heel of taprooted species—especially those that have evolved in dry environments—is excess water around the roots. *Lewisia tweedyi*, that bewitching and enigmatic alpine wildflower from Washington, is a case in point. If sited in loose, stony soil with the top of its fleshy, carrotlike root wedged between rocks but free of soil, it will live for many

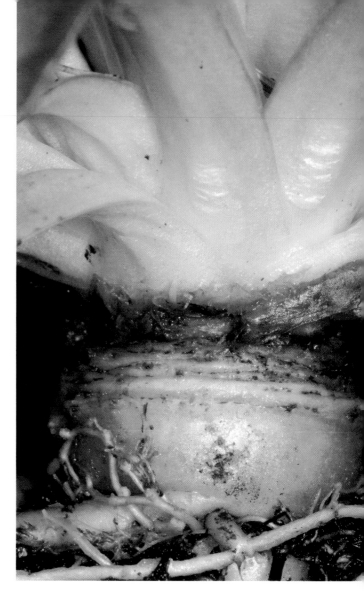

LEFT: *Lewisia* 'Little Plum'. RIGHT: *Lewisia* 'Little Plum' taproot. The large, stumpy taproot of lewisia is irresistible to rot-causing bacteria and fungi, but that can be discouraged by growing the plant in a few inches of loose gravel mulch to keep the root well aerated and dry.

years. If you plant it in even a sandy soil that holds moisture around the top of the root during the hot, humid months, it will quickly succumb.

Though some species retain a fat taproot through their lives, in most crown-forming perennials the dominance of the taproot is quickly lost, as secondary or lateral roots branch off and out from it. After the first year, it is difficult to determine which was first and which came after. Sometimes, these branches also grow corpulent and act much like an unbranched taproot (picture the humanlike form of a ginseng root) but more often attain only moderate girth. These, too, act as food and water tanks for the plant, relying, as does a single taproot, on short-lived, hair-thin feeder roots for the actual uptake of water and nutrients.

Sucking It Up and Spitting It Out: Absorption and Exudation

Plants require a steady supply of water to grow. One large perennial may transpire (remember—humans sweat and plants transpire) a gallon of water during a hot summer day, and an acre of prairie or forest can suck up more than 10,000 gallons per day at the height of summer. An inch of rainfall contributes about 27,000 gallons of water per acre, so even in a climate like mine, where we get three to five inches per month, it is not enough to meet the demands of all those roots. Furthermore, much of the 27,000 gallons flows downslope into ponds, swamps, streams, and rivers or percolates deep into the soil. Plants with a penchant for soggy, low-lying ground or those with deep roots receive more than their share, while all the others have to learn to do with less. Some wetland plants are notoriously wasteful of water. They suck it up like an SUV sucks gasoline because, in their water-rich environment, they have little reason to conserve. Dryland plants are just the opposite, surviving on thrift and conservation in a very unforgiving climate. Just as we are driving more efficient vehicles as the price of gas continues to rise, water shortages and water bans are forcing more gardeners to leave the water-hungry perennials in favor of more drought-tolerant selections. How do some plants manage so well on so little? In part it is because they transpire less than others, and in part it is because they have harder working, more efficient roots.

Water is very predictable in the way it moves around on and in the ground. Of course, it is not so predictable when you are waiting for it to fall from the sky. If you remember anything from high school chemistry, osmosis is the movement of a solvent (liquid) across a semipermeable membrane from an area of lower solute concentration to an area where the concentration is higher. In plain English, purer water wants to move across a membrane into dirtier water (water that contains a lot of dissolved chemicals or salts) until all the water is equally dirty. It is the reason why salt can pull the water from a cod, and it is the way that roots take up water. Water is stored in the soil within pores—the small spaces between soil particles. After a soaking rain, all the pores become filled and the soil is saturated (or *at field capacity,* in the language of soil science). At this point, it is very easy for any root tip or root hair to absorb water, but as the soil dries, it gets increasingly harder because the remaining water becomes both progressively dirtier as it is concentrated and because the soil particles begin to cling to it more and more desperately. Very water efficient species can raise the solute levels in their roots to create more osmotic pressure to pull in every available drop. They in effect have very powerful pumps that can draw water from deep inside the nooks and crannies of the soil. There is a danger that when the soil becomes very dry—especially soil that is naturally salty—the pump can reverse and pull water right out of the roots. Salt-tolerant perennials have a way of closing down the pump when the soil becomes so dry or salty that the flow of water might begin to reverse. On the other hand, salt-sensitive species cannot turn off their pump, and high salt levels will pull water from the roots and kill them. Since inorganic (chemical) fertilizer is basically a mix of salts, you can easily kill the roots of many perennials in this way if you over-

Symphyotrichum cordifolium. Drought stress is hardest on a perennial's fine root system. In the first image, well-watered roots of **blue wood aster** are shaggy with short root hairs and are absorbing water efficiently. In the second image, moderate drought has caused the root hairs to die and the roots to stop growing. This exacerbates water stress by limiting the plant's ability to absorb what little water is left in the soil. Aboveground the plant is wilting noticeably. In the third image, severe drought has killed all the visible roots, leaving only a few structural roots, which must regrow an entire root system if the rains return. This plant has been dangerously weakened by drought, and aboveground leaves and stems have withered.

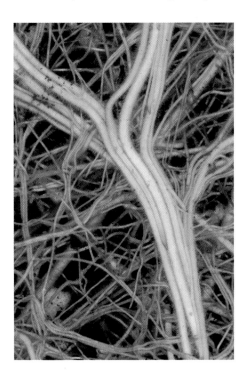

Penstemon hirsutus. **Hairy beardtongue** is a drought-tolerant perennial that is very thrifty in using water and very efficient at absorbing the last bit of water from parched ground.

fertilize—especially during drought, when their root pumps are already straining to keep water flowing in the right direction. You may often hear warnings not to use fertilizer on wilted plants, and for good reason, for you risk pushing stressed roots over the edge—literally killing them with kindness. Wait until the rains return and the leaves and stems are plump and turgid again before fertilizing. If you are feeding container plants, avoid applying fertilizer on hot days when water needs are high or when the soil is dry, as this will make it harder for the plants to take up the extra water they need.

Drought stress also takes its toll on root hairs and feeder roots. As soil begins to dry, root hairs first become less active and eventually wither. If the soil becomes so dry that the whole plant starts to wilt, the delicate feeder roots that provide the bulk of nutrient and water uptake for the plant also shrivel and die. The insidious thing about drought is that once the root hairs and feeder roots become compromised, it is even harder for the plant to absorb water, and the problems compound.

Drought damage has both short- and long-term effects. Immediate symptoms such as root loss, wilting, and dieback create obvious short-term stress that can kill the plant, but the effect of drought lingers even after the plant is no longer wilted. To replace damaged roots and leaves the victim has to dip into food reserves needed for dormancy and flowering. During acute drought stress and recovery, photosynthesis slows or stops, so these food stores may take a year or more to replenish, exposing the stricken individual to higher risk of death after insect attack or a hard winter. Let's say you plant a hibiscus in June and water it well for the first two weeks, then go off on vacation and find the poor thing badly wilted when you return three weeks later. After watering it well over the next three weeks, it appears to recover and even blooms, but then it fails to return the next spring. While cold damage would be the obvious suspect, it is equally likely that drought stress a full six months earlier is to blame. Though perennials establish much more quickly than woody plants, I hand water newly transplanted individuals every day for the first week, every other day for the next, twice a week for the third, and once a week for the next four or five, when it does not rain.

Even well-established perennials—typically those with large leaves that lose water quickly—will wilt temporarily on a very warm, sunny day. This is not a problem as long as the leaves recover later in the day, but it should be worrisome if they are still wilted by morning. The more you can do to minimize wilting and root loss, the healthier your gardens will be in the long term. If your soil is very well drained or you live in a dry climate where drought stress is a fact of life, it makes practical and ecological sense to select drought-tolerant plants for your garden. Not only will you spend less time watering, you will spend less time worrying and less money replacing dead plants.

Water-wise Gardening

I am fortunate to live in a water-rich part of the world where, aside from establishing new plantings, I rarely have to water the garden if I choose my plants appropriately. We receive on average about 45 inches of precipitation annually that is spread out very equally through the year, though we do have occasional droughts like everybody else. All this rain adds up to roughly one million gallons of water per acre per year. Our household uses 100,000 gallons a year from our well, which seems like an impossibly large number considering we do not water the lawn, wash cars, or fill swimming pools. Fortunately, ours is the only well currently drawing from a watershed of about 200 acres of swamp and low woods. This could change quickly if the land behind us is developed or the climate continues to become warmer and drier. In many parts of the United States and around the globe, water use is quickly outstripping the supply. In most of the American Sunbelt, water scarcity is already a fact, and communities must either drastically cut back on water use or on development. Water-addicted lawns and gardens are inevitably the first casualties as water bans sweep though towns and regions during droughts. An oasis of green amid blocks of withered flower beds and brown turf is a sure sign to the neighbors that someone has been violating the ban on outdoor water use. I am sure you have read accounts of neighbors clandestinely videotaping a gardener out illegally watering at night and turning the tape over to the authorities. It does not have to be this way. Our model of what a garden should be—vibrant green lawns meandering through lush flowerbeds and underneath verdant shade trees—is still based largely on English models. Let's face it, few if any places in North America have a climate just like England's. Most of us live in areas that are hotter, colder, or drier than the British Isles, and we can sustain such gardens only with lots of work and lots of water. Gradually, though, as water bans become increasingly permanent, many

gardeners are being forced to either adopt a new approach or hang up the trowel.

The truth of this new reality hit home recently when I was traveling through the Southeast, which has been gripped by a four-year drought that has left pontoon boats stranded on the muddy flats of once-brimming reservoirs. I heard a commercial by one of the big-box retailers alerting homeowners that knowledgeable personnel were waiting to assist them in developing water-wise landscapes full of drought-tolerant

Echinocereus reichenbachii. Like all of its ilk, **lace cactus** is masterful in a dry environment. This lovely species from the Rocky Mountains is winter-hardy to 15 degrees below zero F. as long as it is growing in gravelly soil.

shrubs and perennials. After ruminating for a minute on just what sort of knowledge the underpaid teenager manning the register at said warehouse might impart ("Plant this green side up," "I think it's a geranium-type ornamental tulip or something, but if it dies bring it back and we will replace it no questions asked," and "Sure it's drought tolerant—we never water anything here and it is still alive, right?"), I realized that the drought must really be impacting sales for them to craft a whole sales pitch around it. Xeriscaping has arrived at last.

The word *xeriscape* combines the Greek word for "dry," *xeros*, with *landscape* to denote a style of gardening that seeks to minimize irrigation use by choosing plants that are capable of growing without supplemental water. It was coined and trademarked in 1978 by Denver Water, the water department for the city of Denver, Colorado. Denver Water estimates that the average Denver household uses 150,000 gallons of water per year, with 75,000 gallons of that going to landscaping (the majority used to support turfgrass). An eighth of an acre in Denver's dry climate receives on average about 32,000 gallons of rain a year, and the same area of water-wasting Kentucky bluegrass (*Poa pratensis*) requires 18,500 gallons of water a *month* during the summer to remain green—obviously an unsustainable amount. The same acreage of drought-tolerant native buffalograss (*Buchloe dactyloides*) needs only 3,000 gallons per month. Some drought-tolerant native and nonnative perennials can get by with no supplemental water at all. They have several adaptations for life in a dry climate, including roots that are more resistant to drought injury and more efficient at scavenging the last bit of moisture out of the ground.

Xeriscaping is first and foremost a water conservation strategy, and if adopted nationwide, it could conserve tremendous quantities of drinking water. However, it does have an aesthetic and practical side as well. You may not end up with a facsimile of an English cottage garden, but it will be much "greener" in the ecological sense. Choosing plants that can grow in your climate without irrigation will also make your work easier in the short term (less time dragging the hose around) and in the long term (less replacement, fewer pests and diseases). And, because appropriate species tend to reflect and mirror the natural vegetation of the region, your garden will have a stronger regional identity. To me, lush swards of

OPPOSITE TOP: *Agave parryi.* Agaves have undergone a surge in popularity in the drought-plagued southeastern United States because they thrive without any irrigation.

OPPOSITE BOTTOM: *Salvia coccinea.* The increased interest in water-wise gardening has fostered more widespread use of native drought-adapted species, such as this scarlet sage growing without care in Florida's dry, sandy soil.

bluegrass and sweeps of delphiniums amidst sagebrush and cacti are as appropriate as a pocket-protected techno-geek at a bikers' rally.

Why Are Some Wetland Plants also Drought Tolerant?

Ironically, too much water can also cause drought stress. Roots absorb water most effectively when they are actively growing and respiring. When soils are saturated with water, the oxygen is forced out. Since roots need oxygen to absorb water effectively, water uptake is effectively slowed or stopped in flooded soils. Consequently, you may witness the seemingly incongruous phenomenon of a flooded and wilted field of corn. Wetland grasses and wildflowers have several ways to combat this lack of air during floods. Many that live in permanently wet soils sprout roots from the stem that spread like a net over the surface of the soggy soil, where oxygen levels are highest. Others grow roots with large, air-filled cells called aerenchyma, which act almost like lungs for the root. Oxygen is pumped in from above and stored in these sacks as needed. Still others have simply evolved drought tolerance to weather periods when flooded soils make water scarce.

Since waterlogged soils limit root respiration and water uptake, flooded plants are under drought stress just as much as plants growing in an arid environment. Adaptations such as surface roots and "lungs" are necessary in soils that remain constantly wet, but they are unnecessary if the soil is only occasionally flooded. You do not need scuba gear to bob for apples, and many plants growing in soils that flood then dry simply "hold their breath" by being thrifty when it comes to water use. Rather than try to take up water when soil oxygen is low, they do things to conserve the water they already have, just as a desert plant does during times of scarcity. This includes slowing down metabolism and reducing transpiration loss by leaves. Unlike plants that live in constantly flooded soils, which have evolved elaborate root anatomies for life in water, those from temporarily flooded environments have conventional roots, but modified leaves and metabolisms that are very similar to what you might find in a desert plant. It is for this reason that many wetland plants are also drought tolerant.

Another way to tolerate seasonal flooding and drought, and one that is common among spring-blooming wildflowers such as primroses, shooting stars, and skunk cabbage, is to simply go dormant once the soil dries out. These species have evolved roots that are very effective in flooded soils, so the plants grow lustily in spring when swamps, streambanks, and pond shores are saturated with snowmelt and spring rain. They are not thrifty with water, so when the soil begins to dry, they drop their leaves and retreat underground until the following spring.

Lilium pardalinum roots. Leopard lily roots are easily suffocated in waterlogged soils. After a period of rainy weather, many of this individual's roots drowned and died (brown roots). As the soil dried somewhat and oxygen returned, healthy new white roots began to sprout.

Lysichiton camtschaticum. White skunk cabbage grows naturally in swampy soils and is not at all drought tolerant. It blooms and grows lustily in spring but quickly goes dormant as waterlogged soils dry out during summer.

The Soil Is My Stomach

Roots also absorb most of the mineral nutrients the plant needs. Some of these minerals come from weathered rocks and soil particles, a bit comes from the atmosphere dissolved in raindrops, but the rest is simply recycled from the dead plants and animals that do not need it anymore. One of the ironies about plants is that to get the nutrition they need, they must eat themselves—at least all the dead parts, like leaves, stems, and roots that are shed over the course of the season. Perennials can reabsorb some but not all of the nutrients from leaves and stems as they wither and die. The rest are lost, at least temporarily. From a plant's perspective, the soil is really a big stomach where organic materials are digested to liberate the nitrogen, phosphorus, and all the other elements trapped in dead organic matter that a plant needs for proper growth. Just like our stomachs produce digestive acids and enzymes, roots exude a host of chemicals into the soil, including sugars, vitamins, amino acids, enzymes, and acids. Some of the enzymes and acids act just like those in our stomach to liber-

ate nutrients from organic materials by digesting complex molecules, improving the solubility of certain otherwise insoluble nutrients. Other root exudates retard the growth of pathogens and competitors' roots, but the vast majority of these substances are dribbled into the soil to attract and nourish fungi, bacteria, and a host of other tiny creatures. Just as cows and termites need bacteria to turn plant materials into food, so too do the plants themselves rely on myriad soil organisms to digest their dead leaves and stems so they can eventually access the majority of nutrients found within.

Nectar, excess pollen, and sugary fruits are produced by the plant to attract birds and the bees for pollination and seed dispersal, and sugars, vitamins, and amino acids are exuded by roots to nourish fungi and bacteria that in turn digest organic materials for the plant while also protecting the roots from disease. It is estimated that between 15 and 50 percent of the sun energy captured through photosynthesis by the plant is purposely exuded into the rhizosphere (the hair-thin zone just outside the root) to nurture microorganisms that in turn benefit the plant (for comparison, nectar secretion by flowers has been estimated to use only 2 to 20 percent of the plant's energy over the course of a year). It was a revelation to me that *up to half the plant's energy* is simply leached out into the soil—like pouring sugar water into a pitcher with a hole in the bottom. I have always known that the soil flora and fauna depend in large part on plants for their sustenance—either directly through deposition of dead leaves, stems, and roots or indirectly through animal wastes built from plants—but the notion that plants actively pump food into the zone around their roots is very odd indeed. Unlike the passive recycling of death and decay, exudation is an active process in which the plant lures beneficial organisms to its roots, cultivates them, and reaps the rewards.

Obviously, the rewards must be great if the demands are so high, or natural selection would have stopped this apparent waste a long time ago. Bacteria and fungi benefit plants by cleaving complex organic molecules into smaller, usable ones and by extracting minerals from soil and rock at a slow, steady rate. Root exudates provide the fuel that helps drive this digestion.

First One In, Close the Door

Like settlers on the prairie, soil fungi and bacteria are highly territorial and quickly stake their claim within a particular patch of ground, excluding competing species that try to invade. As a perennial feeds the beneficial fungi and bacteria around its roots, they grow lustily, and as a consequence they exclude pathogenic (disease-causing) organisms that might try to attack the roots. One of the big problems we run into in pasteurized container soils as well as in unhealthy garden soils is an excess of fungal root diseases such as phytophthora, pythium, and rhizoctonia, which are largely kept at bay in field

Phlox carolina. The flowers of this Carolina phlox growing along the Blue Ridge Parkway offer nectar and pollen to bees and butterflies, and underground its roots exude great amounts of sugars and proteins to feed symbiotic bacteria and fungi, which help the plant recapture lost nutrients.

Bark mulch mixed with cow manure feeds your plants as well as beneficial fungi. The hyphae of these mushrooms can be seen threading through the layer of mulch.

soils with a healthy balance of microorganisms, proper pH, and nutrients.

Building a Better Community

Fungi and bacteria, along with larger things like snails, earthworms, nematodes, ants, and rotifers, pitch in with the roots to construct soil that is beneficial for all residents' health and prosperity. Remember that those trillions of organisms in the soil cannot live inside the particles of sand silt and clay that largely comprise it, any more than we can squeeze inside a solid boulder. They all have to shuffle, squirm, and trace through the tiny pore spaces between soil particles. In soil that has been compacted under the weight of feet, tires, pavement, or agricultural abuse, large pores collapse, and the small ones are often choked off from their neighbors so that the soil becomes stagnant, toxic, and, from a nematode's perspective, impossible to wiggle through. Like a football team in a phone booth (remember those?), microorganisms in a compacted soil will slowly suffocate and starve unless they take action. With their 200 pounds per square inch of concentrated thrust, roots begin to open up channels in compacted soil with the help of digging ants, moles, and worms. Root exudates, as well as the organic molecules left over after bacteria and fungi have finished digesting, act as glue that cements small soil particles together into larger ones and will, over time, build the sort of open, breathable soil that allows all to flourish. Unfortunately, though, a soil's wounds are not healed overnight.

Trading Spaces

In a simple and elegant experiment, researchers in Brazil dug up a square foot of degraded, compacted pasture soil and an equal amount of healthy, well-structured soil from an abutting forest and swapped them. Within a year, the sorry square of pasture soil had regained its structure and a healthy population of microorganisms and roots, while the once-healthy square of forest soil became barren and compacted as its compliment of soil flora and fauna died off in the inhospitable new world of the pasture. The diversity of forest organisms had been replaced by one worm species that ran amuck, clogging up the soil with castings and exhausting the food supply.

It is not hard to see corollaries to this in my own yard. We live in a house in the woods, and we did our best to leave well enough alone during construction, but inevitably with the septic system, driveway, foundation, and foundation drain, some of the soil was pretty disturbed. The areas directly adjacent to the woods have healed over quickly, and the native species have returned, but other areas, including the (gasp) lawn and perennial beds, have soil that is still compromised. Whether you are dealing with the aftermath of construction, abusive agriculture, or a chemically dependant lawn, chances are you have a similar situation, too. So what can you do?

The organic gardening movement has for years advocated for the liberal use of composts to rebuild a fractured soil. Good compost adds nutrients, some carbohydrates, and humic compounds to restore soil structure, as well as a boatload of critters to boost compromised populations in the soil (for more on compost and composting, see p. 199). Spreading and incorporating two to six inches of aged compost (compost in which the organic materials have been digested to the point where they are not recognizable as such) can jump-start a soil's metabolism, and a yearly topdressing of an inch or so will keep it chugging along. Mulching with less-decomposed materials will also provide the raw materials for metabolism, and since a specific suite of microorganisms prefers the type of organic material most common in its habitat, use leaves and bark or wood mulch in the woodland gardens and straw or hay in sunny ones.

Recently, increasing attention has been paid to compost teas and the reported benefits they offer. As I understand it, a well-prepared tea adds both organic molecules and nutrients, in addition to substances similar to root exudates. Compost tea is seen as both a fertilizer and an energy drink for the soil flora and fauna. While there is probably some truth to this theory, the waters have been muddied by quite a bit of speculation and questionable science. So the jury is still out as to whether a little tea is better than a big load of compost (at least the tea is easier on the back!). I do talk to more and more people that swear by compost tea as a sort of miracle remedy for a host of garden ills. Some think that the beneficial bacteria in the tea not only help build the soil, they colonize leaves and stems, excluding disease organisms. Compounds excreted by these bacteria may even induce systemic acquired resistance (see p. 153). I am going to try some for myself and see what happens; I encourage you to do the same. (The tea can be purchased at certain retailers, or you can buy the equipment to brew your own.)

The Nitrogen Fix

One of the great ironies of life is that nitrogen—a key element for all life—is the most abundant element in the earth's atmosphere but very scarce in the soil. Nitrogen gas is very stable, but all solid forms that can be utilized by living things (ammonia, urea, nitrate, etc.) are very unstable, so over 99 percent of the nitrogen on earth is locked up in the air as nitrogen gas (N_2). There are no nitrogen-bearing rocks, so until the beginning of the twentieth century, what little earth-bound nitrogen there was at any given time had been captured (fixed) by bacteria and lightning. Bacteria are the only living things that have figured out a way to convert gaseous nitrogen into solid nitrogen. That is, of course, until the beginning of the twentieth century, when Fritz Haber and Carl Bosch invented a process to industrially convert gaseous nitrogen into ammonia and summarily change the course of human history. The Haber-Bosch process requires extreme heat and pressure to convert gaseous nitrogen into ammonia and uses upward of 1 percent of the world's energy annually. Bacteria accomplish the same thing much more elegantly and efficiently, without the pollution and consumption of fossil fuels that are the hallmarks of industrial nitrogen fixation.

Bacteria convert nitrogen gas into ammonia with an enzyme called nitrogenase. The Achilles heel of this enzyme is that it is easily damaged by oxygen, so bacteria must either somehow scrub oxygen from their cells or exist in a low-oxygen (anaerobic) environment to perform their magic.

Nitrogen fixation bacteria-style does also require some energy, which the bacteria get either directly through photosynthesis or indirectly by feeding on organic materials.

Plants need nitrogen to form amino acids, which are the

Baptisia alba with root nodules (top). Though growing in a pot in the nursery, this seedling white false indigo (a species in the bean family) has managed to attract some nitrogen-fixing bacteria to its roots. The specialized root nodules seen at center left in the photograph are little climate-controlled factories pulling nitrogen gas from the air and converting it to a form usable by the plant. This remarkable symbiotic relationship allows plants like this lupine (bottom) in the mountains of Washington State to grow luxuriantly in infertile soils.

building blocks of proteins, and they never have enough. It is the major limiting nutrient for plant growth, so figuring out a way to get a steady, unlimited supply would be quite a trick and would convey a huge competitive advantage. Therefore, a few unrelated plant families have evolved partnerships with nitrogen-fixing bacteria. Perennials with this ability are a boon to gardeners because they need little fertilizer and can actually leach out some of their excess nitrogen for other plants to use. The plants provide energy for the bacteria and house them in special, low-oxygen structures called nodules that form on the roots. The specific bacteria are free-living in the soil and enter the roots by infecting root hairs and penetrating deep inside the root's core. The nodule then encases the bacterial colony and begins pumping in sugars, nitrogen, and hydrogen while scrubbing out oxygen. Ammonia is whisked away as it is produced, to be used by the plant. The legume family (Fabaceae) enlists the *Rhizobium* genus of bacteria to fix nitrogen. It obviously works, as the legume family is the third or fourth largest plant family and includes many garden perennials such as species of *Lathyrus, Lupinus, Baptisia, Tephrosia, Astragalus, Dalea, Trifolium,* and *Thermopsis.* Some shrubs and trees, such as alders (*Alnus*), autumn olives (*Elaeagnus*), bayberries (*Morella*), and California lilacs (*Ceanothus*), employ another type of bacteria—the genus *Frankia*—to fix nitrogen. These two types of bacteria are called actinorhizal species. The only perennial genus that I know of that uses *Frankia* is *Dryas. Nostoc* bacteria are found on wet surfaces and in water, and some aquatic plants—most notably species of *Gunnera*—have formed partnerships with them to fix nitrogen. Many other wetland and aquatic perennials probably take advantage of *Nostoc* by cultivating colonies on their roots and nourishing them with root exudates.

Whether they are on the roots or inside them, these bacteria confer obvious advantages to the host perennials that can utilize them. From a horticultural perspective, then, how can we be sure our plants find the bacteria they need? *Gunnera* has a very open immigration policy when it comes to *Nostoc* species, so you do not have to travel to the Andes to collect just the right microbe to cultivate your massive specimen to perfection. Chances are good that the *Nostoc* inhabiting your pool will work just as well. Legumes are far more specific. There are quite a number of different *Rhizobium* species, and each works most efficiently with a particular legume. You can buy powdered bacterial inoculant for lupines, false indigos, and vetch-

Orontium aquaticum. It is likely that this **golden club**, an aquatic member of the arum family, takes advantage of free-living *Nostoc* bacteria to capture nitrogen.

es, though be sure it is fresh and that you use it quickly. You can either roll the seeds in the powder, Shake 'n Bake style, before sowing them, or add a packet to 2 gallons of water with a drop or two of dish detergent, shake, and water container or garden plants lightly. I routinely see nodules on baptisias and lupines that we raise from seed in pasteurized potting soil, so the bacteria are certainly out there, and perhaps we do not need to worry too much about inoculating the plants (I imagine they find their way into the pot via dust). Though there is no guarantee that the wild *Rhizobium* in your soil will do the

The porcelain-like blooms of *Gaultheria procumbens* (**wintergreen, top**) owe their existence in part to subterranean fungi that aid the plant in its quest for nitrogen. A mycorrhizal cup fungus helps wintergreen scavenge phosphorus as well as nitrogen while protecting the roots from toxic aluminum in the highly acidic soil in which it lives. Unlike the more common AM (arbuscular mycorrhizal) fungi, which penetrate plant roots, this ECM (ectomycorrhizal) fungus wraps around the **wintergreen** roots like a white jacket while also spreading like a web or mat through the soil. Notice both growth patterns in the photograph below.

job as effectively as commercial strains selected for a particular plant genus, they will still help, and over time, they will likely evolve to work more effectively with your particular plants. Because *Frankia* species is not commonly available commercially, we sometimes inoculate actinorhizal plants by digging a spade full of dirt from the base of a wild stand, mixing the dirt with water to form a thin slurry, and watering the container plants with it. This is advisable if you are growing plants for restoration projects or other situations where the nitrogen fixation confers great advantage. Unfortunately, the number of perennials that benefit from association with nitrogen-fixing bacteria is rather low. Most get their nitrogen secondhand from organic wastes or chemical fertilizer. On the other hand, almost all perennials enlist certain fungi to gather scarce nutrients.

My Fungus, My Friend

Plants came into existence after incorporating photosynthetic bacteria into their cells, but they would likely have never left the water without the helping hand of fungi to pull them from the drink. In the sea, nutrients are dissolved and floating around in the water, so it is easy to scavenge them. On land, nutrients are harder to come by and mostly locked up in minerals and organic material. Fungi arrived on land first and figured out how do digest these materials to acquire the minerals they needed. Instead of figuring this out for themselves, the first land plants simply lured fungi to their roots with a sugary reward and let them do the scavenging in turn. The plant shares the sugars and other exudates it makes via photosynthesis, and the fungus shares the nutrients it obtains. It is a symbiotic relationship that has allowed plants to thrive on land. This is the essence of what we call the mycorrhizal relationship between roots and fungi, and estimates are that upward of 92 percent of plants, including most ferns and some mosses, employ it. Interestingly, the cress family (Brassicaceae) and the carnation family (Caryophyllaceae) are

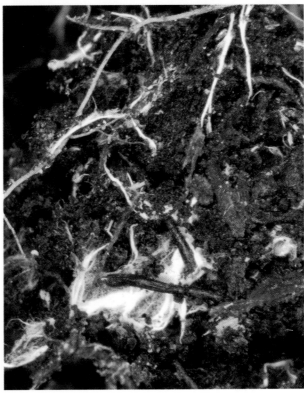

Pterospora andromedea. Woodland pine drops is a member of the Monotropaceae. What you see are the flower spikes; it has no leaves. Instead of photosynthesizing for itself, the plant parasitizes mycorrhizal fungi of certain trees, drawing what it needs from the tree indirectly.

allow it to grow out into the surrounding soil and scavenge nutrients (especially phosphorus), protect the root from invasion by disease organisms, inhibit the growth of competing plants' mycorrhizae, and potentially help with water uptake. Fungal roots are very, very thin and thus have a tremendous surface area, which exponentially increases the absorption capacity compared to larger plant roots alone. Roots can also be infected as they grow through bits of hyphae or pass next to another infected root. The AM fungi do not produce mushrooms and do not appear to reproduce sexually, though they do form spores that are basically copies of the parent. Many species are very widespread worldwide, associate with a large variety of plants, and appear to be little changed from fossils millions of years old.

Ectomycorrhizae (EcM) are a more recently evolved, less-common type of association limited mostly to woody plants and a few herbaceous perennials. Ectomycorrhizae wrap around the root and also spread a large mat of hyphae through the soil and detritus. They produce mushrooms and are generally more host specific than AM fungi. They are also less dependent on their hosts and can survive without them. If you hunt mushrooms, you know that certain species grow in and around certain trees. A few perennials develop EcM, most notably herbaceous members of the heath family, such as some wintergreens (*Gaultheria*), and others in related families such as the Pyrolaceae (*Pyrola, Moneses,* and *Chimaphila*) and the lovely members of the Diapensiaceae (*Shortia, Galax, Berneuxia, Diapensia, Pyxidanthera,* and *Schizocodon*). These all employ species of cup fungi that are very efficient not only at scavenging phosphorus, but also nitrogen; and the fungus also helps protect the root from toxic concentrations of aluminum and other ions that build up in the very acidic soils the plants grow in. These supermycorrhizae have allowed the heaths and related plants to thrive in cold and/or highly acidic soils with toxic levels of aluminum, where few other plants can grow.

Mycorrhizal fungi have also allowed plants in yet another related family, the Monotropaceae, to give up photosynthesis altogether and rely on parasitism for their sustenance. Indian pipes (*Monotropa*) are familiar, ghostly white or yellow plants of woodlands throughout North America. They attach themselves to the hyphae of fungi that are mycorrhizal with trees, drawing off carbohydrate from the fungus that was provided by the tree; so in a sense they parasitize the tree by way of the fungus (this type of fungal parasitism is called heteromycotrophism). I am occasionally asked if it is possible to cultivate the spectrally beautiful many-flowered Indian pipe (*Monotropa hypopithys*). I have established it by collecting the seeds from the dried capsules in fall and sprinkling them around in the woods. The plants appear after a couple of years, but only if one of its fungal hosts is present.

two of only a very few families that have not been found to form mycorrhizal associations.

Mycorrhizal roots are basically a fusion of fungal roots (hyphae) and plant roots—a sort of hybrid structure that is neither plant nor fungus. The most common type of mycorrhizae are endo- or arbuscular mycorrhizae (abbreviated AM). They are the type found in about 80 percent of plants and almost all perennials. Fungi in this group have lived with plants for so long that they cannot survive on their own except as dormant spores. Spores germinate on a plant root, and the hyphae grow into the root tissues, penetrating the cell wall of specialized root cells. The plant gives the fungus sugars, which

This leads to an obvious question: does it help to inoculate plants or soil with mycorrhizal fungi? If you read the claims of Internet hucksters, the answer is YES, YES, oh you better believe it, YES, but I think some healthy skepticism is in order. (One gentleman even claims that his mycorrhizal inoculant allowed him to grow a 42-inch cabbage. I guess no one told him that cabbages, like other Brassicaceae, are not mycorrhizal!) Most perennials employ AM, and these are very widespread in soils. If you are planting a new garden in nothing but unammended subsoil, or are involved in a strip-mine restoration or other restoration of degraded lands, then it may be prudent to purchase one of the commercial preparations. These are primarily spores and hyphae of species of *Glomus,* one of the most common, widespread, and least host-specific genera of AM fungi. However, if you are gardening under anything but these extreme conditions, save your money and invest it in some good compost instead. This will feed the mycorrhizae that are already present.

As far as I know, no commercial sources exist for EcM, but just as with AM types, they will likely be present in a forested area. These types in particular are nourished by rotting wood, leaves, and other plant debris and are most abundant in the layer of duff that forms in woodlands. They are more dependent on conditions external to the roots than most AM fungi are. I have come to believe that the proper mycorrhizae are more essential to success with challenging plants such as Oconee bells (*Shortia galacifolia*) than with most perennials (there is some evidence that, like Indian pipe, *Shortia* species are fungal parasites—at least during the seedling stage). I killed a few Oconee bells and trailing arbutus (*Epigaea repens*) by planting them in nice garden soil before realizing they wanted to be set into undisturbed leaf duff rife with fungal hyphae. Even challenging plants such as spotted wintergreen (*Chimaphila maculata*) will thrive if handled in this way. Applying a liberal layer of rotted hardwood chips or pine bark mulch has allowed me to cultivate some of these challenging genera in more typical garden conditions.

TOP: *Shortia uniflora* var. *grandiflora.* The key to cultivating this lovely Japanese shortia is to plant it in a highly acidic, organic soil containing quantities of rotten leaves and bark to nurture its fine roots and feed the fungus it needs to thrive.

BOTTOM: *Castilleja* in a meadow. Indian paintbrushes are one of a select group of plants that parasitize other plant roots directly. To cultivate this beguiling wildflower, you need to interplant it with grasses or other wildflowers to which its roots can fasten.

CHAPTER 3

LEAVES

Roots and stems have several functions, but leaves have but one true purpose: photosynthesis. Leaves are finely engineered solar-powered factories that manufacture simple sugars on which just about everything else on the planet depends. Leaves are truly at the heart of it all. Since their first appearance on the world stage, leaves have evolved into all manner of shape and even color. The shape of a particular blade is a wonderful balance of photosynthetic efficiency, aerodynamics, and thermodynamics.

The variation in the size and shape of leaves is enormous, but big or small, round or heart-shaped, all leaves have certain things in common. They facilitate the conversion of sunlight into chemical energy via photosynthesis—and the nearly universal primacy of this vital process means that nearly all leaves look more or less like each other. A few perennials, such as the carnivorous pitcher plants (*Sarracenia*), require their leaves to double as insect traps, and some others, such as the familiar florist's poinsettia and the showy mountain mint

ABOVE: *Rodgersia podophylla.* The channeled veins in the leaves of **featherleaf** are visually dramatic, but they are purely functional. They lend structured support and drain rainwater that could encourage disease if it remained.

(*Pycnanthemum muticum*), produce colorful leaves (bracts) as stand-ins for petals, but these are the rare exceptions. Less-colorful bracts are more commonly employed by many perennials to protect expanding shoots and flower buds. These sacrificial leaves do not last for long. On the whole, though, leaves have to hold up to wind, rain, and sun for weeks, months, or even years, so they are designed to be very tough and resilient.

Veins in the Main

The main surface of the leaf is called the blade (lamina), and this is generally rather thin to allow light to pass into and through its tissues. The blade is stretched between a network of veins that serve both to transport water, hormones, carbohydrates, and nutrients to and from the leaf, and to physically support the thin blade in the same way tent poles support thin nylon fabric. Leaf veins (or at least the conductive tissues in leaf veins) are somewhat woody to give them stiffness. This is one of the reasons that many leaf-eating insects avoid the tough, indigestible veins, consuming only the softer tissue in between. Veins, as well as the leaf tissue itself, also rely on hydraulic pressure to remain stiff. Much like the inflatable bouncy houses you see at amusement parks and kids', birthdays, it is pressure that keeps leaves taunt. As soon as you turn

off the blower in one of those inflatables, it collapses into a heap of canvas, and much the same thing happens when water pressure drops in the plant. During periods when roots cannot supply enough water, the pressure drops and the leaf quickly wilts until water pressure is restored. It takes exponentially more water pressure to keep a large leaf stiffened, and this is one of the reasons that very large leaved plants mostly inhabit wet places. Even though the massive three-foot-wide leaves of gunnera (*Gunnera mantica*) are arrayed

LEFT: *Rheum rhabarbarum.* Garden rhubarb enfolds its developing flower buds in bracts, which are simply leaves modified for a protective function. Still, they are green and can photosynthesize like normal leaves as the flower stems develop.

RIGHT: *Sarracenia leucophaea.* White-top pitcher plant sports some of the most highly modified leaves in the plant kingdom. Each insect-trapping pitcher is a single leaf fused along a crease. The leaf tip, the pitcher's cap, is replete with a network of red veins and white windows that lure moths to the plant at night.

TOP LEFT: *Gunnera tinctoria.* The massive three-foot-wide leaves of **gunnera** need equally formidable veins to keep them aloft. Each large vein supports smaller side veins that act in concert to keep the leaf blade taut and circulate fluids. Very large leaves like this require enormous quantities of water to keep from wilting, so **gunnera** must be grown in swampy ground near ponds or pools.

BOTTOM LEFT: *Disporum maculatum.* **Spotted mandarin** displays a more efficient and recently evolved parallel venation than interrupted fern, with small tertiary veins that connect the way roads intersect in a modern city. This pattern facilitates a more rapid flow of liquids and provides more rigidity to the leaf blade than a dendritic pattern would.

TOP RIGHT: *Osmunda claytoniana.* The leaf veins of this **primitive interrupted fern** are arrayed in a simple dendritic pattern, with larger veins branching at the tips like the outline of a tree.

BOTTOM RIGHT: *Arisaema triphyllum* 'Blackjack'. The unusual maroon coloration of this **jack-in-the-pulpit** cultivar highlights the closed loop pattern of its veins. This is a simple answer to the dead-end problem of the more primitive dendritic venation. The looped ends of the smaller veins also provide extra rigidity along the leaf margin.

Evergreen Leaves

Deciduous leaves rely on the mechanical strength of the veins combined with hydraulic pressure for support, but evergreen leaves need a more durable design. They infuse both veins and the tissues in between with lignin (the stuff that makes wood woody). Lignin reinforces the leaf tissues like the threads in rip-stop nylon, reducing the chance of tearing. This is one reason that evergreens do not wilt as readily as herbaceous perennials. The leaves may go a bit pale as the water drains from them, but they do not simply flop down. Evergreen leaves are less likely to irreversibly collapse during drought or when the ground is frozen and water unavailable in the winter. The additional hardening of the evergreen leaf also makes it less palatable to herbivores and more resistant to bacterial and fungal attack. It is worth it for the plant to invest this extra fortification into leaves that must last at least a full 12 months. Evergreen leaves are also a good place to store energy and valuable and easily leached nutrients such as nitrogen during dormancy. In fact, this is one of the main reasons plants remain evergreen. The evergreen plant transfers the energy and nutrients to the fresh crop of leaves as they expand, and this is why most evergreen perennials (hepaticas, hellebores, gingers, coralbells, etc.) shed their old leaves only after the new ones are formed. This is also why you can severely set back an evergreen perennial by pruning off the old leaves prematurely. I always wait until they have browned before removing them, even though then may look tattered and ragged after the winter.

The obvious question then becomes, "If evergreen leaves are so great, why isn't everything evergreen?" Well, evergreen leaves are as much a liability as an advantage. Being more expensive to produce they are also more costly to replace as they are eaten or damaged by the weather. They are more exposed and vulnerable than roots as far as storage goes, and they put a real strain on the plant during times when the ground is dry or frozen (see p. 95). Frozen ground is the real enemy of evergreens. Unless protected under a blanket of snow, they can quickly fry on a cold, sunny day. Gardeners whose ground does not freeze severely in winter can cultivate a wider selection of evergreens that those of us in colder regions cannot, and I believe it is this problem of dehydration rather than a strict sensitivity to cold.

Hepatica nobilis 'Poulette' strain. Rather than risk losing valuable nutrients in shed leaves, this lovely form of the European hepatica retains its foliage all winter. To survive an entire calendar year, its leaves are firm, thick, and waxy. In the spring, the old leaves die off as the new leaves expand and absorb their nutrients and energy.

with a trusslike system of large veins, they need a cool, moist climate and ready access to water to remain inflated (turgid).

Leaf veins are more than just figurative tent poles. They are also highways that deliver the raw materials for photosynthesis from the roots, and truck away the finished products. If you have ever driven around Boston, you know just what a frustrating city it is to navigate. Its roads are arranged like spokes on a wheel with others circling around. It made sense in the 1600s when there were far fewer roads and folks wanted to get quickly to the city from the hinterlands. Nowadays, though, it is easy to become caught in this complicated web of one-way streets that start going north and end going south because we are used to the more efficient grid system found in modern cities and towns. Leaf veins have undergone a similar evolution in efficiency. Fossils of early land plants show leaves with simple venation that consisted of a primary vein originating at the petiole (the stalk that attaches leaf to stem) and branching like a stylized tree into a set of secondary veins. This "dendritic" pattern is considered to be a primitive one, and it is still evident in most ferns and some conifers. It is not very efficient, as the small veins simply dead end at the leaf margin so that the flow is more or less one way. Modern seed plants, including most perennials, have a networked venation in which the small tertiary branches that come off the secondary ones are all interconnected. This pattern looks like a fine grid spread evenly through the leaf. Just like the road system in a modern city, this grid facilitates an efficient flow around the leaf because there are no dead ends. As an added bonus, the grid of veins provides much more even and well-distributed mechanical support for leaf tissues than a dendritic pattern. Grasses, lilies, irises, and others with long, thin leaves employ veins running in parallel up the blade, connected by fine veins that act like cross streets to these "avenues." This pattern is perhaps the most efficient as far as transport and mechanical support.

Canvas Stretched over Poles

Just as the shape of the tent poles influences the shape of the tent, leaf venation patterns help give shape to the leaf itself. I have wondered many times why some leaves are egg shaped and others long and thin or splayed out like fingers on a hand. The evolution of various leaf morphologies is likely a concurrence of physics and ecology, but the result is sure pretty to look at. Leaves evolved as outgrowths of the stem. Primitive leaves are simply a twig with a bit of thin tissue along either side. In modern leaves, the twig has become the midvein and petiole. The most common leaf shape among seed plants is more or less oval—widest in the middle, narrowing to a point at the tip of the blade, with a prominent midvein up the center and branching veins up either side. It has several advan-

tages: low wind resistance, structural stability, and the ability to easily shed water. Water remaining on leaves invites fungal and bacterial attack as well as the growth of algae, and tapered tips concentrate and channel water like gutters. Leaves that have more than one main vein, for example, coralbells, tend to develop a maple-leaf or fan shape. To facilitate rainwater removal, these palmately veined leaves often taper to a point at the tip of each of the main veins, giving the leaf a lobed appearance. One drawback to a large, solid leaf is that it effectively shades those below it. This may explain why some perennials develop leaves with pronounced lobes. The gaps between each lobe (the sinuses) allow light to filter through to the foliage lower down. Another intriguing theory for the evolution of deep sinuses is that they are meant to mimic caterpillar damage so as to repel other herbivores (Niemela and Tuomi 1987). Compound leaves (leaves composed of several leaflets attached to a single petiole) also provide less wind resistance than solid leaves. In palmately veined species such as hellebores, sinuses have become so deep that they separate the lobes of the leaf into distinct leaflets. Because it is composed of several separate leaflets, this type of leaf is called a palmately compound leaf.

Leaves that have one main vein with branches coming off of it are called pinnately veined. When lobed, this type of blade has an oak-leaf appearance. A pinnately compound leaf results if the individual lobes are completely separated as individual leaflets. Typically, each of the leaflets will also have pinnate venation, which means they can also be lobed or even divided once again (bipinnately compound).

TOP LEFT: *Astrolepis windhamii.* **Windham's scaly cloak fern** displays a pinnate arrangement, with pairs of leaflets arranged along a central stalk.

TOP RIGHT: *Rodgersia podophylla.* **Featherleaf** is nearly palmate, meaning that the six individual leaflets attach to the petiole at about the same point.

BOTTOM LEFT: *Hydrophyllum virginianum.* Because the separations between its leaf segments do not extend all the way to the midrib of the leaf, **Virginia waterleaf** is considered to have pinnately lobed leaves. Notice how the slightly offset branching of the veins dictates the arrangement of the lobes.

BOTTOM RIGHT: *Heuchera americana* 'Greenspice'. **Alumroot** displays palmate venation, with all the main veins of each leaf joined together at the base, so the leaves are palmately lobed like those of a maple.

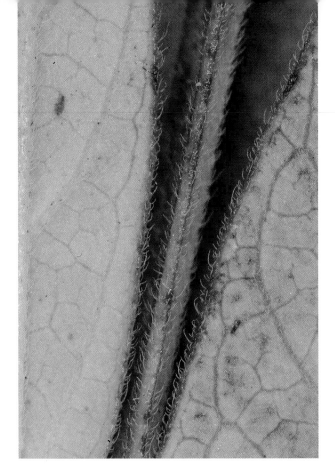

Asclepias incarnata. Seen up close, the leaf margins of swamp milkweed are arrayed with a phalanx of stiff hairs to discourage insect attack. The edge is also rolled slightly for greater strength.

Saxifraga longifolia hybrid. This encrusted saxifrage exudes calcium carbonate from pores along the leaf margins, perhaps to reflect light in its harsh alpine environment, to discourage predation, or to prevent calcium from reaching toxic levels in the leaf tissues.

Arisaema consanguineum and its relatives produce some of the most remarkable compound leaves I have ever seen. The leaflets whorl around the tall, muscular petiole like the spokes of a wheel, and each leaflet is also equipped with an eight-inch threadlike tip that sheds water beautifully.

On the Edge

Leaf edges (margins) vary quite a bit from one plant to the next. Some are toothed, others smooth, and still others lined with fine hairs (cilia). The adaptive significance of different forms is not really known and may be partly just an artifact of the venation pattern in the blade. Swelling or veining along the edge may help to lessen the chances of tearing, and toothy or hairy margins may repel insects by appearing already eaten or by making it physically challenging for a small caterpillar to get in there and chew. Serrated edges may also help to shed water like pointed tips do.

Leaf shape is also heavily influenced by climate. I have mentioned that shade leaves tend to be thinner than those in the sun. Plants from high alpine environments favor small, round, thickened hairy leaves. Plants of dry habitats also favor small, gray, or silver leaves that may also be thickened to store water.

Leaf Arrangement

Most leaves are attached to the stem via a petiole because it gives the leaf some flexibility to jostle for position in the sun. Plants whose leaves lack a petiole (called sessile leaves) have no way of readjusting their location if shaded by new leaves above, but petioled leaves can bend or stretch to move the lower leaf into a better position. Whether they have a petiole or not, leaves attach to the stem singly, in pairs, or more rarely in whorls of three or more. The arrangement of leaves on a stem is very consistent among related species and often within families themselves. Mints, phloxes, and carnations have paired, or opposite, leaves. Usually, if you look down on the

TOP RIGHT: *Penstemon serrulatus.* Cascade beard-tongue has a paired, or opposite, leaf arrangement, which means that the flower stalks that develop in each leaf axil are paired as well. Notice the thick pelt of sticky glandular hairs that protect all parts of the plant.

BOTTOM RIGHT: *Polygonatum macranthum,* fall color. The staggered arrangement of the leaflets on this Japanese Solomon's seal is termed alternate.

BELOW: *Trillium underwoodii,* like all trilliums, has whorled leaves composed of three leaflets attached to the petiole at the same point.

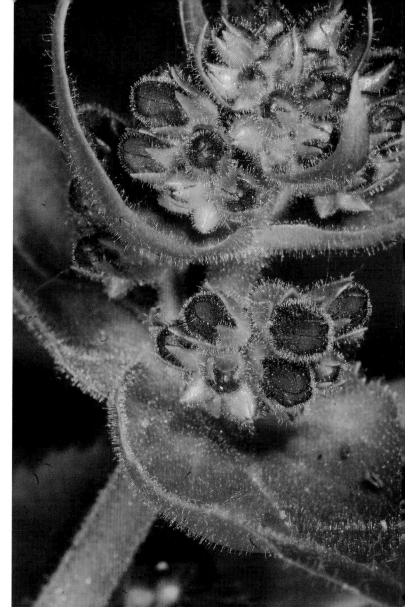

stem from above, the pairs will alternate orientation so as to avoid overlapping the ones directly beneath. One set will point east and west and the next north and south. Plants in the rose family and most in the aster family possess leaves that attach one at a time in an alternating or zigzag pattern up the stem. A few perennials, including many true lilies, produce a whorl of many leaves attached like the spokes of an umbrella to the stem. An opposite leaf and branch arrangement lends a certain regularity to the plant in question, a quality even more pronounced with a whorled leaf pattern. Alternating leaves produce a fuller, more diffuse appearance.

Photosynthesis

Without photosynthesis, life on earth would never have gotten very far. The vast majority of life on the planet depends directly or indirectly on energy captured from sunlight, and captured it is. The photosynthetic process captures the elusive energy in a sunbeam within the chemical bonds of a sugar. The process is written in the simplified equation $3\ CO_2 + 3\ H_2O$ + photons (energy from sunlight) $\rightarrow C_3H_6O_3$ (DHA, a simple carbohydrate) $+ 3\ O_2$. Even more simply put: water and carbon dioxide plus sunlight in, sugar plus oxygen out. I envision these chemical bonds as triggers cocked by the sun and ready to fire when needed. The great thing about this is that whereas sunlight is fickle and unpredictable, this stored energy is there when the plant needs it. The plant may use the energy directly by burning the sugars for food, or indirectly to manufacture all the other molecules necessary to survive, grow, and reproduce. Some of the stored energy passes on to everything that consumes plants and is passed on in turn as they are consumed. The food chain we read about in biology textbooks is essentially a bucket brigade passing the stored energy from the sun from plant to little fish to bigger fish to bear. A little leaks out of the bucket with each pass, but it does go quite a long way.

Without photosynthesis we would have no food and no air to breathe, and honestly, we have bacteria to thank for it. They invented the process, and it was only after they were captured and put to work by primitive algae that the age of plants began. Inside the leaves of early plants, the bacteria gave up their sense of identity and evolved into chloroplasts—the little green sugar factories that give leaves their color.

Sedum nevii. The colorful, needlelike leaves of **Nevius' stonecrop** have a relatively large surface area and efficient venation. These features make them easier to cool than large leaves, a distinct advantage on the hot, exposed rock ledges where this stonecrop finds a home.

Chloroplasts trade their electrons for protons in sunlight to begin the synthesis, obtaining replacement electrons by stripping the hydrogen from water molecules and leaving oxygen gas behind.

This One's Too Big, and This One's Too Small

The photosynthetic process is a finely tuned dance of light, air, and water, and each leaf on each particular plant is designed so that it may proceed with maximum efficiency. Leaves from the same plant growing in the shade are typically larger and thinner than those situated in the full sun. A few large leaves catch more of the dim light that passes through to the forest floor than a bunch of smaller ones that tend to overlap and shade each other, so many favorite, big-leaved perennials such as hostas are shade plants. However, big leaves have many disadvantages, too. If you have ever looked at hosta leaves after a hailstorm, you have witnessed one: big leaves are easier targets for falling objects. They also catch wind like sails do. This is not such an issue in a sheltered forest, but out in the sun it is a major liability. As I mentioned earlier, large leaves are hard to keep pressurized unless water is abundant and transpiration (water loss from leaves) is minimal. Small leaves have more surface area (think of all those edges), so they are more easily cooled. Small or even needlelike leaves, on the other hand, may have an efficient vein pattern and be easy to cool, but they are hard to orient toward the sun without a fair amount of overlap. Very small leaves occur mainly on species growing in dry, sunny environments where light is plentiful but wind and drought stress are paramount concerns. Most perennials strike a balance, producing leaves that are neither extremely large nor extremely small.

A Layer Cake of Sorts

A leaf blade consists of an outer skin (epidermis) surrounding a middle layer called the mesophyll. The mesophyll is a juicy green sponge of chloroplast-rich cells, and it comprises the bulk of the leaf's volume. Leaves formed in shade have a relatively thin mesophyll with chloroplasts clustered near the upper surface of the blade where the meager light is strongest. Some shade leaves may actually have chloroplasts in the outer skin as well. A thin mesophyll means the blade itself is very thin. Sun leaves have a thicker mesophyll, and the chloroplasts are stacked vertically so they can capture as much as possible of the more-intense light as it filters through the spongy tissue. Some arid land plants bury all their chloroplasts deep in a swollen leaf to protect them from the superintense radiation. Even the orientation of the leaf blade changes in sun and shade. Bloodroot (*Sanguinaria canadensis*) growing in shade holds its leaves horizontally to face the light. In

ABOVE: *Cardiocrinum giganteum.* This leaf of **giant lily** was inadvertently sunburned when the plant was moved from shady woods to a sunny plant-sale table. Leaves that are born in the shade cannot adapt easily to full sun.

RIGHT: Many leaves—especially those growing in shade—have reddish undersides because the red pigment helps reflect and absorb the diminished sunlight passing through the blades.

the sun, the leaf is held more vertically so the light hits it at an angle, to shield the chloroplasts from too much light.

One important practical point to remember is that once a shade leaf, always a shade leaf. If you dig up a perennial growing in the shade and move it to a sunny location, the larger, thinner shade leaves will often become sunburned and die. Conversely, if you take an individual that has been growing in the sun and plant it in the shade, its thicker leaves will not function very efficiently. In both cases if the individual is otherwise healthy, it will grow new leaves that are better adapted to the new conditions. Since many shade-loving perennials are raised in the sun in nurseries, it is common for them to undergo a period of transplant shock until new leaves grow.

Like our skin, the epidermis separates the interior of the leaf from the environment. It is covered with a waxy layer called the cuticle that seals in (and out) water. This cuticle may be dull or shiny, clear or opaque. The glaucous "bloom" on agaves and other plants from arid environments is caused by the heavy opaque cuticle that protects the leaf from water loss. Hellebores have a glossy cuticle that both lessens water loss during winter and helps shed excess rainwater that may lead to disease during the growing season. Plants growing underwater

do not need a cuticle, and they will shrivel up almost immediately once brought above the surface. A similar thing can happen if you bring tissue-cultured plantlets out of their sterile, humid environment too quickly, as it takes them several weeks to produce a well-developed cuticle once they are removed from the flask.

Open Windows

The epidermis of the leaf creates a water- and airtight seal. However, the leaf needs to constantly "breathe" in carbon dioxide and "exhale" oxygen during photosynthesis. Leaves breathe through tiny openings, called stomates, that line the upper and/or lower surface of the blade. Stomatal pores are ringed by two guard cells that clamp shut like miniature lips when the leaf needs to slow air exchange. When the pores are open, water vapor as well as oxygen can escape. Otherwise known as transpiration, this loss of water is the "pump" that pulls water up from the roots (see p. 80), but it is very inefficient and in fact is the major source of water loss (up to 97 percent of the water taken up by the roots is wasted through transpiration). Guard cells clamp shut at night and also close

A Better Way to Breathe

When the humidity is low and temperatures are high, transpiration rates increase exponentially. Plants from dry environments cannot simply stop photosynthesizing if it doesn't rain, so they have evolved strategies to circumvent the problem of water loss through transpiration.

Crassulacean Acid Metabolism

Cacti, yuccas, agaves, sedums, and some species in the Portulacaceae such as fame flower (*Talinum* spp.) open their stomata at night when it is cooler and more humid. They bind carbon dioxide on special molecules much like we bind oxygen on hemoglobin in our blood. The bound carbon dioxide can be stored and used for photosynthesis during the day. This type of nighttime carbon dioxide absorption is called Crassulacean acid metabolism.

C4 Plants

The enzyme that begins the manufacture of sugar during photosynthesis is ribulose-1,5-bisphosphate carboxylase/oxygenase, abbreviated as RuBisCO. In most plants, this protein actually picks up carbon dioxide as it comes in to the leaf and reacts with it to form a complex sugar. The problem is that RuBisCO operates inefficiently in the presence of high concentrations of oxygen (which comes into the leaf unavoidably when stomata are open), wasting energy and slowing the rate of carbon fixation, while increasing the amount of time the pores are open and losing water. The initial sugar molecule synthesized by RuBisCO in a high-oxygen environment has three carbon atoms, so this type of photosynthesis is called the C3 pathway. This is the most common type among perennials from cooler habitats.

Some species from drier environments have evolved a more efficient manufacturing process called C4 photosynthesis (so named because the initial sugar molecule synthesized contains four carbon atoms). In this process, RuBisCO is sequestered deep in the leaf tissue where oxygen levels are lower. Another molecule, PEP carboxylase, picks up carbon dioxide as it comes into the leaf and "delivers" it to the sequestered RuBisCO. PEP carboxylase is much faster at scavenging carbon dioxide, and less is needed because the RuBisCO manufactures sugar much more efficiently in the low-oxygen environment deep in the leaf. The net result is that the stomata need to be open for far less time, greatly reducing water loss through the leaf.

C4 photosynthesis is especially advantageous in hot, sunny, dry environments, but it does have some drawbacks as well. Its efficiency drops off in cooler temperatures, and it confers less advantage in a wetter climate, where water loss is not a problem. Therefore, C4 plants are more common in warm, sunny, dry environments, especially if the drought occurs during the heat of summer, while C3 plants are found in greater abundance in wetter, cooler climes. The vast majority of C4 species are grasses and sedges. A few annuals that you might grow in the garden, such as portulaca and gomphrena, also utilize this pathway, but among perennials it is only the grasses such as switchgrass (*Panicum virgatum*), big bluestem (*Andropogon gerardii*), little bluestem (*Schizachyrium scoparium*), muhly grasses (*Muhlenbergia* spp.), maiden grasses (*Miscanthus* spp.), and pampas grass (*Cortaderia selloana*) (Sage 2004).

Sedum oreganum. Oregon stonecrop employs CAM to help it conserve water in its dry, rocky habitat. The ability to bind carbon dioxide at night, when the humidity is naturally higher, means the plant loses far less water through transpiration than a typical C3 plant would.

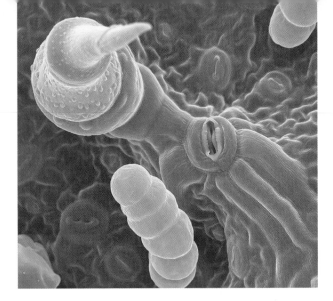

LEFT: A large, stinger-shaped hair guards a mouthlike stomate on the leaf of a *Helianthus* (sunflower) in this scanning electron micrograph. The two guard cells appear as closed lips.

RIGHT: *Clematis ochroleuca.* Curlyheads grows on dry cliffs and slopes, and its thick coating of white hair reflects some of the intense sun to prevent damage to leaf and flower tissues. Hairs like this can reduce leaf-surface temperatures by as much as 30 degrees F on a warm, sunny day.

when the plant becomes wilted. Water loss is reduced during drought but unfortunately so is photosynthesis! This is yet another reason why wilted, drought-stressed plants are more prone to disease, insect attack, and cold damage.

Fur and Fuzz

The epidermis of most leaves is also more or less covered with hairs or glands that serve several functions. The shape, distribution, and size of leaf hairs is one of the key diagnostic characteristics that taxonomists use to differentiate species, and these hairs can also have great appeal to us mammals. Lamb's ears and other gray, fuzzy-leaved perennials rely on this thick pelt to shield the leaves from intense solar radiation and also to reduce water loss through the stomata hidden underneath. Perennials from sunny, dry, or high-altitude habitats are the most likely to sport such protection. Matted silver or white hairs deflect sunlight and thus heat. Shale barren groundsel (*Packera antennariifolia*) from the shale barrens of the Virginias sports smaller leaves and a coat of silvery hairs, unlike its close cousin golden groundsel (*Packera aurea*) from nearby woodland environments. This is important, as in rocky, exposed sites, surface temperatures can approach 140 degrees F on a summer day. Leaf hairs can reduce leaf surface temperatures by as much as 30 degrees F by reflecting excess

heat away. Hepaticas and some anemones have long, furlike hairs on their flower buds. In this case, the hairs act to trap rather than reflect heat. These loosely matted hairs create a small greenhouse effect and can raise leaf temperatures as much as 10 degrees over ambient air temperatures. This gives these early flowering plants a real advantage on cool but sunny spring days, similar to the advantage a warm-blooded mouse has over a cold-blooded toad.

Most hairs, glands, or glandular hairs are designed to discourage herbivory. You can imagine how unpalatable a fuzzy leaf would be, so not surprisingly, all leafy greens we consume are hairless. Glandular hairs contain chemicals that are either foul smelling, irritating, or poisonous. The chemicals are released when the leaf is damaged and the shaft of the gland is broken. Leaves are certainly tempting targets for all manner of herbivores, but they are not powerless to resist.

OPPOSITE: *Adiantum pedatum.* The purpose of the sparse, ribbonlike hairs on the unfurling fronds of maidenhair fern becomes apparent on a foggy morning. The hairs act as gutters that collect and channel water droplets away from plant tissues to eliminate potential breeding grounds for disease.

Hepatica nobilis var. *obtusa.* Hepaticas have long, silky hairs on young leaves and flower buds that catch and retain the sun's heat rather than reflect it. This warms their tissues by as much as 10 degrees F above the air temperature on cool, sunny spring days.

They are laced with an incredible variety of chemicals to deter bacteria, fungi, insects, reptiles, and mammals from chomping on them. These chemicals are further proof that as far as plants are concerned, nothing goes to waste.

Secretory Structures

Unlike animals, plants do not have a digestive system. Solar power is inherently a very clean source of energy, and plants rely heavily on decomposers such as fungi and bacteria to digest organic wastes for them to obtain the minerals and other extrasolar nutrients they need, and this happens discreetly underground. A few insectivorous or carnivorous plants do actually digest organic material—dead bugs, hapless tree frogs, and so forth—but they are the only exception. However, plant physiology is not 100 percent efficient, so they do need to excrete some waste. Woody plants can fill bark or dead xylem with waste, staining the interior of the trunk darker and creating the heartwood so prized by furniture makers. Chemicals such as tannins and turpenes may build up to the degree that they preserve the wood by killing fungi, bacteria, and even wood-boring insects that try to attack the trunk. There is even a hypothesis that cellulose and lignin, the two most important structural carbon molecules plants manufacture, may have originally been just cellular excretions that by chance gave the cell wall more rigidity, a feature that was subsequently capitalized on in a very big way. It is incredible to think that perhaps it was a waste product of excessive photosynthesis that gave plants their "skeleton" and freed them from life as a jellylike puddle on algae. Perennials do not have handy internal waste dumps like trees do, but they do sequester wastes in dying leaves and stems that are then sloughed off. I find it more than a little ironic that the fall color we all celebrate in New England is little more than the plant equivalent of a potty break. In the end, though, plants *excrete* far, far less than animals do, but they *secrete* quite a bit more.

I'm Being Eaten Alive

It is fortunate that plants cannot think. Imagine being conscious of all the things that are out there trying to eat you: armies of bugs with horrible flesh-eating jaws, sinister rabbits with those nightmarish fangs, relentless, invisible bacteria swarming over every minor wound. All these things gnashing and chomping, and you can neither fight nor flee. It is no wonder that plants have created such a vast array of poisons and repellents—without them, they would not stand a chance.

Perennials secrete an arsenal of chemicals that run the gamut from waxes to shed water and deter fungi to aromatic oils meant to make the plant unpalatable and complex alkaloids to poison would-be herbivores like us.

Waxy leaves are most common on evergreen perennials from shady habitats. The glossy leaves of a wandflower (*Galax urceolata*) are certainly beautiful, but they also shed moisture quickly from the leaf surface just as car wax sheds it from the hood of your sedan. Since fungal spores need water to germinate, the wax helps prevent fungal pathogens from getting established and may also deter them from entering the leaf tissue. Wax also retards water loss, so species from dry habitats may also have noticeably waxy leaves.

No, Bug!

Waxes can also help deter insect attacks, but many other secretions do this more effectively. Despite their small size, insects are the biggest plant consumers. Entomologists like to point out that without insects, we would be overrun with plants. I like to think that without plants, we would be overrun with insects! The three main classes of defensive chemicals produced by plants are the terpenes, phenols, and alkaloids.

Terpenes

Terpenes are derived from fat molecules and probably first evolved for functions other than protection. Several are precursors to plant hormones, others are important in cell walls, while still others are the familiar orange, red, and yellow carotenoid pigments that help protect leaves from sun damage. The most familiar insecticidal terpene is pyrethrum, a compound found in the tissues of the pyrethrin daisy (*Chrysanthemum cinerariaefolium*). It and its synthetic derivatives are the most popular insecticides sold today. One problem with poisons is that the plant has to be eaten before the chemical can take effect—a case of too little too late. As a consequence, some terpenes are incredibly volatile (they evaporate very quickly) and aromatic. They act as olfactory warning flags to alert herbivores to the poison before any real damage is done. Menthol, the essential oil that gives mints their characteristic odor, is a terpene. Essential oils such as the gingerlike asarol found in *Asarum* species or the wintergreen oil (methyl salicylate) found in *Gaultheria procumbens* are more than just

Asarum minor. All parts of the wild ginger plant contain the highly aromatic, gingerlike terpene asarol, which is released when anything bites or damages its tissues. If that is not enough of a deterrent, the plant can also release the poisonous alkaloid asarone.

repellents, though; they are a subtle and complex form of interspecies communication. Incredibly, when an herbivore damages plant tissue, volatile oils released into the air can be sensed by other nearby plants of the same or even different species, causing them to increase levels of tannins and other toxic chemicals in their own tissues before they, too, are attacked. The volatiles also attract beneficial insects such as predatory wasps that home in on the scent trail to find and consume the feeding insects.

It is amazing and humbling to realize that plants can communicate with other plants, as well as insects, using pheromones such as methyl salicylate. I liken these aerosol warnings to burglar alarms set off by a plant to alert neighbors to the danger and call the police to apprehend the suspect. It also raises the possibility that a garden collection of plants from all over the world may be the horticultural equivalent of a tower of Babel, where plants cannot communicate with each other or the beneficial insects they evolved with and are instead prey to other insects that are deaf to their chemical cries. It is no wonder we spend so much of our garden time fighting fires, killing intruders, settling border disputes, and attending funerals.

Unfortunately, herbivorous insects have also learned to use these pheromones to their advantage. You have probably noticed that Japanese beetles are attracted to the leaves on your hollyhocks already damaged by other Japanese beetles. The beetles use the volatiles released by damaged food plants to locate their next meal, as well as potential mates that are already dining. Removing damaged leaves and also the beetles at the beginning of an attack can help thwart other pests.

Phenols

Phenols are the second major group in the defensive arsenal, and there is some evidence that they may be *offensive* as well. As with terpenes, it is likely that phenolic compounds first evolved for other purposes. Lignin, as well as red (anthocyanin) and yellow (flavenoid) pigments, are phenols. Lignin is primarily a

structural material, but it also serves a defensive purpose. It is very hard to digest, so many herbivores shy away from heavily lignified tissue. Lignin starts to develop only once a leaf or stem has finished elongating, so young, actively growing shoots have very little, and these, not coincidentally, are the plant parts most favored by grazers big and small.

Tannins are another very important type of phenol that gives most plants a bitter taste. They are important deterrents for mammalian herbivores as well as insects and often build up in tissues that have been browsed. Unfortunately for those of us plagued by unsustainably large deer herds, white-tailed

Cypripedium acaule. The leaves of pink lady's slipper contain the phenolic compound cypripedin, which is chemically related to the compound that causes a skin rash when you touch poison ivy. Fortunately, far fewer people are allergic to cypripedin than to the urushiol in poison oak and ivy.

RIGHT: *Solidago canadensis.* Canada goldenrod dominates this meadow in upstate New York for a good reason. Goldenrods release an allelopathic chemical that inhibits the growth of some competing species.

BELOW: *Aconitum lycoctonum* ssp. *vulparia.* Aconites and delphiniums contain the potent alkaloid aconitine, which, if ingested in high quantities, will disrupt the electrical functioning of the heart and nervous system and lead to a heart attack. Fortunately, the chemical is not absorbed through the skin.

and mule deer have a chemical in their saliva that deactivates the tannin before it reaches their stomach, so they can eat with impunity plants that would kill other mammals.

Tannins break down slowly after leaves die, staining the dead tissues brown. They are related to quinones, another group of aromatic compounds that can cause acute allergic reactions in people for reasons that are not clearly understood. Many have strong antimicrobial properties, and it is probably just coincidental that they cause dermatitis in people. The most familiar to most of us is urushiol, the chemical that puts the itch in poison ivy and poison oak. Some primulas contain primin, which causes primula dermatitis in sensitive folks. Lady's slipper orchids contain cypripedin; plumbagos, plumbagin; and English ivy and ginseng, the chemical falcarinol, all of which may cause allergic skin reactions similar to poison ivy in some people. Even more insidious are the furocoumarins, chemicals produced by gas plant (*Dictamnus albus*) and members of the parsley family, especially the cow parsnips (*Heracleum* spp.), in response to fungus attack. They become active only when exposed to ultraviolet light, bonding with the DNA of your skin cells and causing them to die. The injured area looks burned and then darkened as a result of excessive melanin production stimulated by the chemical. Take care when working around these plants, especially on sunny days.

As I mentioned previously, phenols (as well as some terpenes and alkaloids) are not merely defensive chemicals; they also have offensive capabilities. Allelopathy is the term used to describe the release of chemicals by one plant to interfere with the growth of neighboring plants. These allelochemicals can inhibit cell division, pollen and seed germination, nutrient uptake (either directly or by interfering with mycorrhizal relationships), photosynthesis, and specific enzyme functions. The nature and extent of allelopathy has been hotly debated in

the scientific community because it is difficult to prove outside of the laboratory. I suspect that many highly competitive species synthesize allelochemicals, but the list of perennials with proven allelopathic capabilities is short. This includes catmint (*Nepeta*) and other mints, goldenrods (*Solidago*) and other members of the aster family, euphorbias, and some ferns, such as hayscented and bracken ferns.

Alkaloids and glycosides in common garden perennials

Aconitine	*Aconitum, Delphinium*
Apocynamarin	*Amsonia, Apocynum*
Asarone	*Acorus, Asarum*
Berberine	*Coptis* and members of Berberidaceae
Colchicine	*Colchicum*
Desglucosyrioside, syrioside	*Asclepias*
Digitalin	*Digitalis*
Ephedrine	*Ephedra*
Ergometrine	*Ipomoea*
Harmine	*Passiflora*
Helleborin	*Helleborus*
Hypericin	*Hypericum*
Irisine	*Iris*
Jacobine, seneciphylline	*Senecio, Packera*
Lobeline	*Lobelia*
Lupinine	*Lupinus*
Lycorine	Spring bulbs in Amaryllidaceae, *Galanthus, Lycorus, Tulipa,* etc.
Peltatin, podophylloresin	*Podophyllum*
Phytolaccigenin	*Phytolacca*
Protoanemonin	*Actaea, Caltha, Ranunculus*
Protopine	*Dicentra* and members of Papaveraceae
Prunasin	*Pteridium*
Ranunculin, anemonin	*Clematis,* other Ranunculaceae
Sangunarine	*Sanguinaria*
Senegin	*Polygala*
Valerine	*Valeriana*
Zygacine	*Zigadenus*

OPPOSITE: *Digitalis purpurea* 'Camelot White'. One of the most familiar cardiac glycosides is digitalin, produced by the foxglove. In small doses it has long been used as a drug to treat congestive heart failure.

RIGHT: *Amsonia tabernaemontana.* Damaged tissues of bluestars exude a milky latex that both seals the wound and delivers the potent alkaloid apocynamarin to discourage further attack.

ALKALOIDS

The final group of defensive chemicals is the one that gets the most attention from us. Nitrogen-containing alkaloids and cardiac glycosides are poisons present in about 25 percent of plants, and they are synthesized mostly to discourage mammalian herbivores. In other words, they are especially toxic to people. Strychnine, atropine, coniceine (the alkaloid that killed Socrates), and hydrogen cyanide are all well-known poisons in this group. The majority of plant-derived medicines and drugs are derived from alkaloids and glycosides. Nicotine, caffeine, morphine, ephedrine (from *Ephedra*), scopolamine (in members of the nightshade family), and quinine are all familiar alkaloids that have pharmacological properties in small amounts but are lethal at higher doses. Many perennials contain alkaloids. They are not dangerous to handle because they become toxic only when ingested or inhaled in smoke.

LATEX

Defensive chemicals are usually stored in vacuoles, the empty spaces in cells. In this way they do not endanger the plant itself and become exposed only when the tissue is damaged. Certain perennials, such as *Euphorbia, Amsonia,* and *Papaver,* have special ducts called laticifers containing white latex. The laticifers grow through the tissues like a fine net of capillaries.

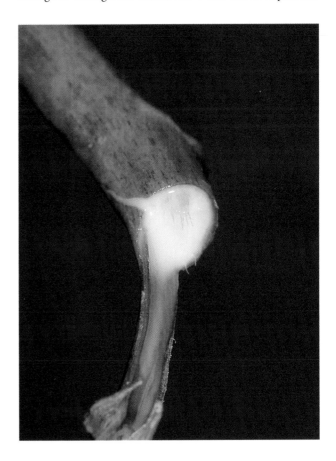

Urtica dioica. The long, needlelike hairs scattered along the stem and leaf petiole of this **common nettle** are filled with formic acid. I imagine most readers have experienced the effectiveness of this deterrent firsthand.

Cystopteris bulbifera. The petiole and rachis of each of these expanding bulblet **bladder fern** fronds is stained red by large amounts of the pigment anthocyanin. As the frond matures, the red is muted by higher levels of chlorophyll, and the stem appears maroon.

When the tissue is injured, the wound bleeds out latex, which seals off the damaged area and also contains terpenes and waxes to inhibit microbes, and alkaloids to discourage mammalian herbivores.

Volatile compounds are also contained in specialized hairs or glands on the surface of leaves and stems that release the chemical when bruised or broken. Stinging nettle (*Urtica dioica*) has small hairs filled with formic acid. When you brush against the leaves or stems, these hairs inject you with a little shot of acid. It is a pretty effective deterrent!

What is the most shocking to me is not that some plants can kill me or sting me or make me high, but our green friends are not the passive, helpless creatures I took them for. It flies in the face of our animalistic bias equating *active* with *moving* (as if to prove this point, a broad-winged hawk just landed in the tree outside my window). Plants cannot run away, but they can actively fight back, and although they cannot speak, they can communicate among themselves and even with other species. I cannot overemphasize the importance of this. Whether it is a plea for help after an insect attack or an advertisement that dinner is served, plants have a complex and highly sophisticated language that surpasses animal communication in its ability to reach across the kingdoms of life. What animal can you think of that can talk to birds, plants, mammals, insects, fungi, and bacteria? I imagine that if plants could think, they would feel sorry for us as we scurry around deaf and dumb to the myriad voices all around us.

All the Colors of the Rainbow

Leaves get their color from pigments diffused through different layers of their tissues. Nearly any leaf contains a variety of colorful pigments, but most of these are obscured by the dominant green of chlorophyll. Red, yellow, orange, and blue pigments may not be visible in a typical leaf, but they do lend each species a particular nuance and hue. If you look around in nature, it's obvious that there are a million different shades of green, thanks to the subtle effects of these nongreen leaf pigments. Under the right circumstances they can also make the leaf appear a very different color. Immature leaves of some species appear maroon or burgundy because the chloroplasts within them are not fully mature, so the red anthocyanins are not yet masked. This is especially true during cool weather and in full sun, as the red pigments contribute both frost and light protection to the tender young leaf tissues. You may have noticed that evergreen leaves often turn burgundy in autumn as levels of red pigments build in response to cold.

TYPES OF PIGMENTS

In addition to chlorophyll, there are three main groups of plant pigments: flavenoids, carotenoids, and anthocyanins. Mixed together as an artist blends paints, they can produce every color imaginable. Plants use pigments in flowers and fruits to lure the birds and the bees, but they also function to protect the leaves from ultraviolet light and insect and microbial attack while aiding photosynthesis.

Flavenoids are phenolic chemicals that probably serve mainly a defensive purpose. They deter fungal and insect pests and may have other roles as well. You have likely heard of flavenoids in reference to their pronounced antioxidant and anticancer properties. Flavenoids are yellow, blue, or purple in color and are most common in flowers and fruits, though also present in leaves. Anthocyanins are a red or blue subclass of flavenoids.

Carotenoids are terpenes that function primarily in photosynthesis. They help chlorophyll both process sunlight and protect the delicate chlorophyll molecule from ultraviolet damage. As such, all leaves contain fairly high levels of yellow and to a lesser extent orange carotenoid pigments.

COLORED FOLIAGE

Occasionally, you might discover plants that have exceptionally high levels of red, blue, or yellow pigments in their tissues. In this case the pigment lev-

els are so high that they actually mask the chlorophyll instead of the other way around, so the leaves remain more or less a red, blue, or yellow color even after the leaves mature. These variants are highly prized by gardeners, so colored selections of many normally green-leaved perennials are widely available. The nongreen colors are most intense and noticeable in younger leaves, during cooler weather, and in full sun for the same reasons mentioned above. Often leaves will start out red or yellow but fade to green as they mature, they are shaded by newer foliage, or the weather warms. Blue-colored foliage is more stable and often enhanced by a waxy bloom that makes the blue appear more gray or white, though it too is affected by environmental conditions. Red cultivars are often called 'Atropurpurea' or 'Rubra', blue ones 'Glauca', and yellow forms 'Aurea'. Though red- and blue-leaved variants still have a good

Clintonia borealis. **Blue bead lily** is aptly named, for the berries are a rich, deep blue when mature. The blue flavonoids in the berries' skin attract birds, which eat the fruit and disperse the seeds.

TOP LEFT: *Liriope muscari* 'Okina'. The ghostly white emerging leaves of this lily-turf cultivar lack any pigment except at their very tips. Albinos like this usually perish because they cannot photosynthesize, but fortunately, as Okino's leaves mature, they gradually turn pale green as some chlorophyll develops.

TOP RIGHT: *Polemonium occidentale*. We found this mutant Jacob's ladder at the Nasami Farm nursery. Its leaves contain only small patches of chlorophyll, so the underlying yellow pigment carotenoid is clearly visible. Unfortunately, the plant lacked vigor because of its reduced photosynthetic capacity.

BOTTOM RIGHT: Some species display remarkable pigmentation only at certain times of the year. The young leaves of *Epimedium* × *omeiensis* (a natural hybrid barrenwort from China) are beautifully marbled in reds and yellows, perhaps to simulate leaf damage and discourage attack. The leaves mature to deep green.

Porteranthus trifoliatus. Depending on the pH of its sap, the anthocyanin pigments in the dying leaves of **Bowman's root** can be pink, red, maroon, or orange.

complement of chlorophyll, yellow selections often have reduced chlorophyll levels and as such may lack the vigor and size of the green-leaved versions (this is because the yellow flavenoid pigments are more easily masked by green chlorophyll, so levels of chlorophyll must be unusually low for the yellow to be seen). As a leaf matures, chlorophyll levels naturally increase, and colored leaves tend to become increasingly green as they age. Of course, many green leaves become brightly colored in the fall as the chlorophyll that masks other pigments begins to fade for good.

Autumn Fires

Why do some perennials color as they do? Surely it cannot be merely for our pleasure. Some woody species such as black gum (*Nyssa sylvatica*) and Virginia creeper (*Parthenocissus quinquefolius*) flush crimson or maroon to attract birds to their ripe crop of fruits, but with perennials, brilliant fall color seems merely a happy accident born of climate and physiology brought together just so.

Chlorophyll is green because it absorbs the blue and red wavelengths of light and reflects back the green. Chlorophyll may be the dominant pigment in most healthy leaves, but individual chlorophyll molecules do not survive long under a punishing barrage of ultraviolet radiation, and so they need to be continually replaced. As the days become shorter and the perennial shuts down for winter, the production of chlorophyll dwindles away. As the chlorophyll fades, the more decay-resistant yellow carotenoids are unmasked. Since they are necessary for photosynthesis and as such are present at high levels in most leaves, most leaves turn carotenoid yellow as they die. These are the pigments that lend bluestars (*Amsonia* spp.) and Solomon's seal (*Polygonatum* spp.) such lovely buttery color in the fall.

Plants lose their leaves by forming an abscission layer at the base of the petiole where the leaf attaches to the stem. In response to the shortening days of late summer, this corky ring of tissue plugs up the sugar-conducting phloem tissues, preventing the sweet by-products of photosynthesis from leaving the leaf. After the phloem is plugged, water can still get to the leaf via the xylem, so it may continue photosynthesizing and producing sugar as long as some chlorophyll remains. Some species—for reasons unknown—convert this trapped sugar into anthocyanins, which are less abundant in the leaf during the growing season. Anthocyanins are sensitive to the pH of the cell sap. Acidic sap makes them show up flaming red and red orange, while in alkaline ooze they are more maroon or pink. Some species, such as Bowman's root (*Porteranthus trifoliatus*), seem to vary the pH of their sap depending on their mood, so their leaves run the gamut from orange and red to pink and maroon. Since this group of pigments is really just a by-product of frustrated photosynthesis, the more photosynthesis, the more by-product; the more by-product, the more intense the coloration will be. Thus, leaves in the sun usually color better than those in the shade. Sunny days combined with cool, not cold, nights also spur photosynthesis, slowing pigment degradation, and accordingly, yielding better color displays. Stress brought on by summer drought may intensify color as well—probably because it gets the dormancy process going more quickly in fall. Fertilizing plants late in the year can decrease the intensity of fall color because a high level of nitrogen and phosphorus in the leaf both encourages chlorophyll production and discourages anthocyanin formation. Autumns characterized by cool, cloudy weather may produce poor fall color, as late-season photosynthesis is reduced markedly under these conditions.

So what is the purpose of fall color? The answer is probably that it is just a lucky combination of the right weather conditions—warm, moderately dry summers; cool, sunny falls; and the process of leaf abscission and carbohydrate translocation. That explains the yellow of most leaves, but why some plants such as Bowman's root or little bluestem go to the trouble of producing seemingly useless red and orange pigments is still a great mystery. Maybe they are just trying to soften the blow of winter after all.

Variegation

Occasionally, a chance mutation in the meristematic cells of an embryo or even the tip of a branch or rhizome in a more mature plant will cause the chlorophyll-containing tissues to appear variegated (striped or patterned in white, yellow, and various shades of green). The affected tissues contain some meristematic cells that can produce chlorophyll and others that do not. Because these two cell types are genetically different, you may hear a variegated plant called a chimera. (A chimera, like Frankenstein, is a composite of two or more genetically different tissues. Fortunately, plant chimeras are usually far more attractive than the creature from Mary Shelley's novel.) Where chlorophyll is absent and not masked by other pigments, the leaf or stem appears white, and where it is present the leaves are green. Zones where these two types overlap are often lighter green or yellow. The pattern of variegation is dependent on the arrangement of the mutant meristem cells. Imagine the apical meristem of the shoot as segregated into a set of layers. Each layer gives rise to a specific part or parts of the leaf and stem. When the mutant cells are evenly spread through part of a layer, the resulting variegation is balanced fairly equally over the two sides of the leaf. (If you fold the leaf along the midvein, the patterning will generally match up.) This type is called periclinal variegation because the mutated cells lie at the tip of the meristem. If the mutant cells are just at the apex of the tip, the leaf will have a white zone in the middle and green along the sides (central variegation). If the mutant cells are in two balanced patches on either side of the tip, the leaf will have a green center with white bands down the side (marginal variegation). A tremendous number of cultivars available from nurseries have periclinal variegation, and for good reason. The patterning is quite striking and relatively stable over time. Nowhere is variegation and its inheritance more studied than among the hostas (*Hosta*). This most popular of perennials is well known for the lovely

TOP LEFT: *Zizia aptera* 'Crazy Quilt'. I discovered this heart-leaved golden Alexanders in a flat of seedlings. The leaves exhibit an interesting marginal periclinal variegation. You can see from this close-up how the absence of chlorophyll (white tissue) is confined to discrete layers within the leaf. Where green and white layers overlap, the leaf appears gray.

TOP RIGHT: *Liatris squarrosa* 'Ivory Towers'. Another seedling discovery, but in this case the variegation is the more unstable mericlinal type. Notice how the white leaves are concentrated along one side of the stem and the mostly green leaves along the opposite side. This cultivar was abandoned because it eventually put up either all white or all green shoots.

BOTTOM LEFT: *Trillium cuneatum*. Many woodland perennials exhibit natural variegation on young leaves as part of their normal development. It is thought that this pattern is meant to camouflage leaves and confuse herbivores.

BOTTOM RIGHT: *Phytolacca americana* 'Silberstein'. Sectoral variegation (here in the leaf of a pokeweed cultivar) causes random stipples or blotches because of scattered patches of green or nongreen tissue in different leaf layers. The leaves of this plant appear mostly yellow because only the production of chlorophyll and not that of the flavonoid pigment is affected. Interestingly, this variety comes true from seed.

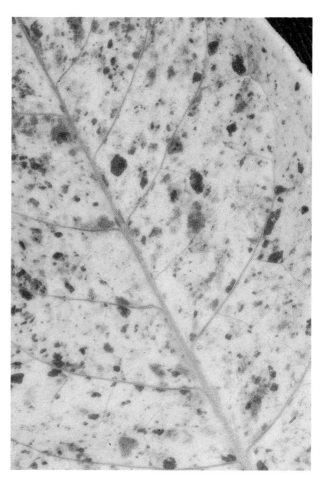

periclinal variegation patterns of various cultivars. Depending on the other pigments in the leaves and in layers adjacent to the variegated zones, leaves can be banded in shades of green, blue, silver, white, or yellow.

The other two types of variegation are far less stable, meaning that the affected tissues can revert back to the all green form very readily. Mericlinal variegation is caused when the mutated cells arise not at the tip of the apical meristem but to one side so that one side of the leaf is variegated and the other is not. Since the white cells are not at the tip, it is easy for them to be left behind as the shoot grows. (Imagine how much more readily a sheet of paper laid across the prow of a ship can remain there compared with one stuck to the side of the hull.) This type most commonly pops up here and there on normal green plants, affecting one section of a leaf or one side of a stem, but because it is both ephemeral and visually unbalanced, it is not very desirable horticulturally. The meristem is composed of several layers, each giving rise to different parts of the leaves and stems. In both periclinal and mericlinal variegation, the afflicted cells are restricted to a single layer of the meristem, but in the final type of variegation, called sectoral variegation, mutated cells spread through the different layers. Sectoral variegation creates wild and irregular patterns or stipples of white and shades of green. It is a schizophrenic chimera that is very unstable but can be very pretty, so a number of sectoral chimeras are on the market. If the mutant sectors reside at the tip of the meristem, sectoral variegation may persist over time. Sometimes, what begins as sectoral variegation will "settle out" on some shoots into one layer at the tip and become periclinal. When we find a seedling or sport with sectoral variegation (a sport is a branch or stem from a normal green plant that has mutated), we pull it aside to watch it for a few seasons. Sometimes the sector will align over the tip of some shoots and stabilize, but more likely it will just disappear after a while. Because leaf variegation is easy to spot, even in young seedlings, we find a few every year at the nursery (we germinate over half a million seeds each year, so even one in a million mutations like this do occur) and we keep an eye on them. Because the tendency to produce chimeras is a heritable trait, when we raise seedlings from a variegated plant, the chance for variegated offspring increases substantially. Of 200 seeds sown from a mericlinally variegated blazing star (*Liatris squarrosus*) I discovered and nicknamed 'Ivory Towers', we selected eight variegated offspring that we will now collect seed from: 1 in 25 is certainly better odds than 1 in 1,000,000. Our hope is to discover a stable seedling from this unstable parent.

Viral infection in leaf tissues can manifest as irregular or striped variegation caused by the death of chloroplasts in the affected areas. Because the virus affects the cells through the whole mesophyll of the leaf, the infected area is often sunken as well as discolored. Once you see it, it is easy to distinguish viral infection from chimeral variegation. Viral infection is incurable, and affected plants should be disposed of.

A number of woodland perennials, such as some lungworts (*Pulmonaria*), jack-in-the-pulpits (*Arisaema*), trilliums (*Trillium*), and wild gingers (*Asarum*), are naturally variegated. This type is called structural variegation in that it is not the result of a chimera but rather represents the natural pigmentation pattern of the leaf. The purpose of this variegation is not known, but it must confer some evolutionary advantage, because structurally variegated leaves contain less chlorophyll than all-green ones, and in a shady habitat, lots of chlorophyll is important. The most likely explanation is camouflage (Givnish 1990). The patterning on the emerging leaves of the whippoorwill trillium (*Trillium cuneatum*) bears a striking similarity to deer hunter's camouflage, and it seems likely to me that it serves to hide the vulnerable leaves from deer and other browsers. The spotting on lungwort leaves may be designed to mimic leaf damage from caterpillars or leaf miners. Adult insects avoid damaged leaves in preference for undamaged ones, so the spotting may provide a real deterrence. Commonly, the intensity and patterning of this variegation, while completely stable from year to year in each individual, varies substantially from one plant to the next. This may help to further discourage predation by confusing the "search image" of the mammal or insect. A third hypothesis mentioned by Givnish is that the patterning on some species may act as a warning to potential munchers that the leaves contain a chemical deterrent or poison (the idea is similar to brightly colored insects advertising their toxicity to birds). The fact that structural variegation is entirely restricted to shade-adapted perennials argues against its possible role in reducing leaf temperature and strengthens the hypothesis that it serves as camouflage. The patterning is much more effective at obscuring the leaf in dappled shade amid a bed of dead leaves in the forest than in the shadowless full sun against a background of green.

CHAPTER 4

STEMS

Stems are not glamorous, but they have two vital roles as far as perennials are concerned: to provide support and structure for leaves and flowers and to translocate (a fancy word for moving things around) water, sugars, and all the other compounds that circulate to and from leaves and roots.

Anatomy of a Stem

When seen in cross section, a perennial's stem is an orderly jumble of structural fibers that make the stem strong and rigid, spongy cells that give it mass, and xylem and phloem pipes that transport liquids. I will talk more about these in a bit. Whether it is growing above the ground or beneath it, the stem is simply a series of segments punctuated by joints (nodes) where leaves, side branches, roots, or flowers are attached. If you look at a very short stem or rhizome, the nodes are very close together. On a tall stem or long rhizome, the nodes are separated by much longer segments. As any

ABOVE: The striking pink flowers of this unnamed peony hybrid were formed the previous fall. Pruning the emerging stems in the spring accomplishes nothing, for it removes the flower buds and stunts the plant.

TOP LEFT: *Chelone glabra* **apical meristem.** Inside the expanding leaves atop this white turtlehead stem lies the tiny apical meristem, where leaf, stem, flower, and vasculature tissues all form from the same tiny undifferentiated (meristematic) cells.

TOP RIGHT: *Symphyotrichum novae-angliae* **stem detail.** The stem of a **New England aster** is interrupted regularly by leaf axils where a single leaf attaches. Within the axil is a dormant bud that often begins growing into a side branch. Eventually, as the day length decreases, these side branches will develop flowers. Like the beardtongue pictured below, the leaves of this aster lack a discrete petiole, so they are considered sessile.

BOTTOM LEFT: *Penstemon australis* **stem.** Because it has an opposite leaf arrangement, **Eustis Lake beardtongue's** side branches are also paired.

Hylotelephium (Sedum) telephium with *Rhus typhina* 'Tiger Eyes'. **Sedum** stems respond to decreasing day length in late summer by switching off leaf production and switching on flower-bud production. This fall-blooming perennial produces stems with fairly short internodes that do not require pruning. Each stem adjusts in length to be equal with its neighbors, so the plant develops a rounded crown.

plant grows, it can control the relative length of these stem segments to grow taller or shorter as needed. If a particular aster is growing by itself on a windy ledge, its stem segments may be only half an inch long, and as a consequence the plant will be short and bushy and less likely to blow over. The same species growing among tall grasses in a meadow might have segments that are six inches long to lift it above the competition. Both may have the exact same number of leaves, but the latter would be 12 times taller. This is also why many-stemmed species such as asters, bee balms, and phloxes develop a rounded shape as stems in the middle of the clump grow taller than those on the edges as they reach for the light.

At every node along a typical stem there is a tiny dormant bud that hides in the nook above where the leaf attaches, and each of these dormant buds can grow into a new stem if the tip is damaged. We can take advantage of this to produce shorter, bushier perennials. If you remove an actively growing stem tip, hormones travel to the dormant bud or buds just below it and spur them into growth. Thus if you pinch back a stem at the appropriate time, several new shoots will arise from it. It takes more resources to feed two than one, so the new stems will grow shorter and more slowly than a single stem would have. A second pinching two weeks later will exacerbate this, so that with some judicious nipping you can force a tall, lanky plant to be a short bushy one. Nurseries do this all the time to make taller plants look better for sale and also to make them easier to transport. It is a bit misleading for the customer, as you may think you are buying a stocky little plant only to have it zoom up to six feet once free of the relentless shears.

What and When to Prune

It is important to time your pruning to coincide with active vegetative growth and not flowering. Typically, we pinch back only those perennials that form their flower buds in the same growing season in which they bloom. To get a leg up on the season, many spring-blooming plants such as peonies and false indigos set flower buds the previous autumn. If you dig up and cut open a little dormant peony shoot in November, then look at it under the microscope, all the leaves and flower buds will be there in miniature: add warmth and water the following spring and the stem simply expands to full size and blooms. Pinching back a peony stem as it pops up in April will do nothing more than remove the flower bud and some of the leaves for that year. On the other hand, most summer- and fall-blooming perennials form flower buds during the same

TOP LEFT: *Porteranthus serrulatus.* Pinching or cutting back certain perennials at the right time of year produces shorter, bushier plants. Here I am snipping off the stem tip of a wild ipecac. Removing the apical meristem allows the side shoots to grow. After two weeks (lower image) three side shoots have taken off where formerly there was only one. Splitting resources among three shoots means they will be shorter than a single one would have been.

OPPOSITE RIGHT: *Symphyotrichum novi-belgii* **'Fellowship'.** This vigorous **New York aster** hybrid will reach four feet in good soil, but it tends to flop over when in flower. Here I have pruned back the stem tips in late June as outlined on the opposite page, and by fall the clumps have become very thick and bushy and are merely 28 inches high. Photographed after a late September rainstorm, the shorter, stockier stems have not toppled over.

growing season after the shoots are already well grown. All that comes up in spring are leafy shoots that grow for a time until changes in daylength, temperature, or other cues trigger them to start making flower buds. For these plants, a nip and a tuck during the spring or earlier summer will not affect blooming later in the season.

Another thing to remember is that because they set buds in the fall, the bloom performance of peonies, daylilies, trilliums, primroses, false indigos, or shooting stars is a reflection of the previous year's conditions rather than the present one's. If the previous year was dry or a late freeze weakened the plant, most likely it set few if any flower buds. No amount of coddling now will get it to bloom any better this season. However, your love and attention this year will be rewarded in the next. On the other hand, the performance of summer and fall bloomers such as coneflowers, asters, border phlox, mints, salvias, and coreopsis depends largely on the growing conditions in the current season. Drought or other problems in early summer will diminish or prevent flowering a few weeks later.

As a rule of thumb, I stop pinching even fall bloomers after the Fourth of July to give the buds time to form. If you continue to pinch an aster into August, you will begin to remove flower buds and greatly diminish the display.

Have You Been Working Out?

Stems are designed to resist the inevitable pull of gravity, but they also need to withstand the wind. If you have ever raised seedlings indoors and wondered why the stems are so soft and

Helianthus stem in cross section. The stem of a young **sunflower** is filled with spongy pith to give it extra strength until tissues mature and harden.

insubstantial, it is because they have never been damaged by wind. Every time a young stem is bent by a gust, small tears develop in its tissues, and each time the tissues heal, they become incrementally stronger. It is roughly what happens in our muscle tissue when we exert ourselves. No pain, no gain. Setting up an oscillating fan will strengthen your indoor seedlings in preparation for a life outdoors, but you may still have to keep them out of the worst of the wind for a few weeks until the stems have stiffened up.

If you divide a large clump of tall stems, the transplanted sections will often fall over because they have been somewhat sheltered by the mass of companions. As a precaution, I cut tall stems back by a third to a half when dividing, which reduces the chance of blowing over while also reducing the leaf area to compensate for a damaged root system. Though it hurts to do it, I also remove visible flower buds and blooms when dividing and transplanting—even when planting out potted perennials in the garden. Flowers have no stomata like leaves do, so they are a huge water drain, not to mention an energy drain on the weakened plant. As a matter of fact, pruning off flowers and seeds from any plants stressed by drought, disease, or other problems is a good idea. It will allow them to direct energy into immediate recovery and also toward surviving the winter.

Hollow to the Core

Most perennial stems have a spongy core called the pith. It is composed of large, loosely packed cells that give young stems extra stiffness and a place to store food reserves. Often the pith disintegrates in older sections of the stem as the diameter of the stem increases and pulls the pith apart, leaving the stem hollow at the core. The pith is not structurally strong, so its loss is not of consequence to the mature stem.

Plumbing

Both xylem and phloem are essentially networks of pipes running from root tip to stem tip. Xylem tubes are bigger and concerned primarily with water transport, while the smaller phloem conducts sugars, hormones, nutrients, and other metabolites.

A heart is a luxury that plants do not have, so how do they pump fluids through their pipes? Water is absorbed through roots by osmosis. As water is forced in, pressure

Iris cristata. On damp mornings after a soaking rain, it is common to see drops of water along leaf margins. This is due to guttation—root pressure forcing excess water out of special cells.

builds up in the roots and forces the water upward in the xylem tubes. On cool, humid nights, when transpiration slows and the ground is good and moist, you may notice drops of water beading up along the edge of leaves. This phenomenon, called guttation, is the simple result of excess root pressure. Certain pores in the leaves act like safety valves that open to release the excess water and reduce water pressure inside the plant before the pipes burst. Root pressure alone is not nearly strong enough to pump water up the stem on a hot, sunny day, though. Water is primarily *pulled* up by the negative pressure that develops in the leaves as water evaporates from their pores. I will not bore you with complicated fluid mechanics, so suffice it to say that plants move water not with a pump but with a vacuum cleaner. As water molecules exit the leaf via the stomata, they create a figurative vacuum that literally pulls the ones just below them up to take their place. Each of these in turn pulls the next in a column that stretches all the way down to the roots. The vacuum is incredibly strong, pulling water to the top of even 300-foot-tall trees without trouble. However, if the soil becomes excessively dry and roots cannot absorb water fast enough, the negative pressure can simply break the water column in a xylem tube—effectively rendering it temporarily useless. With the proper listening equipment, you can actually hear little pops in the stems of drought-stressed plants as the tiny water columns break. Fortunately, once it rains, nighttime root pressure will push out the air bubbles and restore the flow. This is one reason that a nice, gentle all-night rain will do more to restore badly wilted plants than a few passes with the hose. (The other reason is that the slow trickle permeates deeper into parched soil than a quick flood.)

Getting the Sugar Where It Is Needed

Water flows one way up from roots to stems, leaves, and flowers in the xylem, whereas the phloem transports liquids (primarily sugars) from the leaves down to roots and up to young shoots. There are several competing theories regarding the mechanism for transporting sugars through the phloem, but the one that most researchers seem to agree on is driven by simple osmotic pressure gradients. Basically, as leaves or roots pump high concentrations of dissolved sugars into the phloem tubes on one end, they are forced to flow toward areas of lower concentration (where they are being used up) through osmosis. It is an elegant system in that the faster sugars are used up in one area the faster more flow in.

One of my first jobs out of college was working in a lab that studied translocation of sugars in wheat. We placed little tents over individual wheat plants at different stages of maturity and injected radioactive carbon dioxide into the enclosure. After a set amount of time, the tent was removed and the plants allowed to continue to grow for a set length of time. They were collected and dried, and it was my enviable task to carefully separate the dried plants into roots, leaves, stems, flowers, and seeds and grind up these various parts in a little mill. I then weighed each pile of powder, then dumped it into little bottles filled with a euphemistically named, nasty-smelling concoction called scintillation fluid, which absorbs radiation so it can be counted in a large, conveyer-like Geiger counter. Because we knew how much carbon was supplied via the gas, we could get a realistic idea about where the products of photosynthesis end up at different times in the growth cycle. Wheat is an annual, so not surprisingly, most of the carbon ended up in young leaves, flowers, and seeds, but in an herbaceous perennial, most of the stuff winds up in the roots. In the language of plant physiology, tissues that provide the sugar are called sources, and the tissues that use it for growth or convert it to starch for storage are called sinks. One of a perennial's biggest challenges is to coordinate this appropriation of sugar so that leaves and flowers get made, seeds birthed, fungi and bacteria in the rhizosphere fed, and after all is said and done still wind up with enough energy reserves for dormancy.

Stocking Up

If you have ever had any experience with solar panels, you know that they are usually hooked up to an array of batteries that collect and store surplus electricity generated by the solar cells, to be utilized at night or on very cloudy days. Plants capture the sun's energy chemically, not electrically. When chloroplasts are active on a sunny, warm day, simple sugars produced by photosynthesis are carried in the phloem to the carbon sinks—storage organs in various parts of the plant that convert sugars into more stable and space-saving starch compounds. Starches are just long chains of sugar molecules that can be metabolized for energy or synthesized into other molecules needed by the plant. Typically, the younger, mature leaves near the top of the stem shunt energy to the shoot tip and developing leaves. Older leaves send their sugars to the roots, while those in the middle of the stem can send them either up or down. Leaves on one side of the stem are connected with those above and below by the phloem tubes, and these feed the roots on their side.

Imagine how large your batteries would have to be if your solar panels shut down for four to six months at a time. Perennial plants need to sequester large quantities of starch during the growing season to keep them alive during the winter and to provide the considerable energy necessary to leaf out again in the spring. Building up adequate reserves for these two critical tasks is the primary goal of perennials during the growing season. Flowering and seed set will happen

Anemone occidentalis. Photographed in mid-August atop Mt. Rainer in Washington after an especially hard winter, this **anemone** has just emerged from the melting snow and now has only six short weeks to flower, set seed, and store away enough carbohydrates for another ten-month slumber. It is a formidable task with life-or-death consequences.

only when food reserves remain above a critical level. If you could chart the starch reserves in a hypothetical perennial's roots like you can the power remaining in a battery, it might look like the following graph.

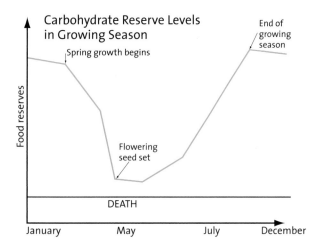

Food reserves peak toward the end of the growing season, after the plant has been photosynthesizing all summer. Once the stems die down for the winter, the roots, crown, and/or rhizomes use some of the reserves for low-level metabolism while the plant is dormant. The big drain on starch reserves comes in spring as the plant harnesses most of its sup-

ply to grow new leaves, stems, flowers, and seeds. Remember that only mature leaves can start producing sugars again, so starch levels do not start to rise until well into spring. Like a car running out of gas, if spring growth demands more carbohydrate reserves than the plant can muster (say, its roots—and their store of starch—were badly damaged by rodents during the winter) the plant will die. Ironically, when is it that we buy, transplant, and divide most of our perennials? We buy them when they are in flower, of course. We are stressing out our plants at their weakest point in the year, as the following graph illustrates:

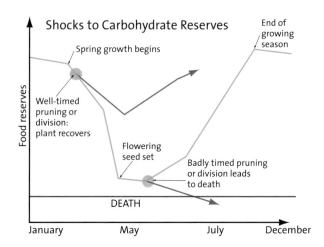

In this example, the same plant suffers a very different fate if divided or pruned in early spring, when most of the reserves are still in the roots, as compared to late spring, when the stores are badly depleted. The first eventually rebounds after using some of its stores to grow new leaves and roots, while the second "runs out of gas" and dies.

To prevent your prized perennials from redlining, schedule surgery for early spring or fall whenever possible, and realize that late-spring and early-summer division and transplanting carry more risk and require more attention to watering, disease prevention, and the like.

Shop in the Discount Bin

Though you may not believe it after plunking down $12 for a potted perennial, it is difficult for nurseries to turn a profit without growing plants in considerable volumes. Most perennial growers produce two, three, or even four crops a year, by pushing them to grow much more rapidly than they would in the garden or the wild. It is amazing how fast most perennials will grow in a greenhouse if they are supplied with all the water and fertilizer they can handle. Being in the business myself for many years, I sympathize with the growers, but I do worry that you, the gardener, are not getting the best possible product with this system. In essence, what sells the best are perennials with a flush of new leaves and blooms, and through manipulation of light, water, temperature, and fertilizer, it is possible to produce what are in essence plants in that initial flush of spring growth all season long. You can buy spring-blooming bleeding hearts in August and fall-blooming asters in June, but what effect does this have on each plant's long-term survival? As the graph above shows, plants in that spring-flush stage are at their weakest—no matter what time of year it is. Low starch reserves are further stressed if the plant is out of sync with the natural rhythms of the seasons. Lush perennials coming out of heated greenhouses too early are vulnerable to late frosts, and others forced to grow too late in the season have trouble going dormant in time for winter. From the plant's perspective, the best time to purchase it would be either just as it is going dormant after a good season's growth in the nursery, or in spring when it is still dormant or just beginning to grow (perennials that are overwintered in pots and sold in spring are called vernalized plants). Of course such plants will either look a bit yellow and moth eaten in the fall or be hardly showing any sign of life in the spring. The difference though is that they have good to excellent energy reserves to produce new roots once transplanted (which, of course, is every transplant's first order of business). A big, leafy, flowering perennial pushed to the limit at the nursery may be tempting on the sales bench, but it will have little or no food reserves to help it put down roots or to deal with that late frost or

Monarda bradburiana. As the heavy dews of autumn set in, Bradbury's bee balm ceases stem growth and begins to withdraw belowground. Though not as tempting as a plant in flower, this large and somewhat tired-looking potted plant will have a much better chance of surviving transplanting than one stressed by flowering and active growth.

unseasonable heat. In the end, often the prettiest-looking plant is the biggest risk. The irony is that you are paying top dollar for the blooming one when the better bargain is usually the slightly moth-eaten specimen or the one that is yet to show much growth. Just as you should never let the faded color of the walls or outdated light fixtures sway you from buying a house that others might pass up, so too look for perennials that are a bit long in the tooth but otherwise healthy. Buy plants before they bloom, if possible, and trim off some or all the flowers of those in bloom to conserve resources, because once weakened, it may take longer for the plant to recover than you might think.

Long-Term Consequences

If a plant is slow growing by nature or under stress from transplanting, heavy shade, drought, insect attack, or other factors, it may not have the reserves to flower every year.

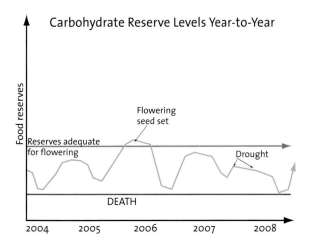

In the hypothetical graph above, growing conditions are only favorable enough for this fall-blooming species to flower in 2005. A severe drought in the summer of 2007 forces it into early dormancy, dangerously taxing reserves so that it barely has enough left to leaf out in 2008. Another bad drought year in 2008 would likely do in the weakened plant. All the consequences of stressors such as droughts, severe winters, or herbivory are not immediately apparent, but they directly affect the food stores of the plant; they can have cumulative, lasting consequences. The individual in this example might need several more years of favorable growing conditions to recover sufficiently to flower again. With lower food reserves, its ability to grow roots and leaves and manufacture defensive chemicals will also be compromised, which can have a cascading effect that may lead to death a year or two in the future, when our memory of the causal event has long since faded. On the other hand, when we fertilize, water, mulch, or squash Japanese beetles gleefully between our fingernails, we are helping our perennials stay healthy by allowing them to sock away higher levels of food reserves than they otherwise could. This insures they will thrive and flower to their utmost. The next time a well-meaning person asks what you *do* all day in the garden, just reply "starch management." That should sufficiently confound them to allow a smooth change of subject.

Controlling Who Gets What

When I picture sugars flowing from leaves to shoots, flowers, or roots as needed, I wonder, "What insures that every part gets its fair share of the pie?" We all know that plants do not have a central nervous system, as we do, but they do have ways of effecting some centralized control over their various body parts. Without this, roots, flowers, shoots, and seeds would all be demanding all the sugar all the time, just like five-year-olds at a birthday party, and with equally chaotic results. It seems that, just like in animals, hormones provide most of the global control necessary for the plant to allocate its resources efficiently and fairly. For example, when days become shorter and nights become cooler in fall, production of the dormancy hormone abscisic acid increases in many plant cells. Part of its effect is to actually slow sugar uptake by young leaves and stimulate roots to gather up more of it to convert to starch. As the leaves begin to request less and the roots request more, the pressure gradient to the latter increases and more sugar flows downward in the phloem. Furthermore, if the roots are really working quickly and removing dissolved sugars from the phloem at a high rate, they will cause a decrease in turgor pressure in their phloem. Think of a garden hose that is hooked up to an open spigot. When the spray nozzle if shut off, the hose plumps up, and when the sprayer is turned on, the water flows out and the hose markedly deflates (loses turgor). This rapid change in turgor is relayed through the phloem in a way that is analogous to the electrical signals sent through an animal's nervous system to alert the source tissue (in this example, mature leaves) to pump in more sugar into the phloem. Plants have a water vacuum instead of a heart and turgor pressure in lieu of neurons, but they are not so unlike us after all.

Green Side Up

One of the most basic things that stems as well as roots and leaves need to figure out is which direction to grow in. This may seem so obvious as to not even be worth mentioning, but it is a huge first step for a seedling, and all subsequent growth depends on the proper orientation of the plant's respective tissues. One of the first clues that an emerging root or a germinating spore has regarding its position comes from a sort of streaming current that flows from the soil through certain cells. It is called the transcellular current and is composed mainly of calcium ions that rush into the developing root tips and out again. Roots and root hairs orient themselves toward the influx of calcium like salmon following the taste of their birth waters upstream. Light is also a simple navigation aid. Light shining on one side of a stem or leaf petiole will cause the cells on the other side to grow more quickly so that the stem curves toward the light source, while that same light will have the opposite effect on a root. But the most elegant method by which stems and roots find their way is by what is called geotropism, or gravitropism. Basically, there are special cells in the various plant parts that contain little starch grains suspended in fluid. Like the snow in a snow globe, the grains

Diphylleia cymosa. It is remarkable that plants have centralized control over the allocation of resources throughout their bodies without benefit of a central nervous system. In spring (top left) expanding leaves demand much of the food stored in the roots. Soon afterward, flowers (left) become the most demanding carbohydrate sink. As seed is shed (top right), the leaves turn yellow as energy flows once again to rhizomes and roots.

free-fall and settle to the lowest point of the cell, where their presence is perceived by special receptors in the cell wall. If the plant is blown over by the wind, the starch grains in the growing shoots are dislodged and resettle in the new downward position, which alerts neighboring cells on the downward side of the stem to stretch, righting the growing tip again. Older shoots and petioles are too stiff to respond to the change in direction, so the older parts of the plant remain horizontal. Thus, if you want to stake or train stems, start when they are young and supple. Older stems and leaves will always look a bit off kilter if staked in a new position.

Plant Hormones

Whether we like it or not, much of our lives are controlled not by our wills but by our endocrine systems. During most of our daily activities, the role hormones play may go unnoticed for the most part. But at certain times, their effects simply cannot be ignored or denied. Take conception and pregnancy, for example. The sheer impossibility of the whole process—from menstruation to ovulation and the resultant spike in desire, followed by conception, weeks of violent retching as the body is overwhelmed by the influx of hormones stimulated by others produced by the growing embryo, then ravenous hunger, mood swings, labor and birth, lactation, bigger mood swings, bonding—is all controlled by hormones. Of course, the brain, pituitary, and other organs control the production of hormones, but in many cases, even this is controlled by yet other hormones. Divine intervention and free will aside, our purpose in life may be to reproduce and pass on our genes, but it is our hormones that make sure the job gets done right. It is the reason why weight loss or abstinence-only sexual education programs, which rely on reason to subdue hormones, are bound to fail. If we could just accept the uneasy truth that our hormones are in charge, there would be many fewer disappointed dieters and teenage mothers in the world.

Endocrine systems are one of the things we have most in common with plants, though without conscious thought, they are much more willing to acquiesce to the hormonal sway than we are. Hormones are the primary means by which the whole organism can maintain some control over its various parts. This is important to stress and represents a profound leap forward in evolutionary terms. The only way plants could climb out of the primordial ooze—to progress beyond mats of single-celled algae—was to develop some sort of more or less centralized command and control network both to guide the growth and development of roots, stems, flowers, and leaves and to make sure that all parts cooperate and work together for the greater good. A mat of single-celled algae is a lawless place where each cell basically does what it wants. As a consequence, mats of single-celled algae are pretty unremarkable

Asclepias tuberosa. Figuring out which way is up is one of the first critical skills a baby plant must acquire. Thanks to special gravity-sensing cells filled with starch grains, these **butterfly weed** seedlings have passed the test.

from a structural standpoint. Hormones provided the language and the laws that allowed plants to move from a state of single-celled chaos to the complex, multicellular civilization we know as a perennial or tree. Plant hormones are of great interest to the propagator, since the art of plant multiplication relies heavily on the use and manipulation of hormones. However, if you have ever pinched back a plant that had grown floppy in the shade or wondered why your coneflower seeds did not sprout, the following information will be quite illuminating. You cannot hope to understand another civilization unless you first study its language and laws.

Plant hormones are small molecules that are either synthesized locally or transported from one place to another. Plant cell walls have a variety of protein receptors, each recognizing and binding with a specific hormone should it pass by. Once bound with the receptor, the hormone may trigger the release of other chemicals that produce the desired effect within the cell, or it may directly switch on or off certain of the cell's genes. For example, if a plant is being shaded, auxin (one of the primary plant hormones) is released by the leaves and picked up by receptors in the stem tips that activate genes that make the stem grow longer (Dharmasiri et al. 2005). In another example, when a rice plant comes under attack by specific bacteria, a hormone is released by the infected cells ordering the genes to manufacture bacteria-killing hydrogen peroxide and additionally ordering the destruction of the very same cells that gave the order. This is not the sort of cellular self-sacrifice you would expect to find in a colony of algal cells.

There are five primary groups of plant hormones: abscisic acid, ethylene, auxins, gibberellins, and cytokinins. The first two are thought of as growth inhibiting hormones and the last three as growth promoters. This hormonal yin and yang maintains balance in the plant and allows it to respond appropriately to emergencies as well as to the predictable seasonal rhythms of its particular place.

ABSCISIC ACID

Abscisic acid (ABA) is a fairly simple terpenelike compound manufactured in the leaves from carotenoid pigments. It is primarily a stress and dormancy hormone that is also important in seed dormancy. When a perennial is under drought stress, the chloroplasts begin to synthesize ABA very rapidly, which causes the stomata in the leaves to snap shut to reduce water loss through transpiration. Concurrently, it stimulates roots to grow and absorb more water. If the drought persists, ABA will slow or stop stem growth and also indirectly trigger leaf drop by encouraging the buildup of ethylene. Anyone who has gardened is aware that plants under strong to severe drought stress will stop growing and begin to drop leaves, and this is thought to be primarily the result of changes wrought in the plant by high levels of ABA. The hormone is also implicated in the immune response to wounding, but its other primary function appears to be in the initiation of dormancy. The lower night temperatures and shorter days of fall trigger

Cornus canadensis. The onset of cold weather last fall triggered a spike in abscisic acid that spurred dormancy in this bunchberry. Now, as the weather warms, the hormone levels have dropped and fresh green leaves begin to expand.

an increase in ABA in plant tissues, which also induces leaf drop and forces crown or stem buds into dormancy. In a dry year like 2007, drought stress exacerbates this effect, and the plants go dormant a few weeks earlier than they typically do in a normal rainfall year. You may have heard that watering and fertilizing your plants too late in fall will delay the onset of dormancy and thus increase the chances of winter damage. In this case, the good growing conditions stimulate the production of growth hormones and *not* ABA, so the plant will keep growing longer than it should. In the nursery we routinely decrease watering in late summer and early fall to stress the plants slightly in order to nudge them toward dormancy. Of course this is a delicate procedure—too much drought will compromise carbohydrate reserves, but a bit of midday wilting will quickly bring about a slowing and hardening off of growth and the first glimpses of fall color. Unless you are out there with the liquid fertilizer every week, established garden plants that are normally winter-hardy in your area will not require this hydro diet, but it is a good trick to keep in your toolshed, especially when planting in the fall. When planting perennials after Labor Day that have been growing lushly in the nursery, I water them in well but then hold back on the hose until I see some wilting. This will both slow or stop top growth and promote the root growth necessary to anchor the plants for winter.

For the propagator, ABA is important primarily because it prevents seeds from germinating prematurely. The majority of perennials native to temperate climates produce seeds that germinate in spring, when the weather has moderated and the promise of a full growing season stretches out before the young plant like an endless string of golden sunrises. This all seems perfectly logical from a planning perspective, but what keeps the seeds from germinating as soon as they fall into the damp earth after they ripen in summer or fall? The seed can tell time, so to speak, in several ways, but the most common involves ABA. As a seed becomes mature, high levels of ABA build up in its tissues to prevent the little seedling from growing as soon as it hits the warm ground. Levels remain high through the rest of the growing season but slowly begin to decrease as the seed is exposed to temperatures below 45 degrees F. After a sufficient number of chilling days or months, the ABA level in the seed becomes very low, allowing the seed to germinate under the sway of growth hormones. Of course the winters are much shorter in Alabama or Spain than in Illinois and Norway, so the number of chilling days necessary to accomplish this varies greatly from species to species and even within the same species over its range. For example, seeds of perennial sunflowers (*Helianthus* spp.) native to the Canadian prairies require a month or more of chilling to germinate properly, while sunflowers from Georgia require little or none.

ETHYLENE

One bad apple spoils the whole bunch because overripe fruits produce quantities of ethylene, the only gaseous plant hormone. Ethylene is a simple hydrocarbon (C_2H_4) that is synthesized in all plant tissues, usually in response to some stress such as flooding, drought, cold, or disease, or to hasten or delay flowering, trigger fruit ripening, or cause leaf drop (senescence). Being a very simple hydrocarbon, it is also an extremely important industrial product, as it can be used as a building block to create all sorts of other organic molecules including plastics such as polyethylene, polystyrene, and polyester; organic solvents such as toluene and ethylbenzene; antifreeze (ethylene glycol); alcohol (ethanol); and even aspirin.

In the world of green plants, not manufacturing plants, ethylene, like ABA, is involved in stress reactions and the dormancy process. One of the most interesting stress-induced ethylene responses occurs after flooding. As I discussed on p. 39, flooding of plant roots and the subsequent decrease in oxygen inhibit water uptake and create a drought situation in the plant. Flooded roots send a chemical message to leaves that cause leaf petioles to bend downward (a phenomenon called epinasty). One theory is that the leaves are thus able to flap up and down in the breeze like pump handles and that this actually does create a vacuum that pulls water into the roots and up the stem. It is an engaging theory, if nothing else, and explains why weeping willows are always weeping: "epinastic willow" just doesn't have the same ring. Ethylene is also important in leaf drop. Levels build in the leaf in response to ABA, causing the layer of cells between the leaf petiole and the stem to harden and separate, cutting off the leaf from the rest of the plant, which then colors, withers, and falls off. The hormone will also prevent young flowers from opening and cause open flowers to wither.

If you breathe small concentrations of ethylene, it produces a mild, pleasurable euphoria, and since ethylene is present in floral scents, especially sweet, penetrating ones, it is possible or even likely that every time you take a big whiff of a lily or gardenia, you are really "doin' drugs, man." Could part of our love affair with flowers be just a Pavlovian response to their mild narcotic effects? Think about it the next time you stop to smell the flowers.

The ancient Egyptians discovered that a ripe fruit will hasten the ripening of green ones when in a closed container, and to this day ethylene is employed by fruit and vegetable

Paeonia suffruticosa. **Perhaps the joy we feel after inhaling the heady scent of a tree peony is partly due to a brief ethylene high!**

growers to color unripe fruit, though as we all know, ethylene cannot give a green tomato that vine-ripened taste! The presence of fairly high levels of ethylene may also explain why, like sweet-scented flowers, ripe fruit is so pleasant to sniff.

Auxins

There are three families of growth-promoting hormones: auxins, gibberellins, and cytokinins. Auxins are concentrated in young growing tissues and especially in growing tips (meristems) of shoots and rhizomes. They promote cell division and elongation in the stem tip and also suppress the growth of lateral shoots lower down the stem. In a branching perennial such as a chrysanthemum, high auxin levels in the main stem tip (apical meristem) of the shoot prevent the lateral buds in each leaf axil just below the tip from growing, as they would rob resources from the stem tip and produce a highly branched, more compact plant. As the stem lengthens, dormant buds lower on the stem become increasingly removed from the auxin-rich tip and are released from dormancy. These stem tips then start synthesizing auxins to suppress their own lateral buds as they grow. Now, though a tall, unbranched plant is better at competing with its neighbors, it is not the sort that makes a good potted mum. Pinching off the stem tip of a mum or any other perennial removes the source of auxin and thus releases the dormant lateral bud or buds just beneath, producing a shorter, more highly branched plant. High levels of auxin also prevent leaf drop, which is one of the reasons why pruning back your plants too late in the season or keeping them growing vigorously into the fall will affect the winter acclimatization process and subsequent winter-hardiness.

Understanding Cold-hardiness

You often hear that the only things we can count on are death and taxes, but as I write this in the last week of September, when the nights are dipping down to the lower half of the brass frog–shaped thermometer I tacked to the porch post, I can add winter to the list. While folks in the tropics swat mosquitoes and sip margaritas on the screened porch, we northerners are stacking wood, putting on storm windows, and changing the oil in the old snowblower. The perennial plants around me are also stocking up and preparing for inevitable cold. Many get their first hint of winter's approach in mid-

Delphinium cultivar with a crested stem. Occasionally the hormone system in a stem goes haywire, skewing the balance of auxins and cytokinins. The crested (fasciated) growth of this delphinium stem results from having several competing apical meristems, rather than one, arrayed in a line atop the stem. This aberration may be caused by insect attack, disease, or a spontaneous mutation.

summer, when the days start to shorten. As we shoot fireworks and roast weenies on the hibachi, the nights start to increase in length a minute or two per day. In a world of uncertainty, you can also count on this, and seeing as plants are already highly light-sensitive things, it is not surprising that the photoperiod, or length of the day, is an excellent calendar. Of course, the farther you live from the equator, the longer your summer days will be. On June 21, the days in Homer, Alaska, are almost 19 hours long, while in Houston, Texas, there are only 14 hours of daylight. By October 21, the days have dropped to just 9.75 hours in Homer, while they are still 11.25 hours in Houston. Plants native to specific latitudes have tuned their photoperiodic calendars to their place over the eons through natural selection: individuals that miscalculate the arrival of winter are quickly dispatched in favor of those that respond to the shortening days appropriately. We used to cultivate a rare species in the aster family called Alabama warbonnet (*Jamesianthus alabamensis*). It is a fall-blooming species, and flowering is triggered once the days shorten to a genetically determined length (this type of plant is called a short-day bloomer). By August 5, the days in Mobile are only 13.5 hours long, which begins the process of flower bud formation at the tips of the tall stems and insures the plant will have plenty of time to grow and bloom before the weather turns cold in December. Farther north in Massachusetts, the day is still 14.25 hours long and does not shorten to 13.25 hours until the end of the month. Consequently, when we have tried to grow Alabama warbonnet, it does not even begin to flower until late October and is more often than not cut down by frost before the first few blooms open. It is not just flowering that is affected by this confused internal clock. The processes that prepare the plant for winter are also inadvertently postponed, with potentially disastrous results. By misreading the daylength in its adopted home, the plant mistakenly senses in September that winter is months away, when in reality the cold may arrive in a matter of mere weeks.

Cold tolerance takes a lot of work to maintain, and plants—even extremely winter-hardy species—lose all cold tolerance during the warm days of summer and then only slowly build it back up again in fall and winter. There is no sense wasting precious resources maintaining cold tolerance when it is not necessary, and even when it is cold, the idea is to stay just a few steps ahead of the chill. Perennial plants go through three stages of winter dormancy: acclimation, midwinter hardiness, and deacclimation. During the summer, even very winter-hardy species that can withstand −50 degrees F in January may be killed by just a touch of frost. Decreasing daylength and then decreasing temperatures (especially night temperatures) spur the production of ABA and ethylene to ready the perennial for winter. Stem growth slows and carbohydrates are redirected to roots as leaves begin to wither. Mature tissues are more resistant to frosts than young, tender ones, so this is a good first step. Excessive fertilization and watering in late summer raises auxin levels that counteract the effects of the dormancy hormones and delay the onset of early acclimation, making your perennials more vulnerable to early frosts as well as more extreme cold further on. During early acclimation, the plants can weather light frosts, and these light frosts as well as temperatures below 40 degrees F trigger further cold tolerance to develop. In this later stage of acclimation, temperatures just above freezing, rather than daylength, are the important trigger. Ice is of course the big danger to plant cells. Since water expands when it freezes, ice crystals can blow cells apart. Cold-mediated increases in ABA induce plant cells to lose some water and increase concentrations of sugars and other cryoprotectant proteins and alcohols. Like antifreeze in your car, these lower the freezing point of water to 20 degrees F or even 10 degrees F. This corresponds to USDA hardiness zones 8 and 7, and many perennials are hardy to these temperatures. After completing this acclimation process, they are able to withstand hard freezes without harm. If we experience a period of cold in fall followed by two to four weeks of unseasonably warm temperatures, plants can actually lose some of their cold tolerance. This happened in much of the Northeast during the winter of 2006/07. We had record warmth in December and January. I

Carex laxiculmis. Ice crystals forming on the outside of this spreading **sedge** leaf may do no harm, but should they form inside, they would slash the cells asunder.

Opuntia polyacantha. Cold-hardy prickly pear cacti withdraw most of the water from their succulent stems in the fall, effectively increasing the concentration of solutes in their fluids and thus lowering their freezing point.

Muhlenbergia capillaris. Hair-awn muhly grass from North Carolina will not survive the winter in southern New England, but seed from locally native Connecticut plants will do fine. Through natural selection, plants evolve the proper cold-hardiness for their particular region.

remember going on a family walk in early January with the air temperature approaching 70 degrees F. In late January, the temperature abruptly fell, and February was very cold, with disastrous effects on many typically hardy perennials.

For perennials to withstand colder temperatures without the benefit of a thick insulating layer of snow, they have to control the formation of ice crystals in their tissues. Very cold-hardy plants (those hardy to USDA zone 3, or –40 degrees F) are able to prevent ice crystal formation in their cells. You have probably heard of planes seeding clouds to produce rain. One technique is to spray silver iodide crystals into clouds. The crystals act as nuclei or nucleation points on which ice crystals begin to grow, and it is these ice crystals that fall as rain once they melt at lower levels of the atmosphere. Ice crystals in cells need nucleation points to begin forming, too, so very cold-hardy plants prevent them forming by removing potential nuclei from the cellular and intracellular fluids. Such fluids become, in effect, supercooled and can withstand temperatures as low as –40 degrees F without damage. Below this tem-

perature, ice crystals will form without nucleation points, and this explains why USDA zone 3 is the lower winter-hardiness limit for even many very cold-hardy species. The list of perennials that can survive below –40 degrees F without snow cover is relatively small, but a few high-alpine and tundra species can weather temperatures around –60 degrees F (USDA zone 1) with a combination of supercooling and cellular dehydration that removes much of the water from cells that the ice needs to grow. Their cellular membranes are also fairly flexible and resilient so they can resist the thrust of ice crystals.

So, winter-hardiness is a combination of first the proper recognition of day-length cues and response to cool temperatures to slow and stop growth and build up food stores. Water content decreases and cryoprotectants increase to shield the plants from the subfreezing temperatures that follow, and very cold-hardy species also prevent ice crystal nucleation and growth. A *Crinum erubescens* (a swamp lily) from South America can withstand temperatures as low as about 10 degrees F by lowering the water content and increasing antifreeze levels, but it lacks the genes to allow supercooling. You can grow some crinum lilies in the warmer parts of USDA zone 6, where the ground does not freeze too deeply, but unless the genus undergoes some major evolution to develop the ability to prevent ice nucleation, it is very unlikely that there will ever be a crinum that will be hardy to zone 3. However, if you are a breeder searching for the cold-hardiest crinum, you would naturally search for plants growing high in the mountains at the limit of the species' cold limits. Natural selection will have eliminated all but the most cold-hardy plants that produce the highest levels of antifreeze or a particularly effective combination of chemicals. Since, as I mentioned earlier, cold tolerance requires a lot of resources, plants from a particular region are only as winter-hardy as they have to be, so when you are looking for cold-hardy cultivars, look for those native to the coldest part of the range. Likewise, if you try a particular cultivar and it fails to overwinter even though the species is purportedly hardy in your zone, it may have originated from a warmer region. Before giving up on the species, try another selection from a more northerly place or higher elevation. One of my favorite grasses is hair-awn muhly (*Muhlenbergia capillaris*), which has become justifiably popular as a landscape specimen in its native Southeast. I tried unsuccessfully to get plants from a North Carolina source to overwinter for us in Massachusetts as they lack the full cold-hardiness necessary to survive zone 5. It was not until I obtained some seed from a rare Connecticut population that I was able to grow this plant as a perennial. Wire-awn muhly is gradually evolving increased winter-hardiness as it moves north, though −15 degrees F seems to be about its current limit. Whether it will be able to evolve even greater cold tolerance may be a moot point, since global warming is extending its comfort zone farther north by the decade.

Corydalis flexuosa. When the first utterly charming **blue corydalises** were imported into the United States from China in the early 1990s, this species was represented in cultivation by only a handful of clones, none of which proved to be extremely winter-hardy. Subsequent imports—like the form pictured here from plantsman Darryl Probst—are far hardier. Cold-hardiness can vary from plant to plant just as it does from one population to the next.

The heat from the earth's molten core radiates up through the bedrock and actually keeps the temperature of the soil substantially higher than the air temperature, especially if it is covered by an insulating mulch or blanket of snow. As a consequence, roots and other belowground structures are not nearly as cold-hardy as evergreen leaves, stems, and buds. Since most perennials retreat belowground for the winter, root hardiness rather than stem hardiness is the critical factor

TOP LEFT: *Helleborus niger.* **Christmas rose** is blanketed by snow until spring. When grown in mild winter climates like those of England or Georgia, it flowers in December or January.

TOP RIGHT: *Penstemon smallii* winter damage. Sometimes you gamble and lose. This **beardtongue** was killed in the unusual winter of 2006, when two months of warm weather in December and January were followed by a stretch of very cold, snowless weather in February.

BOTTOM RIGHT: *Astrolepis sinuata* and **agave.** Dry, gravelly soil prevents excess water from lingering around the roots of these desert denizens and greatly improves their winter-hardiness in cultivation.

determining their ability to survive cold. The ubiquitous groundcover Japanese pachysandra (*Pachysandra terminalis*) is rated as hardy to −30 degrees F, but its roots will die if exposed to merely 15 degrees F. For nursery growers, root hardiness is a major concern, as the roots are far more exposed to cold in a container than they are in the ground. Growers use insulating blankets, minimally heated greenhouses, and other tools to keep pot temperatures from falling below 15 or 20 degrees F. If you garden in the ground, you can still use root temperatures to your advantage when trying to overwinter marginally hardy species. We all know that thick mulches can help retain ground heat and protect sensitive roots and bulbs. Folks with reliable snow cover of more than six inches all winter can often overwinter plants rated a zone or two warmer than they should because snow is an excellent insulator. Planting tender species along the foundation of your house, where heat leakage from inside keeps the soil just a bit warmer, can make all the difference. I once worked at a state research facility that heated all its buildings from one central boiler that distributed steam via underground pipes as needed. The horticulturist was able to overwinter even subtropical plants such as bananas in zone 6 when he planted them atop the buried pipes. This did not say much about the energy efficiency of this centralized system, but it did raise eyebrows on garden tours.

Since cell dehydration is an important part of the acclimation process, waterlogged soils can lead to winterkill. This is especially true for some taprooted or fleshy-rooted perennials, as well as bulbs and species native to desert locations. Excessive water in the soil leads to higher than optimal water content of root and stem cells and subsequent freeze damage. Rock gardeners know the value of a very gritty, free-draining soil when it comes to overwintering water-sensitive species. On the other hand, persistent drought in the late summer and early fall can adversely affect the hardiness of other perennials by interfering with carbohydrate buildup in the roots.

Evergreen plants face additional challenges in the winter. When the leaves of Japanese pachysandra or any other evergreen perennial are exposed to the sun when the ground is still frozen, the leaves heat up and lose water through transpiration, which the frozen roots are unable to replace. The leaves and stems are often winter burned (effectively dried out to the point of damage or death). In my area, it is usually not until late February or March, when the sun has regained some of its strength but the ground remains frozen, that winter burn occurs. The best way to avoid winter burn if you live in

Trillium pusillum var. *pusillum* emerges well after the frosts of late winter have passed.

an area that is prone to it is to plant evergreen perennials and groundcovers where they will be shaded from the southern and western sun in late winter. Since the sun is still fairly low on the horizon at this time of year, a hedge of evergreen trees or a nearby building will often cast shade on an area in February that will be sunny by the time the growing season begins and the sun is higher in the sky in spring. A deep layer of mulch applied in the autumn will keep the ground from freezing as deeply. Additionally, a light mulch of hay or a blanket of a spun-bonded row cover such as Reemay can also be effective if applied over the plants temporarily for shading during the critical two to six weeks in which winter burn occurs. Just be sure to remove the shading as soon as the ground thaws. Some folks swear by antidesiccants or antitranspirants (oil or wax sprays that coat the leaves and lessen transpiration-related water loss), though their efficacy remains in question. Many evergreen perennials can survive one bad year in three, but the loss of their leaves (and the carbohydrate and nutrient reserves they contain) will weaken the plant and may affect flowering and long-term survival.

While the acclimation process and maximum winter lows are important pieces of the winter-hardiness puzzle,

deacclimation in spring is just as critical to understand. With the onset of cold weather in late fall, high levels of ABA will prevent fully acclimatized, dormant perennials from resuming growth even if the weather warms. Once the plant has been exposed to a few weeks of subfreezing temperatures, a spell of unseasonably mild weather will not break dormancy. Only after a genetically predetermined length of cold (anywhere from one to five months below 45 degrees F) do levels of ABA drop sufficiently to allow growth to resume. Christmas rose (*Helleborus niger*) or snowdrops (*Galanthus* spp.) need very little chilling before ABA levels drop, and they bloom at the slightest hint of mild weather in midwinter. If cold returns, the plants will slow or stop growing again and resume when temperatures stay above freezing. Very few plants risk flowering during the winter, and the ones that do are usually from mild maritime or Mediterranean climates with predictably mild winters (this is the case with snowdrops). Christmas rose, on the other hand, is an alpine species from the mountains of Europe. In its native haunts, it is reliably covered all winter in deep snows that do not melt until spring, so it has little need for additional hormonally induced dormancy. In garden situations where snow cover is intermittent or absent, this lack of internal dormancy control may present a problem. Although Christmas rose is a fine garden plant in many parts of the United States, we have trouble growing it in southern New England, where it is often damaged by snowless cold following mild spells. Ironically, it is a more satisfactory plant farther north, where it is significantly colder but snow cover comes earlier and stays longer.

Even the hardiest perennials begin to lose cold resistance once their dormancy period has been satisfied and milder weather spurs them to undo some of their midwinter preparations: antifreeze levels drop, cells rehydrate, and tender young roots and shoots spring to life. Correctly timing the true onset of spring is critical for plants: grow too early and risk being killed by a late freeze; grow too late and risk losing ground to competitors. Poorly timed deacclimation is sometimes a problem when we cultivate plants from very different regions or climates. Though we cultivate our northeastern trilliums very successfully, we lose the gorgeous *Trillium chloropetalum* from California because it begins growing too early during our unpredictable spring and is cut down by frost. The timing of deacclimation, like the other stages of winter-hardiness, is fine-tuned by natural selection. Those plants that get it right year after year are the ones most likely to reproduce and pass on their genetic calendar to the next generation.

In conclusion, to be truly winter-hardy in your garden, a particular perennial needs to possess the ability to read the approach of fall, to build up sufficient countermeasures to combat the damaging effects of ice crystals, winter dampness, and winter burn, and also to read the arrival of spring correctly. As the following graph illustrates, a perennial can fail to survive the winter at any of these junctures. Species 1 acclimated well but lacked sufficient extreme cold tolerance to survive the maximum winter low temperature, which hit in mid-January. Species 2 possessed sufficient cold tolerance to survive the entire season, while species 3 weathered the extreme cold but deacclimated too quickly in spring and perished during a mid-April freeze.

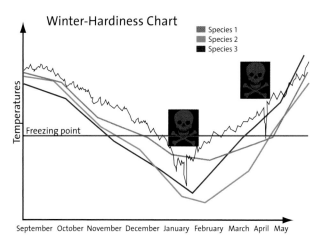

Hypothetical cold tolerance of three perennial species as plotted against actual seasonal low temperatures

Now this is an important point. Hardiness zone ratings reflect *only* a particular plant's ability to withstand extreme low midwinter temperatures. Just because a fully dormant individual rated as hardy to zone 5 can withstand −20 degrees F in January, this does not mean it can read day length or cooling temperatures correctly in fall or emerge at the proper time in spring. Winter-hardiness zone ratings should be used simply as a guide to eliminate completely appropriate species. Even so, remember that hardiness zone ratings are assigned to a species with no regard for the variation in true hardiness that it may exhibit over a large natural range. An *Arisaema triphyllum* 'Black Jack' found in the wild in northern Florida will be unlikely to possess the zone 3 hardiness of another plant grown from wild Vermont seed. It is only through first-hand experience and a lot of dead plants that you can gain a full understanding of how a particular cultivar, species, or genus will behave in your garden.

MORE ABOUT AUXINS

If you have ever applied a broadleaf weed killer to your lawn to control dandelions, plantain, and other weeds, you likely used a synthetic auxin called 2,4-dichlorophenoxyacetic acid

(2,4-D), which was discovered in the 1940s and is still the most widely applied herbicide in the world. It selectively kills dicots but not monocots or conifers, which lack the specific receptors for it. Since hay grasses, corn, wheat, rice, and all the other grains are monocots, it can be sprayed on the growing crops to kill weeds. It enters the plant and binds with auxin receptors, but unlike natural auxin, the plant cannot easily break it down, so it literally grows itself to death. The wisdom of spraying tons and tons of such a potent hormone on the food we eat and the grass our kids roll on is extremely questionable in my opinion.

The most abundant and widely studied natural auxin is indole-3-acetic acid (IAA), which cannot be easily synthesized. However, a closely analogous molecule, indole-3-butyric acid (IBA), can be easily synthesized and is the most common active ingredient in rooting powder or other rooting hormones (some preparations also contain another synthetic auxin called naphthalene acetic acid, abbreviated NAA). The auxins work by stimulating root formation in the stem's core, effectively inducing stem tissue to form adventitious roots where it would otherwise not. Most commonly, the auxin is mixed with talcum powder, which adheres to the cut end of the stem and allows the hormone to be absorbed. Professionals also use liquid preparations in which the IBA is dissolved in alcohol, antifreeze, or water. In this case, the cut stems are placed in the liquid for a few seconds up to a few minutes to allow uptake of the IBA. You might wonder if soaking bare-root transplants in a solution of IBA might help root growth. It appears that soaking for one to two days in a solution containing 250 parts per million IBA does have a stimulating effect on the roots of some species, but the effect is not so pronounced as to make the extra effort worthwhile. (Davies et al. 2002.)

Gibberellins

The gibberellins are a group of over 100 related molecules that promote stem growth by stimulating both cell growth and elongation. If you spray a plant with gibberellins, the stems will stretch alarmingly and eventually collapse under their own weight. It is effectively what happens when you keep a plant in too little light. It becomes tall and leggy because it is producing high levels of gibberellins to lift itself up toward the light (for more on this see the section on phytochrome below). Gibberellins also stimulate seed germina-

Aquilegia canadensis 'Little Lanterns'. This compact cultivar is one third shorter than the average Canada columbine. Its small stature is probably caused by a slight gibberellin deficit.

tion, overcoming abscisic acid and allowing the seed to sprout. Though it is more difficult for the home gardener and propagator to obtain gibberellins than IBA (search for it on the Internet), they are very useful in coaxing certain species to germinate without protracted cold stratification periods. When we want to sprout seeds in a hurry or when we obtain them in the spring and want them to come up in time for the

Vitamin Tonics

There are a few proprietary preparations on the market, such as Superthrive, that are advertised as plant restoratives with purported abilities akin to the patent medicines of the 1800s. Judging by the odor of the concentrate, the mixture probably contains B-complex vitamins like the ones we take in vitamin supplements. B vitamins (especially B_1 and B_{12}) have a hormone-like effect on plant roots, greatly accelerating the growth of excised root meristems in tissue culture experiments. However, this effect of B_1 (thiamine) does not appear to translate to whole plants growing in soil, as whole plants can synthesize their own thiamine as needed. However, like animals, plants cannot synthesize B_{12} (cobalamin), which is important in the synthesis of certain enzymes. Plant roots absorb it from bacterial sources in the soil (bacteria are the only organisms that can create this essential nutrient), and though I cannot find any research to support it, it is possible that soaking plant roots in vitamin B_{12} may promote root growth in an indirect way, but certainly less so than soaking roots in a dilute fertilizer solution would. Should you soak your bare-root transplants in vitamin solutions? Despite testimonials and manufacturers' claims to the contrary, I would have to say no, the research just does not support it.

What about compost teas? Interestingly, animal manure and manure-based compost have relatively high levels of both vitamins B_1 and B_{12} (Mozafar 1994). Perhaps one of the benefits we see after enriching soils with manure stems from the effect of B_{12} on roots, as well as the effects of fungi and bacteria. In recent years, compost teas have eclipsed vitamin preparations as the miracle treatment for many plant maladies. Compost tea is brewed by soaking compost of various sorts and levels of maturity in water kept aerated by mixing blades, bubblers, and the like. The tea is then strained and applied as a foliar spray or root drench. Compost teas are said to work by (1) providing a direct source of plant nutrients, (2) providing beneficial organic compounds necessary for plant and microorganism growth, (3) suppressing certain plant diseases, and (4) helping to build soil structure.

The literature regarding the efficacy of compost teas is even more baffling than in the case of B vitamins. Some proponents make claims that to me seem based more on conjecture and woo woo science than on experimental results. Many reports are really more testimonials akin to the ones you find for vitamin water treatments, but all in all I do feel that compost teas can have some real benefits that recommend their use. For several years I brewed manure tea to use as a fertilizer for my orchid collection. Fresh and dehydrated manures are especially high in plant nutrients such as nitrogen, and teas made from them are a somewhat smelly but effective mild organic fertilizer. However, most compost tea brewers use well-aged compost that has been properly turned to keep it aerated during decomposition (the reasoning is the anaerobic decomposition produces toxic levels of ammonia and other deleterious compounds). Aged compost has much lower levels of the big three soluble plant nutrients (nitrogen, phosphorus, and potassium), as most of it is tied up in the living bodies of the microorgan-

Trillium erectum var. *album*. A five-petaled variant of a normally three-petaled flower.

isms that decomposed it. It may have decent levels of readily available micronutrients, though, along with humic compounds that make them more soluble and available to the roots (these are known as chelating compounds). It also contains compounds similar to the root exudates plants excrete into the rhizosphere to foster microbial populations (see p. 40). Some experiments have indicated that compost teas can have a real disease-suppressing effect—especially against certain fungi. The logic is that high bacterial populations in the tea suppress fungi through direct competition for food, inhibitory chemicals, or by stimulating the plant's own disease response similar to a vaccine. Other experiments found little evidence of disease suppression or found that the tea actually increased fungal activity in the soil. Certainly, the humic compounds and microbial exudates in compost tea can have some positive effect on soil structure by binding finer particles together into larger ones.

I think the reason that the information on compost teas is so often contradictory stems from the immense variability and complexity of soils, microorganisms, composts, brewing, and application techniques, and the various plant species themselves. As far as perennials are concerned, I am confident that the single best thing you can do to decrease transplant shock and increase growth, bloom, winter survival, and disease resistance in you garden is to add liberal amounts of compost to the soil before you plant and continue to topdress with compost mulch every year thereafter. This will give your plants all the possible benefits of teas while also greatly increasing the soil's tilth, fertility, aeration, and moisture-holding capacity while at the same time cooling the soil, decreasing evaporation, and suppressing weeds. For places such as lawns, golf courses, and large existing gardens, compost tea is undoubtedly easier to apply than compost itself. Just as it is easier to pop a vitamin pill than eat lots of fresh vegetables, it is easier to spray on a bit of compost tea than spread 10 yards of the steaming raw ingredient, though in both instances, easier is not clearly better.

growing season, we sometimes soak the seeds overnight in the most readily available gibberellin, GA3. It is available from chemical supply companies as a salt that you dissolve in water, or as a liquid. GA3 is produced by fermenting the *bakanae* disease fungus, *Gibberella fujikuroi*, which causes—you guessed it—abnormally tall and weak growth in rice plants. Concentrations of between 250 and 1,000 parts per million will typically replace cold stratification if you soak the seeds for 24 hours, rinse them, and sow them immediately. Some seeds need the higher concentrations to overcome abscisic acid, but it is better to start out with lower concentration at first, as too much will cause the seedlings to stretch like bean sprouts.

Many dwarf or compact varieties of popular perennials, such as the one-fourth-sized *Aster novae-angliae* 'Purple Dome', have abnormally low levels of natural gibberellins in their systems, so the stems remain short. If you count the number of leaves on a stem of Purple Dome, the number is just about equal that of a typical New England aster. The flowers are just as big, too, but the internodes between leaves and even the flower stems are shorter than normal. Since compact, leafy stems with proportionally large flowers are desirable traits in a garden or container plant, gibberellin-deficient, dwarfed cultivars are very common in the nursery trade. The translation of the Japanese term *bakanae* means "foolish seedling," as rice plants infected with *Gibberella fujikuroi* not only grow tall, they tend not to flower or set seed. High levels of gibberellins in the system delay or even prevent flowering, so levels of the hormone in a perennial's tissues are high when it is growing vegetatively, but they drop precipitously as the plant approaches flowering. Gibberellin-deficient cultivars have less to begin with, and as a consequence they may bloom earlier than their typical counterparts. We have a plant of *Euphorbia corollata* we call 'Short and Sweet' that appeared spontaneously at Garden in the Woods. It is one-third shorter than its neighbors and begins blooming about two to three weeks earlier. Lower than normal levels of gibberellins keep the stems short and also allow the flowers to develop earlier. Biennials such as mulleins (*Verbascum* spp.) as well as rosette-forming perennials such as cardinal flower (*Lobelia cardinalis*) produce very low levels of gibberellins when in the rosette stage, so that the internodes are basically nonexistent. When flowering is triggered by winter vernalization (in the case of mulleins) or long days (in the case of cardinal flower), gibberellin levels surge and the stems rapidly lengthen (bolt).

Gibberellins are used commercially to force seedless grapes to form larger fruits and increase yield and quality of other orchard crops such as apples and cherries. Gibberellin antagonists such as B-nine, A-rest, or Bonsai that inhibit gibberellin formation are widely used by greenhouse growers to keep tall plants such as Easter lilies, poinsettias, and a wide range of perennials short so that they look neat and presentable for sale. This is fine for a throwaway plant like an Easter lily, but it is a bit deceptive as far as garden perennials go. It reminds me of one of my college friends who stopped into a pet store and impulsively bought what the owner described as a dwarf bunny rabbit. Turns out it was just a baby, because it grew to the size of a small dog after a few months. *Caveat hispania emptor* (let the buyer in the land of rabbits beware).

Cytokinins

The final group of growth-promoting hormones comprises the cytokinins, which have an important role in tissue culture. Cytokinins promote cell division and can induce mature cells to begin growing and dividing again—basically cause them to become stem cells. When you place some sterilized plant tissue on a medium containing a synthetic cytokinin such as kinetin, the tissue begins to grow rapidly into a blob of callus, or callus with lots of little shoots sprouting from it. It was the discovery of cytokinins in the 1950s that transformed the science of tissue culture. Natural cytokinins are made primarily in the root tips. Roots that are growing well with adequate water and nutrients manufacture cytokinins that are transported to the stem tips, telling them in effect, "Life is good, let's get growing!"

Lilium canadense in tissue culture. When placed on a sterile culture medium containing high levels of a cytokinin such as kinetin, lily cells begin to proliferate madly and grow into clusters of small plants that can be divided and grown on.

Phytochrome

Plants do not have eyes, thank goodness. Imagine how hard it would be to prune your chrysanthemums if there were a hundred little eyes pleading with you to *stop the madness!* Eyes are really useful for either searching for something or getting out of something's way, as they pick up not only light but patterns and motion. Plants cannot either chase or run away, so for them, the presence or absence of light is the important thing. You might think that chloroplasts would be effective light meters for the plant, but just like solar panels, they need light to make energy so they can work. Solar panels are no good in a cave and chloroplasts are useless underground. Accordingly, seeds and young seedlings rely on a special photoreceptive pigment called phytochrome. Phytochrome is sensitive to red light (a wavelength of 660 nanometers). Exposure to red light for even a few seconds converts it from its inactive form to its active form. Very small seeds (those smaller than a grain of sand) are too small to push up through soil or leaves and other debris. As a consequence, many have high levels of the inactive form of phytochrome in their tissues when they fall from the mother plant. After settling down into the soil, if they become buried by fallen leaves so that no red light can reach them they will refuse to germinate—even when conditions are otherwise perfect. They can remain in this phytochrome-induced stupor for years, decades, and occasionally even centuries until some chance event, such as a fire, windstorm, flood, or the upward thrust of a gardener's shovel brings them to the surface. A few seconds or minutes of sunlight converts the phytochrome to its active form, and the long dormant seed will sprout. If you ever wondered where all those weeds come from every time you till the soil, the fact is they have been lying in wait—perhaps since before you were even born—to reach the light and grow. After our driveway was installed through the woods, I was surprised to see mullein plants growing from the recently disturbed soil. Mullein is a field weed and not something you would expect to germinate in the soil from a 75-year-old woodland. As it turns out, mullein seeds are very long-lived. Of the 50 species placed underground in glass jars of soil in Dr. Beal's famous seed-bank viability experiment, mullein seeds germinated well at the 120-year test in 2002 (Telewski and Zeevaart 2002). The mullein along my drive probably matured during the Great Depression when this part of my woods was last cut. And its progeny may stay dormant until my great-great-grandchildren come of age. Think about that the next time you let your garden verbascums go to seed.

Phytochrome is also important for larger seeds that germinate under the soil. Moderate levels of inactive phytochrome stimulate gibberellin production that makes them continue to stretch and stretch until they poke through the soil into the light. Red light then converts the phytochrome to its active form, which slows gibberellins, and the seedling greens up, becomes stockier, and starts to grow more leaves. This is not an all or nothing equation: low light may allow some continued stretching (etiolation) as the seedling reaches for more light. This is because far-red light (light with a wavelength of 730 nanometers), which is more abundant in shade, actually causes active phytochrome to change to inactive again. The weak stems that result are prone to breakage and sunburn if moved into brighter light. You may have experienced this if you have ever germinated seedlings on a windowsill and then tried to plant the seedlings in the garden. Though starting seeds on the kitchen windowsill is certainly therapeutic toward the end of winter when we all crave the sight of growing things, you will end up with stockier, healthier seedlings if you wait and sprout them outdoors in the sun and wind once the weather has warmed.

Phytochrome is also important for older plants because it helps the leaves and stem length to continue to adjust in thickness and size as light conditions change (as the plant becomes more shaded by its neighbors, for example). It also helps many species sense the length of the day in order to time flowering, growth, and dormancy (see Understanding Cold-hardiness, p. 90). Finally, because there is proportionally more far-red light than red light in the weaker fall and spring sunlight than there is during summer, it may even help plants to tell the seasons. All in all it is a simple yet very elegant way of seeing that has served our green friends well.

Tellima grandiflora. If covered with soil, the tiny seeds of **fringecups** will not sprout. I cover them with a light layer of coarse sand, which lets in enough light to convert phytochrome to its active phase.

CHAPTER 5

FLOWERS AND SEEDS

Why is it that we are drawn to flowers? There is no ready genetic answer to this question, since from a survival point of view, flowers are about as useful to humans as seaweed—sometimes edible in a pinch, but that is about it. It is a paradox that something so apparently useless to us resonates so deeply. A world without flowers would be like a world without music: they speak to a fundamental human need for color and beauty that defies scientific explanation, yet the language of flowers is one that we all understand.

In evolutionary terms, flowers are a fairly recent invention (scientists estimate the first flowers developed 130 to 250 million years ago) and the way they just suddenly appeared on the world stage has long confounded evolutionary biologists. The first land plants—mosses, liverworts, clubmosses, and ferns—reproduce by spore rather than seed. While a seed is a tiny plant, a spore is only a single cell that must find a place to sprout and grow. When a fern spore germinates, it grows into a little green tuft called a gametophyte that is basically the fern's functional equivalent of a flower. When it is large enough and the weather is favorable, it releases little swimming (flagellate) sperm that move a few millimeters through a

ABOVE: *Rudbeckia subtomentosa* 'Henry Eilers'.

Thalictrum thalictroides 'Semidouble Pink'.

Aconitum uncinatum. The hooded flowers of **wild monkshood** provide ready shelter for any passing bee.

film of water to find egg cells to fertilize. These grow into what we think of as a fern or clubmoss plant. We are so used to the idea of motherhood that spore reproduction is a bit hard to get our heads around, but the fern growing out in your garden reproduces by sending out vast quantities of fairy dust that sprout little fern "flowers" all over the place—each one a mother and father in turn for a separate brood of baby ferns.

Spores are nearly microscopic, so though few survive the trip, journey they do. One of the things we take for granted as animals is mobility. We can move around and so can our offspring. Though we may not like it, our kids can move hun-

dreds or even thousands of miles away to find greener pastures. For plants, mobility is a true challenge. Once a land plant has started to put down roots, it is very unlikely that it will ever move more than a few yards in its lifetime. A plant's only opportunity to find a better place to settle down comes when it is still a spore, pollen grain, or seed. Spores are incredibly light and can travel thousands of miles on air currents before settling down to grow into the "flowers" that will spawn new plants. This is a fern's one big opportunity to travel and it explains in part why so many ferns are very widespread worldwide. Seed plants (or flowering plants) have not one but two

TOP LEFT: *Asarum arifolium.* Pollinated by ground beetles or flies, the remarkable blooms of arrow-leaf ginger are lined with distinctly mammalian-looking fur, and the marbled flesh gives off the slight odor of carrion to close the deal.

BOTTOM LEFT: *Adiantum pedatum* spore. There are 200,000 maidenhair fern spores on the tip of this pocket knife. These tiny single-celled particles can travel vast distances but need very specific conditions to germinate and grow.

BOTTOM RIGHT: *Cymophyllus fraserianus.* Most sedges are wind-pollinated, and the flowers are a drab brown or green, but the unique Fraser's sedge has evolved stark white flowers to attract insects.

opportunities for migration: the transfer of pollen from one plant to the next, and the movement of the seed itself to new ground.

Bring On the Bugs

Long distance movement of pollen confers a huge evolutionary advantage over the few-millimeter breaststroke flagellate sperm can manage, and it is for this purpose that flowers evolved. A flowering plant can effectively spray its genes over several acres or square miles via its pollen, which powers the evolutionary process at a rate that ferns or mosses could never achieve. An acre is about 25 million times the area of a square centimeter, a square mile about 16 billion times as large; so think of all the potential partners a flower has access to in comparison with a fern spore. The first flowering plants, such as cycads and conifers, relied on the wind to move their pollen. The wind can be very effective if you are 100 feet tall or grow out in the open, but it is not so effective for long-distance dispersal if you are the size of most perennials. Early seed plants such as magnolias made a huge mobility leap

Stylophorum diphyllum with bee. A small bumblebee is so distracted by the bounty of pollen in this **celandine poppy** that it is hardly bothered by my camera lens.

Thalictrum pubescens. **King of the meadow** is an insect-pollinated **meadow rue** with stiff, upward-facing anthers to facilitate landing and pollination.

when they evolved flowers designed to attract mobile creatures to move pollen for them. Beetles, gnats, and later bees, moths, butterflies, flower flies, birds, and bats will move your pollen effectively no matter what the speed and direction of the wind, so if a flowering plant's objective is to spread its pollen as far and wide as it can, attracting these assistants becomes priority number one. The incredible diversity of showy blooms we can choose from to grace our gardens is simply the product of an unprecedented advertising war that has been raging for 100 million years to get these creatures' attentions. Lucky for us, the birds and the bees share our taste for bright colors, patterns, and forms. What a boring world it would be if they were all colorblind!

With the exception of grasses and their relatives, very few of the perennials we cultivate are wind-pollinated.

Certainly, a host of wind-pollinated perennials are out there, but the blooms, like those of most grasses, are small, green, and about as aesthetically inspiring as a pile of overcooked egg noodles drizzled in old fryer oil. The showy and colorful parts of peonies, daylilies, coreopsis, and most other garden perennials are the petals and, to a lesser extent, the pollen-bearing anthers, but there is much more to a flower than that.

What Is a Flower?

If you examine a typical insect-pollinated bloom such as a phlox, it comprises five components: the ovary and its eggs, sepals, petals, stamens (male sex organs), and pistil(s) (female sex organ). The number of each component is fairly consistent among related species. Phlox and many other perennials have

TOP RIGHT: *Thalictrum dioicum,* male flowers. In contrast to king of the meadow, **early meadow rue** is wind-pollinated, so its anthers hang down on thin filaments to sway in the breeze.

five sepals and petals, but flowers with three and four of each are also common. A flower usually has only one pistil and anywhere from 3 to 12 or more stamens.

Humble Origins

Flowers are really modified shoots. The ovary, (the flower's womb) is a modified stem, and all the rest of the flower parts evolved from leaves. The sepals are usually the most leaflike part of the flower. They surround the petals like a protective jacket as the bloom grows and thus lay behind or below the petals when the flower opens. You may hear the whorl of sepals collectively called the corona, while the whorl of petals is called the corolla. The sticky sepals of a peony are green and photosynthetic like leaves, though many flowers such as

orchids and lilies have sepals that are brightly colored and resemble the petals (when the petals and sepals are colored the same they are collectively called tepals). Just to confuse things further, so it seems, plants in the buttercup family (Ranunculaceae) have colorful sepals and nonexistent or at best insignificant petals. For most perennials, though, the petals provide the main advertisement.

Double Flowers

Double flowers are very popular among gardeners, for instead of three, four, or five petals, double blooms have as many as 50. Double appears to be a bit of a misnomer! What *is* a double flower? Imagine a flower like a set of nested bowls. The female sex organs become the innermost bowl, followed by the male organs, then the petals, and finally the sepals as the largest or outmost bowl. In rare individuals that produce double flowers, the innermost two bowls (the sex organs) develop as colorful petals (or sepals) instead. Fully double flowers have no sex organs, only petals, so the blooms are completely sterile. Some double blooms even preserve this nested shape, so

LEFT: *Paeonia 'Yellow Emperor'* is a semidouble **peony** that has traded some but not all of its male parts (stamens) for extra petals.

BELOW: *Anemone nemorosa* **'Double White'.** Like the peony above, this semidouble **wood anemone** has converted some of its sexual parts into a boss of petal-like organs.

OPPOSITE TOP LEFT: *Trillium simile.* In this side view of the **trillium** known as **sweet Beth,** the flower stem (pedicel) supports first a whorl of three green sepals, then three white petals, then six anthers, followed by a fluted garnet ovary tipped by a three-lobed stigma.

OPPOSITE TOP RIGHT: After the **trillium** is pollinated (*Trillium foetidissimum* is pictured here), the ovary swells into a fruit filled with large seeds. In this picture some of the seeds (small brown flecks to left of center) failed to develop—probably because of poor pollination.

OPPOSITE BOTTOM: *Sanguinaria canadensis* **'Multiplex'.** If you peel open the many petals of **double bloodroot** you will find no sexual parts in the center. The pistils and stamen seen in the single bloodroot on page 159 have been transformed into petals.

flowers are either missing or inaccessible beneath the excess puff of petals. Like a TV without a picture tube or a pencil without lead, double flowers are useless from both the plant's and pollinators' point of view. Double flowers do appear occasionally in the wild, though their tremendous evolutionary shortcomings mean they are fairly rare and do not persist very long. If by chance someone happens upon one of these rarities and propagates it by cuttings, division, or tissue culture, it may find a ready home in gardens. A case in point is the double-flowered bloodroot *Sanguinaria canadensis* 'Multiplex'.

one whorl of petals appears stacked inside the next. More commonly, though, some of the innermost organs develop normally so the flower can set seed. These partially double flowers are called semidouble and look like a typical bloom that has twice or three times the normal complement of petals. Seedlings raised from a semidouble mother are often either semidouble or completely double themselves. Double blooms are found in just about every family of perennials, though for some reason they are more common in some clans. The buttercup family, rose family, aster family, and peony family all have more than their share of double cultivars.

Fully double flowers obviously cannot produce pollen or seed, and in many cases the nectaries present in normal

As far as I know, this is one of only two or three fully double forms of this species ever discovered. It was found amidst a stand of typical wild bloodroot in 1916 by one Guido von Webern on his property in Dayton, Ohio. It was a weak little plant, but he nurtured it into a fine specimen, eventually sending a division to the Arnold Arboretum in 1919. The Arnold Arboretum staff named the plant before the division eventually died, as did the original clump in Dayton. Mr. von Webern also sent a division to the Montreal Botanical Garden, and by luck there it was propagated and then distributed to various public and private gardens. Over the years, our nursery alone has propagated and sold thousands of *Sanguinaria canadensis* 'Multiplex', all divisions of divisions of divisions of divisions of that original plant. Without question it is the most popular and abundant bloodroot cultivar in gardens. Thus, though it was clearly an evolutionary dead end, this showy rarity has by virtue of its appeal to gardeners become the most successful and widespread individual in the history of the species, and all without producing a single seed!

What Is Your Favorite Color?

Brightly colored or patterned like the floral equivalent of highway billboards, petals are certainly effective advertisements tailored to the tastes of their chosen customer. Individual pollinator species seem to prefer different colors and sizes of flowers. Bumblebees gravitate toward blue and yellow flowers, while honeybees and solitary bees prefer white. Hummingbirds are attracted to intense primary colors such as red or blue, and beetles will flock to white or maroon blooms. However, bumblebees can often be seen visiting red bee balm (*Monarda didyma*), and honeybees swarm over blue salvias (*Salvia* spp.) and lavender (*Lavendula officionalis*). There is so little consistency in part because naïve pollinators can quickly

OPPOSITE: *Trillium grandiflorum* **'Multiplex'.** Since fully double flowers cannot set seed, forms like this stunning double showy **trillium** command high prices in the trade.

TOP RIGHT: *Spigelia marilandica.* The tubular shape and vivid red color of **Indian pink** are sure signs that it is pollinated by hummingbirds.

BOTTOM RIGHT: *Actaea racemosa.* Honeybees love the shaggy white petalless flowers of **black cohosh** because they can dance back and forth collecting food on a pollen-covered rug.

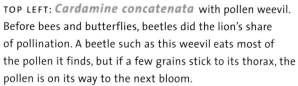

TOP LEFT: *Cardamine concatenata* with pollen weevil. Before bees and butterflies, beetles did the lion's share of pollination. A beetle such as this weevil eats most of the pollen it finds, but if a few grains stick to its thorax, the pollen is on its way to the next bloom.

TOP RIGHT: *Monarda didyma* 'Jacob Cline'. What hummingbird can resist shocking red bee balm?

BOTTOM RIGHT: *Polemonium reptans* with digger bee (*Andrena* sp.). Before European honeybees arrived and displaced them, small solitary bees like the one pictured here on Jacob's ladder were the primary pollinators for a number of wildflowers. Now that honeybees are in trouble, the native bees are making a comeback.

learn which flowers produce the best nectar or pollen rewards and which are not worth the time. You probably have had your share of bees buzzing around your clothes to investigate their food potential or had a hummingbird become trapped in your garage after flying in to scope out a red gas can or orange traffic cone. It does not take long for either to learn that clothes and gas cans are poor sources of food.

COLORED LIGHTS

Light is simply energy, and it is only through the magnificent work of our eyes and brain that we can "see" this energy at all, let alone break it into myriad different colors. I take my sight so for granted most of the time that I do not stop and think much about it, but it is only by the luck of natural selection or, if you have a more theological bent, the hand of the creator that we can see the beautiful colors of flowers. However, there is quite a bit more light than meets the eye that we cannot see. You cannot see the microwaves shooting around in your kitchen appliance, nor can you see the infrared beam coming from the night-vision lamp on your video camera. Neither can I see the ultraviolet (UV) rays that turn my lily-white skin blistering red if I forget to apply the sunscreen. As we fair-skinned types know, UV light is able to penetrate cloud cover or the leaf canopy better than visible light, so you can get sunburned even in the shade. Therefore, flowers in the shade or amidst foliage will be better lit by UV than visible light, and as a consequence, many insects have evolved the ability to see UV light as well as the colors of the rainbow that we can perceive (what we term rather anthropocentrically the visible spectrum). It is hard to know exactly what a bee sees when it looks at a flower, but UV camera lenses capture flowers under UV light as shades of purple and black. Basically, the more a flower or part of a flower reflects UV light, the purpler or blacker it will appear. (If you photograph someone by means of a UV lens after he has liberally smeared sun block on his face, he will appear a ghoulish purple black.) When seen under UV light, many flowers display striking patterns not evident under visible light. These dots, bars, and blotches undoubtedly help the pollinator find and navigate into the flowers more effectively.

WHAT THE BEE SEES

Bees use a combination of visible and UV light to find flowers, but they suffer from a peculiar color myopia. It is estimated

TOP: *Potentilla anserina.* In visible light, silverling appears uniformly bright yellow, but under ultraviolet light (below) it takes on a striking two-toned pattern that helps guide bees to the center of the flower.

that for a bee to see the color of a flower from three feet away the bloom would need to be about a foot in diameter (Spaethe et al. 2001). Though some of us might wish otherwise, there are very few flowers of that size around, so bees find flowers from a distance by looking for colors that contrast with green. The bees fly around looking for contrast then zoom in for a

TOP: *Digitalis* × *mertonensis*. The coalescing spots in the center of a perennial **foxglove** flower resemble paving stones leading to a nectar treat.

BOTTOM: *Hemerocallis* 'Pemaquid Light'. Maybe bigger *is* better. Large flowers like this tetraploid **daylily** cultivar are easy for passing bees to see.

closer look. As it turns out, white flowers are the easiest for the insect to detect by contrast. Additionally, flowers that have rings or patterns of UV-absorbing (light) and reflecting (dark) pigments create higher contrast than those that are consistently one or the other. If you have ever wondered why most small flowers (those under a third of an inch in diameter) are usually white, it has to do with bee myopia. Since the bee would almost have to land on a small flower in order to determine its color, high-contrast white is the plant's best choice.

I have not done a disciplined study of this, but it is my observation that there are proportionally more white wildflowers—even larger ones—in woodland and shade habitats than in sunny habitats. I surmise that once again, it is the higher contrast of white against green that makes them easiest for bees to find in shade. If you doubt this, walk around the garden at dusk and notice how the white flowers seem to jump out at you. Bees can distinguish the color of larger flowers from a greater distance, so blue or yellow blooms tend to be an inch or larger. Yellow and especially lemon yellow is the easiest color for bees to see, so it is not surprising that in sunny environments where color is more useful than contrast, yellow flowers are abundant.

THE BIGGER THE BETTER

We like big flowers over small ones, too, so it is no accident that plant breeders tend to select for flower size in addition to color and plant habit. While wildflower types like myself often poo poo larger flowers as unnatural and bee unfriendly, could it be that to a bee, bigger is better too? A bigger question (pun intended) is the effect that breeding for different colors has on the bees. Do bees see mauve or pink daylilies as easily as they do the "wild" orange or yellow ones? I do not know the answer. I have noticed bees staggering around aimlessly on hybrid oriental lilies. Remember that the lines and spots in flowers are designed to guide the pollinator toward its reward, much like landing lights guide aircraft home at night. I suspect that in some instances, the reshuffling of lines and spots that results when two species are bred will produce an indecipherable pattern that leaves the bee flying around unsure where to land. Fortunately from both the bee's and flower's perspective, insects are fast learners, so they should be able to figure things out eventually. This begs a larger point: what effect do our garden hybrids have on the world of the birds and bees? I will address this question in a bit.

Composite Materials

Many of our favorite perennials are in the daisy or composite family (Asteraceae). This wildly successful group of plants, which includes the asters, coneflowers, chrysanthemums, sunflowers, black-eyed Susans, and coreopsis, has embraced the concept that bigger is better in an innovative way that largely explains their success. Each composite flower is composed of tens or hundreds of small blooms amassed in a disk or cone at the center of the flower that is surrounded by a circle of sterile ray flowers in which one of the petals grows monstrously large (it is the flower equivalent of a fiddler crab's claw). The result is a "flower" of impressive size to attract the notice of foraging bees or other insects. Once the pollinator alights, it is able to drink from and pollinate dozens of tiny individual flowers. Flowers that are close together will look larger than if they are spread diffusely apart. Many of our other favorite garden perennials, such as phlox and astilbe, cluster their colorful flowers together in a similar fashion to create one apparent uberbloom.

Once a bee or butterfly lands on a flower, the petals' collective job is nearly done. Though many petals and tepals are arrayed with dots, lines, or blotches (nectar guides) to guide the insect to the honey pot, some flowers go one step further.

Echinacea 'Sundown'. Up close, the cone in the center of a coneflower bloom is revealed as a bristle of tiny brownish flowers (lower third of image) composed of five anthers and a long, forked, tonguelike stigma. The red and orange bristles must provide a foothold for the insect and prevent it from crushing the delicate flowers. As these tiny flowers are pollinated, new ones (seen as pale green bumps in the middle of the cone) will replace them. An individual composite bloom can flower for several weeks.

TOP: *Symphyotrichum laevis.* The flowers of **smooth aster** change from yellow to reddish purple after pollination. The bees quickly learn to go to the yellow ones and ignore the red ones.

BOTTOM: *Symphyotrichum novae-angliae* and honeybee. New England asters are easy for a bee to land on and are well stocked with nectar. It is no wonder that asters are real favorites of bees and butterflies.

The fertile flowers in the disk of a well-pollinated aster flower turn from yellow (highly bee visible) to red (bee invisible). This clever switch allows the bees to forage more efficiently and pollinate more aster blooms per minute. (Competitive bees are even ranked by their blooms per minute, or BPM, score, and asters are banned from international competitions as they confer unfair advantage and skew the BPMs of bees in aster-rich regions.)

A Currency of Pollen and Scent

The world of flowers, birds, and bees is really a vast service economy built on a currency of pollen and nectar. Most plants offer their assistants a decent wage for an honest day's work, but as you might expect, this floral economy has its share of cheats and deadbeats. Lady's slipper orchids (*Cypripedium* spp.), for example, rely on a clever bait and switch to attract bees and get them to perform their services for free. The bee is lured by the large, artfully colored blooms and enticed inside the pouch by yellow blotches and glistening nectar that are nothing more than an artifice of pigment and wax. The bee thus becomes trapped inside the pouch and must climb out the back using a series of well-placed hairs as a ladder. This escape route puts the bee in line with the anthers, and as it passes underneath, the back of its head is dabbed with a sticky packet of pollen placed so it is just out of reach. If the bee, once fooled, enters another flower, it will transfer its pollen

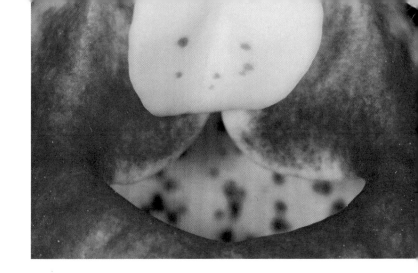

TOP: *Cypripedium reginae.* The unfortunate bee that tries to feed on a lady's slipper flower is greeted by a winsome smile before finding itself trapped and forced to go out the back way on an empty stomach.

BOTTOM: *Lilium pyrophilum.* The downward-facing orientation of this rare sandhill lily has evolved so that hummingbirds must fly in from below and bump against the long anthers as they move toward the center. The even longer female stigma is then poised to receive some pollen from the next bird that happens in.

and pollinate the bloom before getting another dab of the yellow stuff, but more often than not the bee learns its lesson quickly and refuses to visit another lady's slipper. As a consequence, lady's slipper pollination rates can range as low as 5 percent in a given season. It seems that in the economy of pollination, crime does not pay.

It appears likely that during the earlier years of floral evolution, pollen was the primary reward for the visitor. When compared with seeds, the energy investment a plant sinks into pollen is relatively low, so each flower can afford to offer some as an incentive. It is a protein-rich foodstuff that bees and other insects depend on to nurture their bodies or those of their young. However, insects cannot live by protein alone, so plants also produce sugary nectar to lure them in. Nectaries (nectar glands) are usually located at the base of the petals or sepals, but nectar may also ooze from the petals or even leaves, leaf petioles, or stems. Floral nectar is pretty sweet stuff containing from 12 to 50 percent sugar along with a few amino acids for protein (to put this in perspective, pure maple syrup contains at least 66 percent sugar).

My Pollen, My Pollen

After navigating to the center of the bloom, the pollinator will harvest pollen and/or nectar. Pollen grains mature inside a pouchlike anther that sits atop a long filament. When the pollen is ripe, the pouch or sack splits open and exposes the mealy yellow treasure within. Each pollen grain is basically equivalent to a single sperm cell, but instead of a little tail-like creature, pollen under magnification looks like little balls or prickly sea creatures, mediaeval weaponry, asteroids, or spongy blobs. Each is a little packet of genes encased in a hard shell that protects the contents during shipping and that is also fitted with a unique protein fingerprint—a bar code, if you will—that makes it recognizable to another of its species. More on this in a bit. Pollen that is spread by insects or birds is sticky or gooey so it clings to hair or feathers.

Are Garden Hybrids Bad for the Planet?

You're kidding, right? On the surface at least, this may seem like a silly question when we have more immediate issues such as global warming or a child's high fever on our already burgeoning plates. Still, it is one of the issues that raises the hackles of conservationists who in turn anger gardeners; a telltale sign that there is more to this question than might meet the eye.

I am intimately involved with and interested in North American native plants and the role they play in the larger ecology of their place. Still, I appreciate many exotic plants because, like a good wedge of Ukrainian goat cheese or a cherimoya fruit from Ecuador, I enjoy their novelty. I also find it fascinating to compare closely related species from different regions. I have

gained a much deeper appreciation for evolution and the mad, marvelous diversity of life through such simple comparisons, and I also have a keen interest in the role natural hybridization plays in all of this. However, I do feel a particular connection to the local species that I share the land with because they are part and parcel the fabric of my life, as closely woven into my memories and identity as the music I love or the friends I have come to know. A blousy hybrid or beguiling exotic may appeal to my senses, but it is the local plants that feed my soul.

I realize that a youth spent tramping around in the woods learning to recognize the trees and the bees by sight does not qualify me as a typical Gen Xer, and that based solely on this, some might classify me as a tree-huggin' commie, just as I might characterize them as knuckle-dragging spider stompers in turn. So it escalates. The whole question of hybrids, not to mention native versus exotic plants, seems to quickly degenerate into polemical arguments and oversimplified, black-and-white declaratives when conservationists and horticulturalists try to resolve important issues such as the potential invasiveness of certain nursery plants. While I know a few folks that feel horticulture itself is evil, and a few others that believe that they should be allowed to grow anything or do anything to their environment no matter how potentially destructive, I know that most of us fall somewhere in the middle. Gardening by its very nature connects us to our land and the plants we share it with, and I would wager that few gardeners want to intentionally do harm to the land of plants they care deeply about.

I am trying as best I can to tread lightly on the land and the earth in general—a real challenge for someone born in the age of plastics—because I do believe that a more sustainable way of life depends foremost not on government action but on the personal choices we make every day. It is not always easier or less expensive to live a greener life, so it is important to have an ethical framework within which I can weigh choices and make decisions and that gives me the will to keep on carrying on.

Echinacea 'Orange Meadowbrite'. Though it boasts a very unusual color, this **coneflower** hybrid involving three different parent species lacks vigor.

The Precautionary Principle

In the United States, we have developed a legal and ethical system surrounding environmental issues that puts the burden of proof on the victim or their agents. One must prove beyond any reasonable doubt that global warming is real, genetically engineered crops are hazardous, or that toxins in certain plastics will cause your gonads to shrivel. Until then, the carbon dioxide is free to flow, the gene splicing can proceed apace, and the toxins may continue to leach out of the teething ring your infant is now mouthing. It is a system that unabashedly puts the rights of the individual or corporation above the rights of the citizenry and the environment. In Europe (and increasingly the rest of the world), the burden of proof falls to the person, corporation, or government that is engineering the suspect crops or manufacturing the plastics to prove beyond any reasonable doubt that they are not harmful, which is a monumental difference. At the root of this second position is the Hippocratic oath to "do no harm." Of course this idea is far older than Hippocrates and lies at the root of most of the world's religions. In terms of environmental policy, it means simply that if there is good reason to suspect a problem, we should proceed with caution until those fears are proved false. It is important to stress that random speculation or public hysteria is not enough to prevent a company from manufacturing something. However, once a potential problem has been identified through good science, the manufacture is suspended until the problem can be fully investigated.

If the smoke detectors go off in the middle of the night, do you roll over and drift back to sleep until you are overcome by smoke, or do you get up and check to see if there is a problem? We all follow the precautionary principle in our day-to-day lives, but many in America will argue against this "socialist, antibusiness" idea as an environmental policy until our seacoasts are gone and invasive organisms have reduced the biodiversity of the continent by a hundredfold. It is completely illogical that a policy that has led to a cleaner, healthier environment and a higher standard of living in much of Europe would be so roundly trounced in the United States, but such is the strength of our capitalistic embrace. We have been duped, folks: told by the government and the corporations to just ignore that thick black stuff that has set the smoke detectors a beepin' while we suffocate in our sleep.

What does this have to do with gardening, you ask? The precautionary principle and the tenet to do no harm can help guide small choices as well as large ones. Before smuggling those potentially diseased lily bulbs in your dirty underwear, setting out known invasive species like purple loosestrife in your garden, or applying preemergent herbicides to your perennial beds, before doing anything that gets that little angel of conscience all worked up on your shoulder, ask yourself honestly, "Is the risk worth the gain?"

I am an optimist at heart, so I prefer to make gardening decisions not just in an attempt to "do no harm" but more posi-

Coreopsis 'Moonbeam'. One of the most enduringly popular perennials over the past 25 years, moonbeam coreopsis is a sterile hybrid that was found in a garden. Because it sets no seed, it blooms heavily for months during the summer.

tively, to "do more good." Would planting a hybrid Asiatic lily like *Lilium* 'Karen North' do any harm? I doubt that it would, but would it do more good to plant a local species like *Lilium canadense, Lilium pardalinum,* or the rare and beautiful *Lilium pyrophilum,* each one increasingly beleaguered in the wild? Does the aesthetic appeal of a sterile, double-flowered daylily outweigh its negligible value as a food source for pollinators when compared to a single-flowered variety? When searching for a groundcover, does it make sense to plant strawberries (*Fragaria* spp.) that you can eat over vinca (*Vinca* spp.) that you (and everything else) cannot?

No, garden hybrids are not by nature bad for the environment. Sterile hybrids such as *Coreopsis* × 'Moonbeam' flower for months and put all the energy they would otherwise devote to seeds into nectar production that keeps all manner of insects satisfied in my garden during the summer. In gardening, as in life, there are no easy answers, and there are certainly lots of choices. It is my hope that this book will provide you the knowledge to help make these choices wisely. If we all strive to do the best we know how, to do the most good we can, our gardens and our world will be a better place.

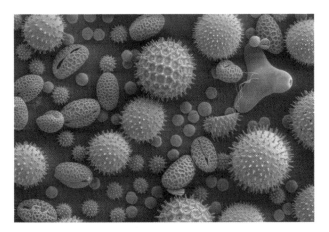

TOP LEFT: *Tradescantia* 'Betty Lowerer'. **Spiderwort** flowers have six stamens, each composed of a fringed purple filament and a folded yellow and black anther. The yellow color comes from the pollen, which is typically this shade but can also be pink (page 18, top right), orange, or blue (page 160, top right).

TOP RIGHT: *Solidago* 'Little Lemon'. **Goldenrod** is still blamed for causing hay fever, but its sticky, insectborne pollen is not to blame for your itchy nose and watery eyes.

BOTTOM LEFT: Under the scanning electron microscope, pollen grains from common garden perennials such as sunflower, mallow, lily, and evening primrose look like deep-sea creatures.

Wind-borne pollen is dry, and since the chances of a microscopic pollen grain blowing off into the wind and hitting its tiny target are very small indeed, wind-pollinated plants such as grasses produce loads of the stuff, much to the chagrin of allergy sufferers. Unfortunately, the protein bar codes on pollen are misread by many of us (including yours truly) as something threatening and harmful, which triggers the familiar allergic responses of watery eyes, runny nose, and earth-shuddering sneezes all meant to drive the purported marauders from our bodies. One thing is clear: the problem pollen for us is the wind-borne variety, not the sticky, insect-dispersed stuff that is engineered to stay put. In a sad case of guilt by association, some insect-pollinated perennials such as goldenrods and asters are blamed for hay fever just because they happen to bloom when grasses and other wind-borne offenders such as ragweed are engaged in a bacchanalian fit of pollen production. So let's be clear—*goldenrod or any other exclusively insect- or animal-pollinated flower will not trigger allergies,* or to put it another way, if you see the birds and the bees, it won't make you sneeze! You may object to goldenrods on aesthetic grounds, but at least you can rest assured that they will cause you no physical discomfort.

Once a pollen grain lands on the sticky stigma (the receptive part of the female reproductive organ), it presents its protein bar code and is either accepted or rejected. Rejected pollen is shunted aside, while accepted grains are flooded with nurturing hormones that induce each grain to germinate and grow a long tube that tunnels down through the stigma and

The Strange Case of the Sex-Change Arisaemas

Jack-in-the-pulpits are well known for their peculiar ability to change sexes from year to year. It is a phenomenon that is quite foreign to us humans, destined from conception to be either one or the other, but it makes perfect sense as a reproductive strategy, and I only wonder why more species have not evolved this way. Since producing pollen is a much less costly endeavor than growing a passel of seeds to maturity, it is not surprising that smaller, weaker, or more highly shaded or stressed plants develop as males and only a small minority (20 to 35 percent) become female or bear both male and female flowers each season. I will always remember one unfortunate graduate student I worked with at the University of Connecticut whose thesis involved a study of jack-in-the-pulpit sex change (or as she called it, gender diphasy). She collected a number of male and female corms and grew them for a year in the greenhouse. As you might imagine, after a season under our care the plants all came up female the following year! She lost a year of work but learned a valuable lesson—we horticulturalists like to spoil our plants! I heard that the next year, she confined her work to the woods.

Arisaema triphyllum, female flower (left) and male (right). A black fungus gnat is pollinating the lower male flowers.

the neck of the pistil and all the way to the ovary, where it finds an unfertilized egg, burrows in, and squirts in its complement of genes. Amazingly, this bar code sensor is so accurate that many perennials can actually recognize not only that the pollen came from another of its same species, but also that it *did not* come from one of its own flowers. Inbreeding can be harmful in plants as well as in people, especially because plants cannot only father children with their mothers, they can father offspring with themselves! A few perennials such as jack-in-the-pulpits (*Arisaema*) prevent inbreeding by being either male or female (dioecious).

It Takes Two to Tango

Many perennials rely on pollen bar-coding to weed out their own grains. For this reason, if you have only one plant of a certain species of, say, coreopsis, it will never set any seed unless a particularly industrious bee brings in some from another garden or nearby wild area. This is advantageous in one sense, as the plant will bloom longer and harder when not distracted by childrearing. On the other hand, if you want the plant to seed itself around, or you like to watch goldfinches pick the seeds off stems, you will need to get hold of another individual of the same species. Of course, many perennials can pollinate themselves, and others will accept pollen from a closely related species (see Plant Breeding, p. 120), but as a general rule, I always like to plant at least two or three of everything if I desire seed. Remember, too, that most cultivars—the plants with clever names in quotes like *Dicentra* 'Langtrees' (fringed bleeding heart)—are clones. Whether you plant one or a hundred 'Langtrees', you will be unlikely to ever see a seedling unless you have some other fringed bleeding hearts around. Many garden perennials never set seed for other reasons. These hybrid plants inherited a jumbled complement of genes that effectively made them sterile. Popular cultivars such as the hyssop *Agastache* 'Black Adder' bloom and bloom, producing nary a seed, even if another hyssop lingers nearby. Plant breeding has become big business, but much of it is so straightforward that you can do it yourself.

Behind Closed Doors

Unlike ferns, which have sex in the open, so to speak, flowering plants keep it all cloistered inside the ovary, which is basically the floral equivalent of a womb that nurtures the fertilized seeds to maturity, filling them with food stores for their journey and allowing the tiny plant (embryo) inside each seed to grow sufficiently that it can survive the trip. In animal terms it is like the difference between a turtle who lays her eggs and departs, and the fox whose offspring gestate inside of her (and

(text continues on page 124)

Plant Breeding for the Home Gardener

(Or How to Make Thousands in Your Spare Time!)

I know that there has been quite a bit of press lately about genetically engineered plants and their potential threats to the environment. Add to this some of the (to my tastes) eccentric and overbred perennials that have come and gone in recent years, and I can see why many people cringe slightly at the thought of plant breeding. This being said, humans had been breeding plants in a casual way for at least 10,000 years before the Austrian monk Gregor Mendel made his famous discoveries about inheritance in sweet peas in the 1860s. Wheat, potatoes, corn, and just about every single food crop we grow are the product of selective breeding. It is natural to save the seeds of the plant that has the biggest or tastiest fruit, grows more vigorously, or keeps best in storage. And it is just as natural to pass on those plants that have the most colorful flowers, best disease resistance and vigor, or any other superior characteristic. You do not need a Ph.D. in molecular genetics to do some basic plant breeding, and the results are often surprising.

Geranium maculatum. A red-leaved seedling is very obvious in a flat of **white-flowered wild cranesbills,** which completely lack red pigmentation.

Polemonium reptans 'Stairway to Heaven'. This chance seedling in a flat of typical spreading **Jacob's ladder** has proven to be very popular among gardeners.

It is very hard today to find perennials for sale that are not the product of some selection and/or breeding. Even if you go out and collect seeds from the wild—which ones do you gravitate to? If you are like me you collect from the biggest, brightest, most vigorous plants, and in doing so you are selecting for certain traits that you find desirable. If you then keep and plant the seedlings that best display those same traits (and why wouldn't you?), then you can consider yourself a backyard breeder in the most basic sense. We raise hundreds of thousands of seedlings in the nursery every year, and I regularly pull aside unique seedlings. Variegated seedlings are particularly easy to spot, and we have a number of different ones in our trial beds. Most turn out to be rather unexciting in the end, but very occasionally, a plant proves to be a real standout. A case in point is the variegated Jacob's ladder 'Stairway to Heaven' (*Polemonium reptans* 'Stairway to Heaven'). I noticed it in a block of seedlings back in the late 1990s and pulled it aside. After five years we introduced it and began to collect royalties. To date the New England Wild Flower Society has collected well over $200,000 in royalties from this one plant! I only wish I had found it in my own garden: I could have nearly paid off our house. Now a one-in-a-million plant does not come along every day, but some of the most popular garden perennials such as *Coreopsis* 'Crème Brûlée' appeared spontaneously in gardens and owe their fame and fortune to intrepid and observant gardeners (in this case Long Island, New York, horticulturist Lois Woodhull). As I mentioned earlier, coreopsis are self-incompatible (they ignore their own pollen), but they will freely accept pollen from other coreopsis species and hybrids. What this means is that if you have a collection of several different coreopsis growing in your garden, some seeds that are produced will likely be hybrids between the different types. The justly famous *Coreopsis* 'Moonbeam' arose in just this fashion. It is a bastard seedling, so to speak; no one really knows who the father is, so you see it listed as several different species. It is surely one of the 10 best perennials ever introduced for a couple of reasons: it is vigorous and hardy, and best of all, it blooms for several months during the summer, which is a very rare thing among true perennials. It blooms so long because it is a sterile "mule" that cannot set seed. In plants, as in horses and donkeys, a hybrid is often sterile because the set of chromosomes it receives from one parent is slightly different from the one it gets from the other. Mismatched chromosomes do not divide evenly, and as a result, the poor plant cannot produce viable seed or pollen. So, it puts all the energy into flower production that other plants put into growing seeds, and it blooms and blooms and blooms. Not all hybrids are incapable of reproducing, but sterile hybrids appear much more commonly in gardens than in the wild because we tend to both isolate a species from others of its kind and surround it with closely related species it would not encounter in the wild. Though they are evolutionary dead ends, they do make for good garden plants for reasons that go beyond mere proclivity to bloom.

You may have heard the term *hybrid vigor* before. One of the simple truths of genetics is that diversity is good, homogeneity is bad. Inbreeding produces offspring that are genetically homogeneous and more likely to display rare, often deleterious traits not seen in the larger population. They are more likely to grow to the same height, bloom at exactly the same time, or suffer from the same rare genetic abnormality. Thus the population as a whole is more vulnerable to, say, a stretch of rainy weather that keeps the bees indoors when their flowers are all in bloom. Outbreeding (pollination by an unrelated individual of the same species) and to an even greater degree hybridization between different species produce the opposite effect. Seedlings as a group are more diverse and thus more adaptable in an unpredictable universe. In the example of bloom time, a few might flower weeks ahead or behind the pack, so the effects of bad weather on pollination are minimized.

There is more to hybrid vigor than this, though, but it requires a little understanding of genetics. I am not a geneticist, so I will keep it simple for both our sakes, because even if you do not want to launch into serious plant breeding, it is useful to know the basics so you understand why your fancy blue-flowered phlox begets magenta seedlings. What Gregor Mendel discovered back in 1860 is that every characteristic or trait, such as flower color or height, is controlled by one or more genes. In the most basic case, a plant has two copies of each gene, one inherited from the mother and one from the father. One form of the gene is the dominant form and the other is recessive. If a seedling inherits either one dominant and one recessive or two copies of the dominant gene, the dominant form of the trait is displayed. Only if the seedling inherits two copies of the recessive form will the recessive trait be seen. This is clearer when described graphically using blue lobelia (*Lobelia siphilitica*) as an example.

White flowers in *Lobelia siphilitica* are the product of a recessive gene. Only individuals with two copies of the recessive form (written here as ww) will be white. If you cross-pollinate a rare white-flowering plant that appeared in your garden some-

how with a standard blue-violet-flowering plant, which has two copies of the dominant gene (BB), all the offspring (called the F1 generation by breeders) will inherit a w from the one and a B from the other. The B will dominate in this F1 generation, and all the seedlings will bloom blue. Now, if you grow two of these

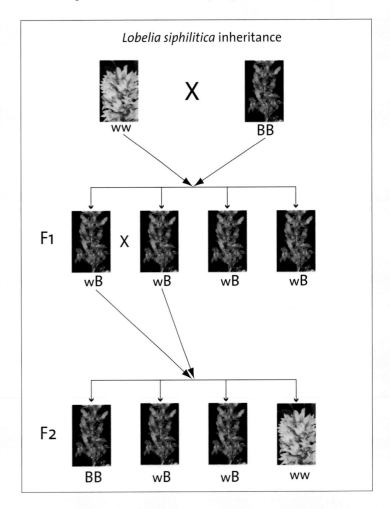

Lobelia siphilitica inheritance

blue F1 seedlings and cross them, 25 percent of the seedlings will inherit two copies of the recessive gene and thus have white flowers. Finally, if you then "backcross" one of these white-flowered seedlings with the original white-flowered parent, all the resulting seedlings will have white flowers (assuming, of course, that the bees have not snuck in with some blue pollen!).

As if this were not complicated enough, many traits are controlled by the two, three, or four independent genes. So, while the chance of getting a white-flowering lobelia in the F2 generation is 1 in 4, it would climb to 1 in 256 if four different genes were involved, and with such a genetic jumble you might expect to see a few other rare color forms such as pale blue or even true blue pop up here and there as well. This is the case with our eye color, and it explains why there are so many different shades of the common eye colors blue and brown and so few of the rare eye colors such as true green or violet. A breeder who is trying to breed a compact, disease-free, white-flowered lobelia has an even tougher road, as this rare individual would need to have just the right combination of, say, 16 genes, making the chances of finding one as low as 1 in 65,536! It is no wonder that plant breeding is a long and slow process. To increase the odds of finding that one special plant, breeders continue to cross siblings to produce F3, F4, and even F5 generations because, just as shown in the chart above, rare recessive traits are more and more likely to show up in highly inbred lines. Herein lies the paradox of much plant breeding. If you think about it in animal terms, an F4 generation occurs when parents, grandparents, and great-grandparents were all sister and brother. Generations of plant incest mean very rare undesirable recessive traits as well as desirable ones are more and more likely to show up in the same individual. It is the plant equivalent to the slack-jawed, humpbacked simpleton son drooling and slavering up there in the attic, who can nevertheless compose music that sounds as if it comes from heaven itself.

It is no wonder that unusual flowers such as blue border phlox or red daylilies are often weak and disease prone, as the inbreeding necessary to uncover such a rare recessive trait brings with it many other debilitating ones that are suppressed by dominant genes in the vast majority of the population. Have you ever planted a blue border phlox such as *Phlox paniculata* 'Blue Paradise' only to have it turn a rather unexciting magenta after a few seasons? The phlox has not actually changed flower color, as many people think. Rather, it has been overtaken by its own more vigorous seedlings. When 'Blue Paradise' is planted next to another cultivar such as the vigorous, white-flowered 'David', the muddied tide of inbreeding begins to flow the other

way as a flood of unrelated genes enter the pool. The seeds produced from such a pairing will have fewer recessive traits, so they are likely to produce plants that are both more vigorous and closer in color to the typical wild border phlox. These more vigorous seedlings spring up around the base of 'Blue Paradise' and quickly overtake it; the parent is actually choked out by its more fit and vigorous offspring. Though it might appear that the original plant has just changed color, it has in fact been the victim of unintended matricide.

Plant breeders commonly attempt to circumvent the paradox of inbreeding in two ways: breed a weak but special plant with a "wilder" one in hopes that a few seedlings with the special traits *and* increased vigor will appear, or purposely hybridize one species with another. Whereas *Coreopsis* 'Crème Brûlée' was a spontaneous (or, more accurately, bee-created) hybrid, many popular garden perennials are the products of planned marriages. The advantage of hybridization is that you can get some pretty unusual seedlings in only one or two generations because the genes of the parents are so different to begin with. Hypothetically speaking, it might take six or seven inbred generations to get a true blue border phlox if you stay within the species, but if you cross another blue phlox species, say, wood phlox (*Phlox divaricata*), with the white *Phlox paniculata* 'David', you are likely to have many blue-flowering ones in the first, or F1, generation. Cross a few of these that more strongly resemble the larger border phlox, and you can conceivably have a plant that can pass as a blue border phlox in only the second generation (well before the deleterious effects of inbreeding have

LEFT: *Iris siberica* breeding. The folks at Joe Pye Weed Garden in Carlisle, Massachusetts, grow out thousands of Siberian irises from controlled crosses to find a handful of exceptional new plants. Wouldn't you love your backyard to look like this in June? RIGHT: *Phlox paniculata* 'Blue Paradise'. Though striking in color, this highly line-bred garden phlox is very susceptible to powdery mildew; you can make out a bit on the leaves in the background.

Tiarella × 'Cygnet' is a patented hybrid between eastern and western **North American foamflowers.**

you are technically in violation of federal law. The U.S. patent office states it thus: "Grant of a patent for a plant precludes others from asexually reproducing or selling or using the patented plant" (www.uspto.gov/web/offices/pac/plant/#4). Now, I do not think home gardeners need to fear a visit from the FBI if they divide a few protected plants. The intent this flurry of patenting and trademarking (trademarks can be renewed indefinitely, whereas patents expire after 20 years, so breeders are adopting the former to secure long-term control over their "brands") is to allow the originator of the plant to control how it is produced and marketed and to allow said originator to collect royalties on the "invention." A case in point is the hardy delphinium *Delphinium* × 'Bartwentyfive'—not a true red but really more of a salmon pink. The breeders of the plant deliberately gave it a nonsensical name so folks have to use the trademarked name Red Caroline Delphinium (and pay a fee) if they hope to sell the plant.

But, this situation has two sides. I and the New England Wild Flower Society, along with a number of backyard hybridizers and gardeners, have benefited from plant patent royalties, and it is certainly fair to reward the inventor should he or she succeed in producing a red-flowering delphinium after many years of work. However, many home gardeners have the sense that large corporations and Big Brother have teamed up to squeeze the joy from gardening in the name of maximum profit. There is an element of truth in this, as the exponential rise in branded plants is concurrent with a massive consolidation in the industry since the early 1990s. Gardening is big business, and these days it is largely brought to you by big business, too.

taken their toll). In practice it is not that easy, for as I discussed above, when you combine two different species, the offspring are often sterile mules. Breeders use unbelievably heroic measures akin to those used in human infertility clinics to get these sterile plants to breed. The result of high-tech innovations such as embryo rescue is that for better or worse, some very unlikely pairings are now possible, and some hybrids finding their way into gardens would never have been possible 20 years ago.

The payoff for all this work is a patented, trademarked species de novo that may be worth millions to the originator. In the past two decades, we have witnessed a transformation in the perennial industry as patented and trademarked clones have largely replaced wilder forms and heirloom varieties. Technically, if you buy a patented plant, you are not allowed to propagate it in any way. If you divide one to fill in a few holes in your garden or root a few cuttings to share with a friend,

Delphinium 'Bartwentyfive'. The name is not the most evocative in the world, but nonsensical patent names are becoming much more common for plants so folks will use the more legible (and renewable) trademarked name.

go on to eat the turtle eggs). This is a huge advantage and in practical terms explains why, unless you live in a particularly damp climate, you will find many more seed plants volunteering in your garden than mosses or ferns.

Seeds

A typical perennial seed contains a fully formed little plant complete with the beginning of a root system and one or two leaves (the seed leaves or cotyledons). Since this tiny plant has no access to sun inside its protective shell, the mother plant surrounds it with a store of food that sustains it until it can sprout and begin to photosynthesize for itself. Once a seed is released from its ovary, the umbilical cord is cut, and it is a race against time in which it must find a suitable place to germinate and grow before it runs out of stores and dies. Seeds like those of mullein, which can survive in the earth for decades or even a century, do so by slowing down their metabolism so much that they are practically dead. Drying seeds after you pick them, as well as storing them in the refrigerator until you need them, slows down their metabolism too, and both are vital if you want to maintain seed viability (see chapter 10 for more on harvesting seeds).

TOP: *Agastache* 'Black Adder' with *Vanessa atalanta.* This hybrid hyssop is sterile; like *Coreopsis* 'Moonbeam', it flowers for several months and does not seed in, as hyssops are notorious for doing.

BOTTOM: *Dicentra eximia.* Fringed bleeding heart is self-incompatible—in other words, two individuals must be in proximity to each other to produce seed.

Polyploidy

Every normal (diploid) cell has two sets of chromosomes—one contributed by the male parent and one by the female. When cells divide, the chromosomes cleave in half and then each half reconstitutes itself so that the two daughter cells have the full set. This is a remarkable and delicate operation, splitting apart and reconstituting the genes, and sometimes mistakes occur. Very rarely, a cell divides improperly so that one daughter cell gets all the chromosomes and the other gets none (needless to say, this cell is a goner). The remaining cell now has not two but four sets of chromosomes, having become what is called a tetraploid. (*Ploid* means literally "having chromosome sets," so *tetraploid* means having four chromosome sets. Polyploidy is a generic term indicating anything more than the normal two sets. Triploid and hexaploid plants are polyploids with three and six sets, respectively.) If a tetraploid cell originates in a particular shoot tip, that shoot tip may go on to develop and grow but usually this does not amount to much. However, if the mistake occurs very early during embryonic development, the whole plant will be tetraploid. Tetraploids differ from their normal siblings in certain ways: flowers are larger, stems thicker, leaves darker green. Overall the plant may appear to have increased substance and vigor, at least in the best-case scenario. Bigger or more colorful flowers, sturdier stems, vigor, and size are all prized by gardeners, so many naturally occurring tetraploids have been selected by horticulturists over the years. You can even induce polyploidy by treating seeds with colchicine, a toxic chemical found in the autumn crocus (*Colchicum* spp.). Colchicine prevents the chromosomes from separating into two sets during cell division, and if you soak the seeds in it, a few will likely grow up to be polyploid. This has long been a favorite technique of plant breeders aiming to produce bigger, more robust perennials.

Though it may seem counterintuitive, polyploidy has a central role in creating new species in the wild as well. Every species has a specific number of chromosomes that may or may not be the same as that of its near relatives. When two related species with different numbers of chromosomes cross to form a hybrid, the hybrid will often be sterile because the pairs do not match up properly during sexual division (much like the well-known example of the mule—a sterile hybrid of the horse and donkey). The simple explanation for hybrid sterility is that the jumble of chromosomes received from the two different parents do not line up neatly and evenly. Like a deck with only 51 cards, if the parental chromosomes are mismatched, they will not split evenly in half during division. (You cannot play with 25.5 cards.) However, if a chance hybrid offspring has double the number of chromosomes (add another deck of 51 cards to make 102), then its cells could divide evenly and it would grow normally. This rare individual cannot mate with its normal parents (153 divided by 2 is 76.5) so it becomes reproductively isolated from its kin and is on its way to becoming a new species. One of the most famous examples of this is wheat (*Triticum aestivum*), which appeared as a chance natural tetraploid hybrid of two other species. Remarkably, fully half of the plant species alive today originated as such polyploid hybrids that continued to evolve.

Polygonatum biflorum var. *commutatum*. The tetraploid giant Solomon's seal is a magnificent woodland wildflower with stems topping six feet in length.

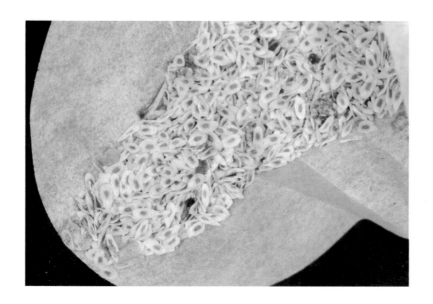

TOP LEFT: *Viola pubescens* seed capsule. As the shell of the violet capsule dries, it squeezes the seeds out, shooting them up to 15 feet.

TOP CENTER: *Actaea pachypoda* berries are even showier than the flowers, and they color up in summer when the shade garden is mostly green.

TOP RIGHT: *Aralia racemosa* berries. Birds love the berries of wild spikenard.

LEFT: *Asclepias incarnata* seed. Like a plane full of paratroopers, **milkweed** seeds are poised for flight.

BOTTOM LEFT: *Gentiana clausa.* The tiny seeds of **bottle gentian** are produced by the thousands.

A Garden Sown

Unless you collect seeds for propagation or are cultivating the minority of species that produce showy fruits or seed heads, your interest in seeds is likely twofold: how to prevent certain plants from seeding in everywhere and how to get others to seed around at all.

Discouraging Plants from Self-sowing

Certain perennials are notorious for self-sowing or self-seeding. Plume poppy (*Macleaya cordata*) is a robust species that takes the biological imperative to reproduce, reproduce, reproduce very much to heart. Plant one and soon you will have many, and boy are they tough to get rid of. Many popular perennials, such as violets or many members of the aster, grass, mint, and poppy families, will seed in exuberantly if conditions are right. It may be difficult to prevent this entirely, but beyond the obvious advice to avoid planting them, there are a few things that help. First, as discussed earlier, weedy species often have small seeds, and small seeds typically need light to germinate, so a yearly layer of mulch applied in spring will thwart some of the previous seasons' bounty. Second, plants that are self-incompatible (that will not accept their own pollen) will not produce seed if they have no partner. Third, you can remove the developing seeds after flowering (a procedure erroneously called deadheading, for as we know, those seed-filled heads are anything but dead!). This is an easy task in theory, but in practice it requires diligence to time pruning after flowering but before the seeds are mature. (You can tell seeds are mature by the color of their seed coat. Immature seeds are green or white, while mature ones are typically tan, brown, or black so they are camouflaged in the soil.) If you prune off the spent flowers and developing ovaries, the plant may even flower again. Remember that seeds can live for years in the soil before germinating, so it may take quite a few seasons to eradicate all the progeny of a garden thug once it has been removed.

Encouraging Plants to Self-sow

Aside from doing the opposite of the advice given above—cultivating the soil around your plants to stir up small seeds, planting at least two of everything, allowing seeds to mature before pruning back perennials—there are a few more things you can do to encourage your plants to self-sow. It may seem rather silly to have to intervene in a process—self-sowing—that is by definition supposed to happen on its own, but remember that in the wild only a small percentage of seeds ever grow to maturity. Most are eaten before they sprout or fail to gain purchase in a favorable spot once they do. If only one

in a thousand trillium seeds succeeds in nature, you cannot expect to see more than a handful of seedlings coming up each year from even a sizable colony (the average trillium capsule contains 15 to 50 seeds). If all you have in your garden are a few plants, then you will be lucky if you ever see a trillium seedling without your assistance. You can greatly increase the odds by collecting the mature seeds before something else does and then planting them in a suitable spot free of compe-

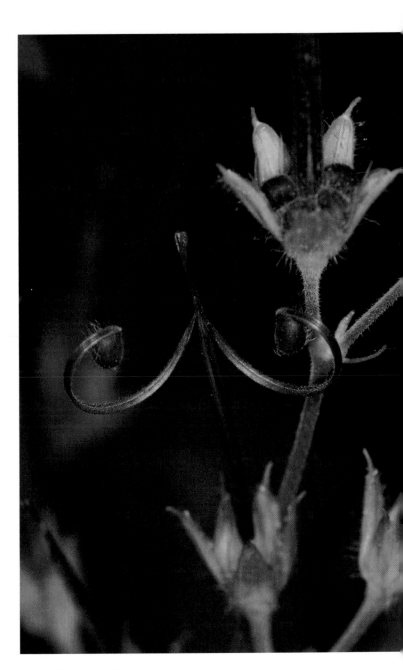

Geranium maculatum. Like violets, geraniums have explosive seeds that are launched via curling catapults. Don't be surprised if you find geraniums coming up some distance from your original plants.

tition somewhere else in your garden. Small seeds may be merely scattered about atop bare soil, but seeds larger than this letter o are best scratched into the soil. To increase your odds, scatter a lot of seeds in a small area rather than a large one. I am not sure why this matters, but I have found that it does. Finally, and most importantly, learn to recognize young seedlings so you can weed out those you do not want and encourage those you do. (I am developing a collection of seedling images on my Web site, www.williamcullina.com, just for this reason.)

Whether you are trying to encourage or discourage them, seeds and seedlings are the remarkable culmination of a process that begins when the first flowers unfurl and the bees go to work. Each seed is a miniature facsimile of its mother jacketed in a protective shell and (if it is lucky) stocked with enough food to survive for months or years until it can put down roots, raise up leaves, and begin the process anew. It is a true sign that your garden has come of age when it is populated by the children and grandchildren of the original patriarchs and matriarchs you brought home from the nursery or the meadow and lovingly set out all those years ago. A garden of generations is the mark of a gardener who truly understands his or her bit of earth and the flowers most appropriate for it.

Helleborus orientalis. **Hellebore** seeds are heavy and mostly fall down below the parent, though a few may be carried off by ants. These can be pricked out and transplanted to a place in the garden where their chances might improve.

CHAPTER 6

PESTS AND DISEASES

Do you obsess over the slug holes in your hosta? Can you rattle off the names of five insecticides in less than three minutes? Does the thought of powdery mildew spreading relentlessly though your phlox make your skin crawl? They are not my favorite subjects, but pests and diseases are something that every plant and every gardener have to contend with. Before I launch into the perennial gardener's equivalent of the *Physicians' Desk Reference,* though, I feel some philosophical perspective is needed.

Despite an array of defensive hairs and chemicals, camouflaged leaves, and myriad other strategies for self-preservation, every plant will be eaten by something. Well, almost every plant. Some of the most serious exotic invasive species became popular precisely because nothing eats them. As a consequence they grow phenomenally well and crowd out indigenous plants that spend a good portion of their photosynthetic budget making toxins and repellants and replacing lost leaves, flowers, stems, and roots. Species such as purple loosestrife (*Lythrum salicaria*) are tempting garden plants

ABOVE: *Mantis religiosa.* The European mantis is a familiar and formidable insect predator with undeniable charisma.

TOP LEFT: *Hibiscus moscheutos* flower under assault from Japanese beetles.

TOP RIGHT: *Lythrum salicaria.* Once a popular garden perennial in the United States because it grows very vigorously and suffers from few pests, purple loosestrife grows *too* well in much of this country, escaping gardens and becoming an invasive pest in many wetlands.

BOTTOM LEFT: *Trillium grandiflorum* deer damage. Finding the telltale signs of deer damage on a prized trillium feels like a punch to the gut.

because they look so unblemished and grow so lustfully, but without any insects, mites, fungi, bacteria, viruses, nematodes, reptiles, amphibians, birds, or mammals to keep them in check, they have run amok in northern wetlands from the Maritimes to the Great Lakes.

The next time you notice those slug holes or mildew blemishes try to be grateful, not grumpy, because these critters are keeping all that greenery at a manageable level (not to mention providing the basis for the food chain on which we all depend). I know this is easier said than done, though.

I am not an horticultural hypochondriac by nature, but I am very parental toward my prized garden perennials, so I get quite an itchy trigger finger when I see my trilliums ravaged by voles or my hepaticas riddled with crown mold, and it is all I can do not to run for the shotgun or the spray gun and begin blasting away. In principle I know that plants are the foundation of the food chain, but it is hard to see my newly planted treasures become gourmet takeout for the local deer herd. While the image of me firing birdshot into vole holes is still fresh in your mind, let me say that I have never actually gone quite this far (probably only because of the collateral damage it would cause to the plants). I have poisoned, trapped, and speared the furry little rodents in vain attempts to stem their ceaseless appetite for my choicest plants. I have

TOP: *Vanessa virginiensis* butterfly nectaring on sedum.

BOTTOM: I grow pussytoes (*Antennaria* sp.) partly to attract the spiny caterpillars of the American lady butterfly (*Vanessa virginiensis*), even though they make the plants look a bit ragged when feeding.

OPPOSITE: *Allium rosenbachianum.* At the New York Botanical Garden the yellowing leaves of ornamental onion are cleverly hidden behind a low boxwood hedge.

TOP LEFT: *Bufo americanus.* Who needs pesticides when you have the American toad? Once I stopped poisoning slugs in the garden, I noticed that the population of toads began to skyrocket while the number of slugs went way down.

TOP RIGHT: *Epargyreus clarus* (silver-spotted skipper) on *Lychnis alpina.*

also, I am hesitant to admit, shot a few deer after all attempts to discourage them failed.

After our nursery cat almost died from eating warfarin-laced vole bait, I gave up on rodenticides, just as I have slowly given up the host of deadly preparations available to kill just about anything that eats plants. I have also hung up the deer rifle and have turned to plastic deer fencing and less-palatable species instead—at least for now. I do occasionally use baking soda on the hepaticas or horticultural oil spray to knock back aphids on the butterflyweed, but by and large I have adopted a live and let live (live and let die?) attitude as time has gone by.

It is certainly healthier for us, our loved ones, and the natural world when we hang up the spray tank for good, but it does require a certain constitutional fortitude to let the sick plants die. I was recently talking to a famed garden writer and expert horticulturist about her maturation as a gardener. In her 40-odd years tending the soil she evolved first into a dedicated plant collector who had to have one of every rare and choice thing available amassed into a jumbled collection that nurseryman Tony Avent famously calls "drifts of one." From there she became an aesthetic perfectionist obsessed with picture-perfect design and flawlessly beautiful perennials flowing in a seamless sea of well-composed color from one property line to the other. As both she and her plantings have matured, however, she is entering a third stage that puts the emphasis on simplicity and suitability. She is giving up all those fussy plants and plans that populated her gardens for years in favor of a more reserved palette that is easier on the eye and on the back. As part of this shift, she tolerates a certain level of destruction, though she has forgone the holey hostas and the mildewed bee balms in favor of plants less afflicted. I believe that if you stay with it long enough and see enough plants die, you reach a point where you stop fighting nature and just grow with it. I am sure the Buddhists have a better word for it, but I will call it acceptance.

I am a bit of a plant collector at heart, though my many moves over the years have tempered this tendency markedly. I am sure if you have ever tried to move a large collection of plants, you know what I mean. This is the hardest sort of gardening, because not only does the desire for the next great corydalis prevent one from enjoying all the plants already in the garden, there is always the problem of where to squeeze that self-same corydalis in once you do acquire it, not to mention the gut-wrenching despair you will experience when it succumbs to crown rot. Buddhism has a word for this insatiable desire: *tanha*. Ironically, though, when you assemble so many plants from so many places in one small area, diseases spread like strep throat through a preschool, and insects spread like lice in a haberdashery (now there is an unpleasant thought). Also, when you are constantly bringing in new perennials from all over the world, you can quickly amass a collection of exotic pests and diseases that hitchhike their way into your garden. In the end it is this sad fact that spells the end of many plant collections and the mad passion to collect them. Many times I have heard versions of the sad refrain, "I used to have such a marvelous collection of _____ until that blasted _____ came in from _____ and killed them all."

Picture-perfect gardens are also a source of considerable stress, though if pictures are truly your aim, modern digital image correction is a wonder. Not enough flowers on that foxglove? Open the image with your photo-processing software and add some more. It is now shockingly easy to remove the dents and wrinkles from garden photographs. I would hope that unlike the faces of certain celebrity divas, most garden magazine centerfolds are not retouched, but the reality is that if you seek your inspiration solely from blousy, buxom garden books, your own garden will always look a bit threadbare in comparison. In the magic world of photographs, every garden is frozen at its peak of bloom in golden hour perfection, but gardens, like people, have their good and bad days. Even the most sumptuous look a bit pale in the harsh light of midday (especially when its 100 degrees F, has not rained for

Biological Controls

To combat the spread of purple loosestrife, four European insects that feed on the plant—two beetles that eat the leaves, a weevil that munches roots, and another that devours flowers—have been released around the Great Lakes and northeastern United States. Though there is some concern that the insects will feed on indigenous relatives such as *Lythrum alatum* and *Decodon verticillatus,* the program has been dramatically effective in reducing levels of purple loosestrife in many wetlands. Some debate the wisdom of introducing one exotic organism to combat another, but biological rather than chemical control—especially when it encourages natural predators—is by and large a far safer, ecologically friendly, and effective way to manage pest species in your garden.

weeks, and you have been too busy to get at the weeding yet). So leave that hose in the path and do not fret over slug holes in the hosta; you can always make them disappear with a few clicks of the computer mouse and enjoy garden perfection from the comfort of your easy chair.

Seriously, though, gardens are meant to be an escape from all the little worries of life, not sources of worry in and of themselves. Regardless, for the serious gardener, this is easier said than done, so I think it is prudent to have some under-

LEFT: *Metriorhynchomiris dislocatus.* The red-bordered black plant bug is an innocuous native species that relies on wild geraniums for its food. It is never present in numbers that threaten the plants.

RIGHT: *Lilioceris lilii.* Asian lily leaf beetle, however, is a newly and accidentally introduced pest that can be devastating to wild and cultivated true lilies.

TOP: Black vine weevil damage on *Heuchera villosa* (hairy alumroot). The weevil larvae tunnel through and kill the stems and crown.

BOTTOM: Nematodes can be plant pests as well as predators of insect pests. I spotted this large, unidentified species crawling through the grass.

standing of the various pests and diseases that affect perennials so that you can decide how and where to pick your battles.

Common Insect Pests

There are millions of different insects in the world, and perhaps half derive all or part of their sustenance from plants. Some, for example, Japanese beetles, seem to eat anything they land on, but most of the insects that feed on the leaves, stems, roots, and flowers of our perennials are fairly species specific, dining only on one family, genus, or even species. In most cases, it is the generalist feeders—especially introduced species such as Japanese beetles and black vine weevils—that are the biggest problem in gardens. Insects that are brought to North America on purpose or by accident are by and large our biggest pests, as the indigenous plants have not evolved defenses against them and there is a dearth of predators that have evolved to eat them. Even specialized insects such as the Asian lily leaf beetle (*Lilioceris lilii*) have proven to be devastating once established in the brave new world of North America. Native insects, especially those that are highly host specific, such as the wild indigo dusky wing butterfly that feeds on *Baptisia* species or monarch butterflies that dine on milkweeds, are rarely a problem because the plants have some defenses against them and there are predators that recognize them as food. Where this type of insect may become a problem is in large monocultures that are rarely encountered in gardens. Where have you seen a perennial garden containing several hundred false indigos and not much else? A diverse garden of many species that have been chosen to thrive in the site where they are planted is much less likely to suffer from severe insect attacks. Remember that healthy plants have the extra resources they need to produce chemical or physical deterrents and toxins, whereas stressed plants do not. Furthermore, many insects can recognize stressed plants by their color or taste, so a perennial in trouble will actually attract more pests to the garden. Therefore, rule one as far as insect control goes is to move or discard any perennials that are simply not thriving where they are.

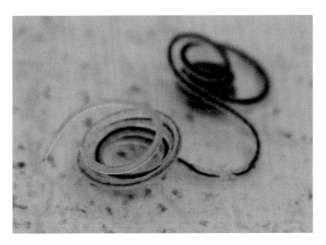

CHEWING INSECTS

Black Vine Weevils

Black vine weevil (*Otiorhynchus sulcatus*) is a serious pest of ornamental plants that was first introduced from Europe in the nineteenth century and has established throughout the United States and southern Canada. The small, gray black adults feed on foliage, but it is the root- and crown-feeding grubs that are particularly destructive to certain perennials. Black vine weevils, along with closely related strawberry root weevils, can do tremendous damage to members of the saxifrage family (Saxifragaceae) such as coralbells, though they also feed on lobelias, jack-in-the-pulpits, asters, and other members of the aster family (Asteraceae) such as coneflowers and black-eyed Susans, in addition to astilbes, epimediums, hostas, lilies, phloxes, and sedums. Badly affected plants will simply topple over as most of their roots or rhizomes are gone. I have had reasonably good results using one of several parasitic nematodes that come impregnated in a sponge that you soak in water and then use to water susceptible plants on a damp or rainy evening. Several nematodes are available to control the half-inch-long white grubs. In my part of the world, they do need to be occasionally reapplied to remain effective. Adults come out at night to feed, so search for them on susceptible plants with a flashlight if you suspect a problem.

Japanese Beetles

Japanese beetles (*Popillia japonica*) entered the United States around 1910 in New Jersey, possibly in a batch of iris rhizomes imported from Japan. They have spread relentlessly westward over the last 100 years and are now across the Mississippi River and headed over the Great Plains. The larvae (grubs) feed on the roots of grasses, so the more turf or meadow you or your neighbors have, the more beetles you will find in your garden. Adults have amazing resistance to plant chemical defenses, so they can feed on a wide range of species. Favorites include members of the rose (Rosaceae), aster, and mallow (Malvaceae) families, which include many popular garden perennials. The most effective long-term control can be achieved by establishing bacterial milky spore disease *Paenibacillus* (formerly *Bacillus*) *popilliae* in lawns and other grass-dominated areas. Milky spore bacteria are applied as a commercially available powder to the surface of lawns. The spores wash down to the root zone and are consumed by and kill the grubs. Every infected larva releases more spores that infect more larvae. It takes several years for the disease to take hold, but once established it persists for decades. If the population of grubs plummets, the spores remain dormant in the soil until numbers increase. Milky spore is amazingly effective once it gets going, but you may have to convince your neighbors to apply some, too, if you live in a lawn-rich neighborhood. In the short term, release of parasitic nematodes such as *Heterorhabditis bacteriophora* can reduce numbers of the insect until the disease acheives control. When I was a kid, we used to set out traps to lure the insects with pheromone and bait attractants. However, research has demonstrated that the traps actually bring more beetles to your yard than they eliminate. You are better off providing the traps free to your neighbors—especially the ones with monstrous lawns—as a community service. Adult beetles home in on foliage damaged by other feeding beetles, so pinching off partially eaten leaves may have some small deterrent effect. I have also trained my son Liam in the art of beetle mashing. As you undoubtedly

Popillia japonica. Japanese beetles are one of the scourges of the perennial garden, but biological controls really do work to keep their numbers at tolerable levels.

know if you have these pests in your garden, they drop off the leaves once alarmed, so you can catch them in a can or hand held discreetly underneath.

Earwigs

Earwigs, with their familiar pincerlike hind parts, are nocturnal insects that hide in mulch and soil during the day and climb up and munch on leaves at night. Like so many of our garden pests, they were brought to the United States from Europe accidentally and are now established just about everywhere. It is very educational to head out at night with a flashlight and investigate the critters that are munching away in your perennial garden. You may be surprised at what you will find. If you are really plagued by earwigs, roll up a section of newspaper and leave it out under the plants in the afternoon, and shake out the earwigs hiding in it the next day. A number of commercial earwig traps are on the market, but I have made my own with a tuna can. When you open the tuna, do not cut the lid completely off. Save the juice from the tuna and mix it with enough vegetable oil to fill the can one-fourth of the way and leave it out in the garden. Those earwigs love the smell of tuna!

Caterpillars

Because caterpillars turn into butterflies and moths, most folks can tolerate a few lost leaves on their perennials if a caterpillar is to blame. Hundreds of different caterpillars feed on perennials, and many are fairly host specific. Many folks interested in butterfly gardening take advantage of this fact

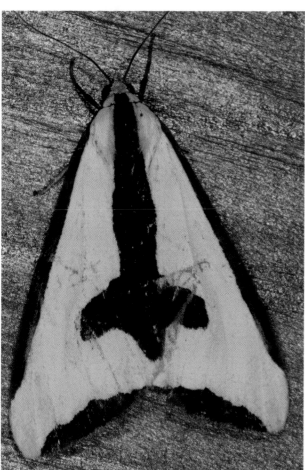

If you plant it, they will come. Native plant species are host to many native insects, and I welcome them into my garden. Plants in the aster family host butterflies as well as the caterpillars of many moths, including *Schinia arcigera* (top left), *Eusarca confusaria* (top right), *Derrima stellata* (bottom right), and *Haploa clymene* (bottom left). One of the most satisfying parts of gardening with natives is watching the biological diversity of your yard begin to increase rather than decrease as is happening in much of suburban America.

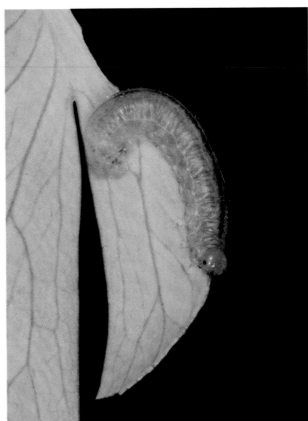

LEFT: *Cucullia convexipennis.* An owlet moth caterpillar shares a goldenrod with a few aphids. Goldenrods support a greater diversity of insects than just about any other perennial.

RIGHT: *Pristiphora aquilegiae.* Columbine sawfly can be a voracious feeder, consuming all the leaves of your garden columbines before you even notice it.

and plant perennials such as pussytoes that are larval food plants for specific butterflies (in this case the American lady butterfly). Generally, caterpillars come and go in one to three generations per season depending on the species and latitiude. Therefore, damage may be locally severe for a week or two, but then the plant recovers as the insects pupate. *Bacillus thuringiensis* (Bt) sprays are employed primarily against crop-eating caterpillars such as corn earworms and cabbage whites but are effective against a wide variety of caterpillars. In my experince, though, chemical control is rarely if ever necessary in a healthy, pesticide-free garden. In fact, one of the things I most enjoy about gardening with perennials is watching how the diversity of moths and butterflies increases as my gardens mature and diversify. One of the few exceptions is iris borer

(*Macronoctua onusta*), a small native moth whose caterpillars bore into and weaken or kill iris rhizomes. Damaged plants will look yellowed and begin to die in summer, and if you cut the rhizomes open you will see small tunnels where the pink, grublike caterpillars have fed. The best defense is good sanitation. Eggs overwinter in dead foliage and stems, so clean up your irises thoroughly in the fall, and remove and destroy afflicted plants.

Sawflies

Sawflies look like caterpillars, though they lack the suction-cup rear legs of caterpillars. Two particularly destructive ones are the columbine sawfly and the hibiscus or hollyhock sawfly. Both appear out of nowhere in large numbers and skeletonize

TOP: *Chrysoperla rufilabris.* Green lacewing is a diligent aphid predator.

BOTTOM: Aphids on *Dicentra eximia* (fringed bleeding heart).

leaves (eating all but the veins). Bt is not effective against sawflies, so hand picking or selective use of a pyrethroid insecticide is the best control.

SUCKING INSECTS

Aphids

Aphids are ubiquitous insects that every gardener is familiar with. Though they all look similar—small, soft-bodied, green, black, orange, or tan insects that congregate in large colonies on tender new growth—there are approximately 1,350 species in North America. Many perennials host aphids, though members of the aster, rose, phlox, mallow, honeysuckle, and milkweed families are especially prone to aphid attack. Aphids feed by inserting a needlelike stylet into the plant's phlom. The osmotic pressure in the phlom actually pushes the sugary fluid up into the insect. Aphids are primarily after protein in the phlom, so most of the sugars are processed and secreted out their rear in the form of honeydew—as euphemistic a word for excrement as you are likely to hear. The next time I change the twins' diapers I am going to call it "collectin' the honeydew." Many ants "farm" aphid colonies, protecting them from predators and licking up the honeydew in return. Aphids reproduce amazingly fast because during most of the season they do it without sex. Eggs that hatch in spring are all female, and these quickly mature into adults that begin to give birth to live young that grow from unfertilized eggs. All the offspring are female, and these soon begin to birth more females. Only as the weather cools are a few males born, and these mate with females to lay fertilized eggs that will wait out the winter, then hatch out a new generation of females. Under ideal conditions, a population can double every three days. Thank goodness that so many things feed on aphids or we would have no plants left! Everyone knows that ladybugs and ladybirds feed on aphids, as do lacewings, hoverflies, plant bugs, parasitic wasps, crickets, spiders, and harvestmen. Spraying broad-sprectrum pesticides to control aphids is futile, because the predators will die along with the aphids and take far longer to recover. Small, soft-bodied, and delicate, aphids are easily killed by detergents such as insecticidal soaps or fine, horticultural oil sprays that have less effect on predators. Their stylets are very thin and fragile, so to protect them they secrete a protective coating that stiffens the stylet like a sheath as it

travels into the plant. If you blast the aphids with a strong jet of water from the hose, you can actually bend or snap off this stiffened stylet, rendering the poor aphid mouthless. I use this technique to control bad outbreaks and leave the various predators to control the rest.

Aphids damage plants directly by siphoning off phloem, especially from tender new growth, but they are also one of the main vectors for plant viruses. When an aphid inserts its stylet into the phloem, it first spits out a bit of saliva that prevents wound clotting in much the same way that mosquito saliva prevents blood clotting in people. The saliva or stylet may contain viruses picked up from neighboring plants that are thus set free to infect a new host: more about the debilitating effects of viruses to come. Sugar-rich honeydew may also attract molds that carpet foliage and reduce light for photosynthesis.

Thrips

Thrips are tiny winged insects that feed much like aphids, though they often hide within flower buds or developing shoot tips, making them both difficult to treat and particularly damaging because small injured areas on tiny developing leaves and shoots expand into large distorted lesions or spots as the plant tissues expand. Thrips are more mobile than aphids, so they are even more effective vectors for plant viruses. Other than relying on biological controls, there is not much we can do to control thrips except avoid the use of broad-spectrum insecticides that kill their natural predators. In the nursery at the New England Wild Flower Society, we have an influx of thrips and green leafhoppers every June when the surrounding hayfields are cut. The insects descend on the nursery once their food source in the fields has been removed. We use insecticidal soaps and ultrafine oil sprays to help control both pests, but it is an incomplete remedy. Luckily thrips are usually not a severe problem in perennial gardens.

Leafhoppers

Leafhoppers are ubiquitous insects that feed like aphids and thrips by sucking plant fluids. There are 100,000 species of leafhoppers in the world, and more are being discovered every year—especially in the tropical rainforests where they abound. Leafhoppers are rarely a problem in perennial gardens, though they can potentially transmit viruses just as aphids do. Larval stages can be controlled with ultrafine horticultural oil sprays.

Plant Bugs

Plant bugs are generally host-specific insects that are true bugs without the shell (carapace) covering their wings that beetles have. Damage shows up as small pits or stipples on foliage but

A leafhopper species.

is usually not severe enough to require treatment. Four-lined plant bug is one of the most common in gardens and loves species in the mint family.

Other Sucking Insects

In greenhouses, whiteflies, scales, and mealybugs are serious pests, but though they are present in outdoor gardens, natural predators keep them in check and they are rarely a serious problem. Spider mites and other related plant mites can sometimes cause significant damage to outdoor perennials, especially in hot weather when the plants are under stress. Leaves that have a stippled, faded look and, in bad infestations, even a fine webbing are signs of spider mite infestation. For all of these insects and mites, insecticidal soap and ultrafine horticultural oil sprays provide control should it become necessary.

Mollusks

For most folks who garden in the shade, slugs and snails are premier garden pests and need little introduction. There is something inherently repulsive about a little shell-less snail oozing a yellow slime that is next to impossible to wipe off your fingers. However, it may come as a surprise that those slimy slugs munching holes in your hosta are probably introduced species brought to North America accidentally. Yes, just like black vine weevils, Japanese beetles, and earwigs, as well as most of our weeds, worms, and pest birds, we have international commerce to thank for our slug problems! There are roughly 73 species of slugs in North America, and of these 22 are introduced (Turgeon et al. 1998). The most pernicious garden pests are the gray field slug (*Deroceras reticulatum*) and dusky arion (*Arion subfuscus*), both brought here from Europe long ago and now widely established in North America. The greenhouse slug (*Lehmannia valentiana*) is also a pest in nurseries as well as gardens in warmer parts of the United States. This is a "weedy" mollusk in that it reproduces very quickly and thus the population builds up rapidly during damp summers. Of the 51 native slugs, most are found along the Pacific Coast (like the colorfully named warty jumping slug, *Hemphillia glandulosa*). In general they are retiring creatures that rarely cause serious harm, and many are rare, local, or endangered. One species, the meadow or marsh slug (*Deroceras leave*), can be a problem in damp, shady gardens. There is some debate as to whether this is a native or introduced slug (yes, there is a whole world of terrestrial mollusks out there if you ever get bored with plants). It appears that, as with agricultural weeds and earthworms, European slugs compete much better than native species in disturbed, human-dominated environments.

Slugs eat by rasping off plant tissue with a ribbonlike mouthpart, and they need to eat several times their body weight daily to survive. They overwinter as adults or eggs, and the weedy species can lay several broods of eggs per season. Most slugs begin life male then become female as they get larger. Slug courtship rituals involve elaborate chases and dances involving copious quantities of slime, culminating in a dramatic semen exchange. Slugs are generally more of a problem in gardens than snails for one simple reason: snails need a ready source of calcium to build shells, and this element is often in short supply, so large-shelled snails have a harder time finding suitable terrestrial habitat. Without shells, slugs are more vulnerable, but they can grow large in places that lack calcium. Slugs are primarily a pest of herbaceous plants since they can crawl away from the ground only for as long as it is

damp. A slug stranded in a tree after the sun comes out risks desiccation and death.

Some commercial baits (molluscicides) are available for controlling slugs, and you may have also tried baiting them with beer. Beer is irresistible to slugs, and they will crawl into

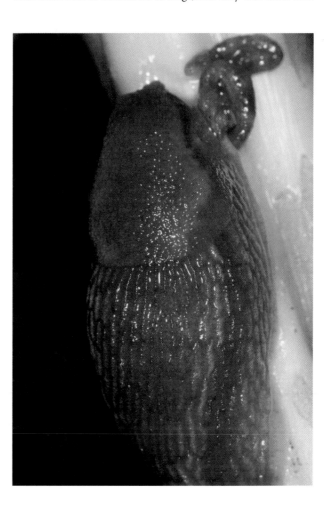

TOP: *Arion subfuscus*. The dusky slug, a very familiar resident of gardens, hitchhiked here from Europe at least 175 years ago and is now widely naturalized.

BOTTOM: *Agriolimax reticulatus*. The European field slug is widely naturalized in the United States.

Foliar nematode damage on *Anemone nemorosa* (wood anemone) shows up as irregular, deeply pigmented areas.

shallow saucers of it and drown. We began baiting slugs in the nursery with a molluscicide one year, though, and our population of toads plummeted. I do not know if we inadvertently killed the toads or if they went elsewhere once the slugs disappeared. Of course, once we stopped baiting, the slugs came back like gangbusters without all those fat toads on patrol. Hence, we have decided to tolerate a level of slug damage to encourage healthy populations of predators such as toads, snakes, and birds.

Earthworms

Undoubtedly you have learned that worms are a sign of healthy soil, but as is the case with slugs, the dominant garden worms in the United States and Canada were introduced from Europe and Asia. European night crawlers (*Lumbricus terrestris*) have been here quite a long time and are abundant both in regions where native worms exist, as well as the zone north of the glacial boundary where they do not. More trou-

bling for me has been the more recently introduced Asian wiggly worm (*Amynthas agrestis*), a big, aggressive superworm that breeds like aphids and turns forest detritus into worm castings at an alarming rate. In affected areas, there is nothing but a three- to six-inch layer of worm castings left in the woodland floor by the end of the growing season. In northern forests dependent on a deep layer of humus and its associated populations of symbiotic fungi, this worm can have devastating effects. The castings make the soil so loose that many perennials simply fall out of the ground. There is no effective control other than to treat the area with powdered sulfur at the rate of about 1.5 pounds per 100 square feet to lower the pH (these worms like a near-neutral soil pH). Of course this has negative impacts on woodland plants that prefer higher pH soils, so it is not always an effective option. I have tried electric shock and mustard-seed teas to no avail. Mixing in sharp sand (also called builder's or concrete sand) does seem to reduce problems around plant roots, but again this is often not feasible except on a small scale. These worms spread as eggs or as adults in nursery soils, so they are easy to accidentally introduce into gardens. You can identify them because they come out of the ground wriggling like little snakes when you disturb the surface. Fishermen tossing out leftover bait have introduced them as well as other species into wilderness areas.

Mammals

Mammals are certainly more appealing to the eye than most insects or mollusks, but they are also some of the most destructive in perennial gardens. Largely this is because of their size, wide-ranging preferences, and longevity. Whereas a sawfly outbreak may last two weeks and be confined to one or two species, a resident deer herd will need to feed extensively all year round. It is also harder to control mammals in that while most folks feel no hesitation in squashing a Japanese beetle or spraying mildew with fungicide, far fewer can pull the trigger on a doe-eyed deer or set out a snap trap at the entrance to a vole tunnel.

Deer

Whenever I give a lecture about plants these days, the issue of deer resistance always comes up. The animal in question is almost always the white-tailed deer, a highly adaptable species that inhabits all of North America south of the Arctic Circle except for the drier areas of the southwestern United States and California (the mule or black-tailed deer is primarily western and can be a problem in certain areas). Estimates I have read put the pre-European settlement population of white-tails in North America at around 40 million animals. Due to relentless hunting in the seventeenth through nineteenth centuries, the population dipped as low as 500,000 by 1900 before legislation was enacted to protect the species from extinction. White-tails rebounded exceedingly well over the last century and are now estimated to exceed 15 million animals continent-wide. This is still less than two-fifths the population that inhabited these lands prior to European settlement, so what is the problem? The problem is that deer like to live around people. Head up to the north woods of Maine and you will be lucky to see one, but drive through a suburban neighborhood in New Jersey and you can easily spot herds of 5 to 10 feasting on shrubbery and perennials during the middle of the day. In parts of New Jersey, Pennsylvania, and New York, as well as other more settled areas, deer densities are two to three times what they would likely have been in precolonial times. So while the total population is still much less than the continent supported 350 years ago, certain regions are hosting far more deer than they ever did historically. If you were to design the perfect place for deer to live it would include a variety of open and wooded habitat, a diverse array of potential forage plants from grasses and forbs to shrubs and trees—preferably well fertilized and watered for maximum palatability and nutritional content and supplemented with feeding stations filled with corn, sunflower seeds, or other tasty treats—a well-planned network of trails and corridors to move to and from foraging and resting grounds, a dearth of natural enemies such as wolves and cougars, little competition from other larger grazing animals such as moose and buffalo, and finally increasingly milder winters, which are the toughest times for deer. Of course this describes suburbia perfectly. Our pampered gardens, lawns, farms, and bird feeders provide plenty of sustenance, roads and trails allow easy movement, predators and competitors have been eliminated, hunting is often prohibited, and global warming is making things easier in the winter. It is no wonder that suburban deer have two or three fawns per year compared to zero to one in wilderness areas. Life is good. Now if we could only get rid of cars, then it would be perfect.

If you are unfortunate enough to live in deer nirvana, then coping with browse damage is a way of life. The only sure way to have a deer-proof garden is to fence the whole thing with strong 8- to 10-foot fencing and remember to always shut the gate. The availability of relatively inexpensive black plastic mesh deer fencing in recent years has made this an attractive option where it is feasible or permitted by zoning. However, once some folks start to fence out deer, their neighbors have to support even more because the females do not migrate far from their birthplace. It becomes much like the situation I found myself in at our previous residence. All the neighbors had dogs, so every time I dispensed with one woodchuck, another would move in to take its place. Mine was the only

Delphiniums contain powerful alkaloids that discourage deer browsing. This is not to say your deer won't sample them now and then.

has greatly reduced deer browsing in the garden, but it does require diligence and adaptation. Hunting is not possible in many places, and neither is fencing, so the next best choice is to focus on plants less palatable to deer. This is far easier than applying repellent sprays, which may be temporarily effective but are very labor intensive to apply.

Deer-Resistant Perennials

I hesitate including a list of deer-resistant perennials because I am certain that there is a deer somewhere that will willingly eat just about any plant on the list. I know the deer in my neighborhood like joe-pye weeds (*Eupatoriadelphus* spp.) even though they regularly appear on deer-resistant plant lists. Likewise, they leave Japanese painted fern (*Athyrium nipponicum* 'Pictum') alone even though some resources tag this as

dog-free, woodchuck-friendly place on the block. From years of watching deer, it has become obvious that they are not only creatures of habit, but often predictable in their movements. If you cut a trail through dense woods, they will begin to use it. If you block a trail with fencing or strands of monofilament fishing line, they will reroute somewhere else. I have taken advantage of this on our property, where deer populations are moderate. I have cut trails around the cultivated portion of our land and partially fenced off the cultivated areas. Additionally, I regularly scent-mark the boundaries of this off-limits zone (beer and other diuretics are very effective for enhancing scent production). A few places I put up several strings of 20-pound-test fishing line to close off old trails. This

highly palatable. Fawns learn what to eat and what not to eat from their mothers, and just as with people, every deer has its own preferences. White-tailed deer undergo seasonal changes in their digestive systems so that in spring and summer they can digest the fresh new growth of forbs and grasses, while in winter they can handle woody twigs and tough evergreen leaves. This, combined with a natural curiosity, leads them to try all manner of plants. Typically when they encounter an unfamiliar plant they will nibble a bit, then if they survive, they will come back in a day or two for more. I have not seen research on the subject, but it is plausible that certain populations of deer evolve resistance to certain plant toxins that are particularly abundant in their area. Complicating things further is the fact that different plants within the same species may have very different levels and types of chemical or physical defenses. There has been little if any research to attempt to selectively breed perennial varieties with high deer resistance, but this would be straightforward to do, at least in theory. Lastly, deer would rather poison themselves than starve, so if population pressure is high enough, they will even eat normally resistant plants. So take this or any list as a guide and try to remember the next time that your hosta is nipped down to the crown or your lily buds disappear just as they are about to open that we have no one but ourselves to blame.

DEER-RESISTANT PERENNIALS

Anemone (*Anemone*)
Angelica (*Angelica*)
Astilbe (*Astilbe*)
Autumn crocus (*Colchicum*)
Baby's breath (*Gypsophila*)
Balloon flower (*Platycodon grandiflorus*)
Bear's britches (*Acanthus*)
Bee balm (*Monarda*)
Bellflower (*Campanula*)
Bergenia (*Bergenia*)
Blazing star, gay feather (*Liatris*)
Blue flag iris (*Iris versicolor*)
Bluestar (*Amsonia*)
Bugleweed (*Ajuga*)
Butterfly weed (*Asclepias*)
Candytuft (*Iberis sempervirens*)
Catmint (*Calamintha* and *Nepeta*)
Checkerberry (*Gaultheria*)
Cinquefoil (*Potentilla*)
Clematis (*Clematis*)
Columbine (*Aquilegia*)
Coneflower (*Echinacea*)
Coralbells, alumroot (*Heuchera*)
Crown imperial (*Fritillaria imperialis*)
Cyclamen (*Cyclamen*)
Daffodil, jonquil (*Narcissus*)
Delphinium, larkspur (*Delphinium*)
Epimedium (*Epimedium*)
Evening primrose (*Oenothera*)
False hellebore (*Veratrum*)
False indigo (*Baptisia*)
False Solomon's seal (*Maianthemum*)
Feather fleece (*Stenanthium*)
Flax (*Linum perenne*)
Foxglove (*Digitalis*)
Fringed bleeding heart (*Dicentra eximia*)

Ginger (*Asarum*)
Globe thistle (*Echinops*)
Goatsbeard (*Aruncus*)
Goldenrod (*Solidago*)
Hellebore (*Helleborus*)
Hens and chicks (*Sempervivum*)
Hyacinth (*Hyacinthus*)
Hyssop (*Agastache*)
Knautia (*Knautia macedonica*)
Knotweed (*Centaurea*)
Lamb's ears (*Stachys byzantinus*)
Lavender (*Lavandula*)
Lily of the valley (*Convalaria*)
Lungwort (*Pulmonaria*)
Lupine (*Lupinus*)
Monkshood (*Aconitum*)
Mullein (*Verbascum*)
Onion (*Allium*)
Pachysandra (*Pachysandra*)
Partridgeberry (*Mitchella repens*)
Peony (*Paeonia*)
Plumbago (*Ceratostigma plumbaginoides*)
Poppy (*Papaver*)
Prickly-pear cactus (*Opuntia*)
Primrose (*Primula*)
Queen-of-the-prairie (*Filipendula*)
Russian sage (*Perovskia*)
Sage (*Salvia*)
Siberian iris (*Iris sibirica*)
Snakeroot, baneberry (*Actaea* including *Cimicifuga*)
Sneezeweed (*Helenium*)
Snowdrop (*Galanthus*)
Soapwort (*Saponaria*)
Spiderwort (*Tradescantia*)
Spurge (*Euphorbia*)
Squill (*Scilla*)

Saint John's wort (*Hypericum*)
Stonecrop (*Sedum*)
Thyme (*Thymus*)
Tickseed (*Coreopsis*)
Waxbells (*Kirengeshoma palmata*)
Wood mint (*Lamium*)
Wormwood (*Artemisia*)
Yarrow (*Achillea*)

GRASSES AND SEDGES

Feather grass (*Nassella*)
Fescue (*Festuca*)
Maiden grass (*Miscanthus*)
Reed grass (*Calamagrostis*)
Sedge (*Carex*)
Switch grass (*Panicum*)

FERNS

Christmas fern (*Polystichum acrostichoides*)
Cinnamon fern (*Osmunda cinnamomea*)
Hayscented fern (*Dennstaedtia punctilobula*)
Interrupted fern (*Osmunda claytoniana*)
Japanese painted fern (*Athyrium nipponicum* 'Pictum')
Maidenhair fern (*Adiantum pedatum*)
New York fern (*Thelypteris noveboracensis*)
Ostrich fern (*Matteuccia struthiopteris*)
Royal fern (*Osmunda regalis*)
Sensitive fern (*Onoclea sensibilis*)
Wood fern, shield fern (*Dryopteris*)

Raised stock beds like this discourage voles because they have difficulty climbing the sides to get at the plants.

A meadow-vole tunnel through turf. Unlike pine voles and other woodland species that feed on woody plants as well as perennial rhizomes, roots, and bulbs, the meadow vole prefers to eat field grasses if they are available.

Voles

Twenty-three species of voles are native to North America. Close relatives of mice and rats, they feed primarily on perennial roots, leaves, and rhizomes, as well as the bark and stems of woody plants. Moles, on the other hand, feed mostly on insects, mollusks, and worms. Moles are constantly blamed for damage inflicted by voles, but other than creating feeding tunnels in your lawn, they generally do not harm plants. They may, however, provide tunnels for voles to co-opt and use. Meadow voles and the closely related prairie voles are mostly grass-eaters, though they will attack perennials, too. In my area, pine voles are by far more destructive in gardens. This eastern woodland vole prefers the rhizomes and tubers of woodland perennials to grasses, and it can wreak havoc on the woodland garden. Voles are incredibly prolific, reaching sexual maturity in 8 to 12 weeks and able to have four broods per year—winter, spring, summer, and fall. By the time a female is on her fourth brood, she will likely be sharing the space with her great-great-granddaughters born to the females of her first brood that year. Availability of food is the primary limiting factor to vole reproduction, so when they move into a garden filled with choice perennials such as trilliums and orchids, they set up shop and breed until the food is exhausted. It is common to see a few voles in the garden in the fall only to realize in spring that they have been at it all winter and there is nothing left. I do not have experience with the other 20 vole species on the continent, so I do not know how voracious they are in gardens, but I find that when it comes to pine voles in particular, I have to be aggressive during the summer and fall to keep the population from burgeoning under the snow in winter. Many natural predators feed on voles, so the populations tend to rise and fall from year to year, and clans will migrate into new territory in search of food. Voles move in shallow tunnels or depressions created as they feed and move along. They love soft earth like that found in new gardens, compost piles, and thick layers of mulch, as it makes the digging easier. I prefer not to use poison baits for several reasons (collateral death of other mammals and birds being paramount), but I do often set out snap-type mouse traps baited with a mixture of peanut butter and rolled oats sweetened with a dab of molasses. The voles feel exposed in the open, so put the traps under some sort of canopy that allows for clearance of the spring. I cut large plastic nursery pots in half vertically and put each half over a trap. This also reduces the chance of harming birds or stepping on the trap yourself. There are a variety of repellents on the market, including fox and bobcat urine, that are touted as effective. I have not tried any so I cannot offer any help there, though one friend says

OPPOSITE: If all else fails, plant your tulips in a bed of juniper where the voles and squirrels will have trouble getting at them.

the urine did reduce vole predation. At Garden in the Woods, we constructed raised beds using 2-inch by 10-inch lumber so the surface of the soil was at least six inches above grade, and this very effectively discouraged the voles from getting into our choice breeding and seed stock. The pine voles at least are not good climbers, so when they meet an obstacle only a few inches high they turn and tunnel elsewhere. This gave me an idea that I have yet to try. I plan to construct a low-perimeter fence out of hardware cloth or some other fine-mesh, durable metal fencing. A one-foot-high length buried half its height would in theory provide an effective barrier along the lines of the wooden beds, and it would be a cinch to install and negotiate. I have built hardware cloth boxes with chicken wire tops (to allow stems to exit) to accommodate the roots of favored plants such as trilliums, orchids, and lilies, and this is generally effective. With thick leather gloves and a good pair of tin snips or wire cutters you can fashion a box using a properly sized cardboard one as a model, and then stitch it together with galvanized wire. The cages do need some attention in early spring to make sure the emerging stems do not get caught up in the chicken wire. Bury the cage so the top is at grade and then plant the specimen into it, backfilling with the soil you excavated to set the cage in place. Other folks insist that blending in crushed oyster shells or a similar fine, sharp grit around the roots of vulnerable plants will discourage voles.

Since writing this section, I have talked with several people who swear by the small, ultrasonic rodent-repelling devices that you stick in the ground (mostly marketed for use against moles). One woman I spoke to said after installing a few of the solar-powered devices in her woodland garden, the

voles and vole damage disappeared. The units are not very expensive, so I plan on trying out a few this season.

Fungal Diseases

While some fungi are highly beneficial and even necessary for certain plants' survival, a host of other fungi earn their keep by feeding on living plant tissues. Fungal diseases are the most common problems I and most others face when growing perennials, whether these attack roots, stems, flowers, or leaves. Fortunately most fungal diseases are straightforward to either prevent or treat, and the ones that are not will probably kill the plant anyway, so you don't have to worry about them, either!

With a few exceptions, fungus diseases are opportunistic, that is they take advantage of stressed plants coupled with favorable environmental conditions. Thus, the most important thing you can do to prevent fungus problems is to pick the right plant for the right place and keep it growing well. Drought, flood, excessive heat or cold, insect attack, improper soil pH, poor fertility, poor soil structure, and poor genetics (i.e., a cultivar bred for its big colorful flowers, not vigor or disease resistance) all weaken a plant's resistance to fungal attack.

ROOT-ROT FUNGI

Several groups of soil-borne disease fungi afflict the roots of plants. The most common are *Pythium*, *Fusarium*, *Rhizoctonia*, and *Phytophthora*.

Fusarium wilt is familiar to tomato growers, but it is also a problem in nurseries and perennial gardens. There are a number of *Fusarium* species and many are harmless decomposers. Only a few cause diseases in plants, usually manifesting as either persistent wilting of foliage even when soil moisture is adequate, or stem-tip dieback (also caused by a lack of water). *Fusarium* enters through small feeder roots and grows upward. As the plant tries to fight the infection, xylem tissues of roots and stems become clogged, effectively turning off the tap so water cannot get from roots to leaves. *Fusarium* takes advantage of both drought stress and waterlogged or excessively warm soils, so

Artemisia schmidtiana. Silver mound artemesia with cottony stem rot (*Sclerotinia* sp.), which plagues this species in hot, humid weather.

Meconopsis × *sheldonii* is a hybrid between two blue poppies from the high Himalayas. Though more vigorous in the garden than its parents, it is still vulnerable to disease in all but the coolest summer climates.

proper watering can go a long way toward preventing the disease. If your soil is heavy and prone to waterlogging, fusarium wilt as well as other root diseases are more likely. In this case, either plant species tolerant of wet soils, or dig in sand, gravel, or gypsum grit to help the soil drain more freely. High soil temperatures are especially common in containers. I continue to marvel that almost all nursery containers are black or dark green instead of heat-reflecting white or tan. I believe many nursery problems could be avoided if growers and customers could accept plants in light-colored pots. In the ground, a one- to two-inch layer of organic mulch will keep soil temperature down while reducing evaporation. *Fusarium* spores can infect seeds, so one way to limit the disease in seedlings is to soak the seed in 3 percent hydrogen peroxide (the kind you can buy over-the-counter in the pharmacy) for 15 to 20 minutes. Verticillium wilt is another common disease that afflicts stressed plants in a similar way. Symptoms include leaf drop, stem-tip dieback, and wilting. Both fusarium and verticillium wilt are difficult to treat, but proper culture and removal of sick or diseased plants will greatly reduce their impact on perennials.

Pythium and *Phytophthora* are common root-rot disease organisms in perennials. Technically they are not fungi but belong to an entirely different branch on the tree of life called the oomycetes, but they look like fungi and act like fungi, so most people still call them fungi. (In case you are interested, fungi strengthen their cell walls with chitin, making them more similar to animals and insects, whereas oomycetes such as *Pythium* use cellulose and are thus more closely related to plants.) *Pythium* and *Phytophthora* require abundant moisture and low levels of oxygen to thrive and are thus most prevalent in waterlogged soils or stagnant greenhouses. Well-drained soils and nursery container mixes allowed to dry at the surface between waterings will discourage them. Low or high pH also inhibits many species, and plants adapted to either will be more resilient at the proper pH. For example, an acid-loving species such as Himalayan blue poppy (*Meconopsis* × *sheldonii*) can fight off infection if the pH remains below 5.5 (very acidic) but becomes more vulnerable as the pH climbs toward 6.5 (slightly acidic) and the pathogen grows more vigorously. Warm soil temperatures will often exacerbate the disease as well, and since this species is a cool-climate plant to begin with, the heat will further stress it. You get the picture.

The genus *Rhizoctonia* contains several true fungi that cause root as well as rhizome and crown rot in perennials and are mainly a problem in greenhouses where crowding, high humidity, and soil splashing from irrigation encourage the disease. Spacing plants, watering only in the morning and on sunny days, using a free-draining soil mix, and careful disposal of sick or stressed plants will all limit the disease without having to resort to fungicides.

A very promising way to treat all three of these diseases involves the use of another genus of soil fungi called *Trichoderma*. These common fungi parasitize the disease-causing fungi and oomycetes, severely weakening them and preventing outbreaks of disease. You can buy commercially prepared cultures of *Trichoderma* and inoculate potting mixes, which greatly decreases root diseases in the nursery. In the garden things are a little more complicated, as the soil is likely to harbor wild strains of *Trichoderma* and a host of other organisms. Research on the addition of specific aggressive strains of *Trichoderma* to garden soils has shown some effect against diseases, but a more effective technique is to maintain a healthy, balanced soil to begin with. In much the same way that encouraging beneficial insects by planting nectar sources will in turn control insect pests, feeding the beneficial soil flora and fauna a healthy diet of good compost will control fungal diseases. Beneficial insects need both nectar and prey insects to complete their life cycle, and beneficial soil organisms need organic materials as well as prey fungi to thrive.

FOLIAR FUNGAL DISEASES

Leaf diseases are common in perennial gardens, and unlike root and rhizome rots they are not as easily controlled with good cultural practices. I see leaf diseases as the colds and flu of the perennial world—basically a fact of life that we all have to live with to a certain extent. Luckily, most leaf diseases are not fatal and can be managed with a combination of proper plant selection and watering—and, if necessary, organic fungicides. The most common fungal leaf diseases of perennials are powdery mildew, downy mildew, botrytis, and rusts. I am sure you have had to deal with your share of all of them.

Powdery Mildew

Powdery mildew is a generic name for a number of related fungi that infect the leaves of plants. The powdery mildew that attacks roses is not the same one that afflicts phlox, but the symptoms and treatment are still the same. Everyone is familiar with the whitish or grayish, fuzzy growth that covers the upper surface of leaves on susceptible species such as phlox, columbine, lupine, chrysanthemum, black-eyed Susans, and bee balm. The disease begins when spores sprout on wet foliage and grow out as a white mat of fungal roots (hyphae) that force their way inside the leaf and feed off the tissues. Fungal hyphae are fragile things, so powdery mildew is usually only a problem when the humidity is consistently high. Late summer and fall are ideal, as cooler night temperatures cause dew to form at the same time the plants are beginning to die back for the year. Older leaves or stems that have already flowered are more prone to attack than young ones, as are individ-

Powdery mildew on *Clematis albicoma* (whitehair leatherflower).

uals under stress from drought or other problems. Because it is such a common disease among perennials, breeders and nurseries have selected cultivars of particularly susceptible species that show resistance to powdery mildew, and these are readily available. If possible, avoid watering your garden in the evening or on cloudy days, to keep foliage drier. Pruning out and disposing of badly infected stems may do some good, but the spores are everywhere in the air, anyway, so I personally feel it is not worth the effort. In fact, powdery mildew does not overwinter well in colder areas and simply blows in from farther south each summer to infect our gardens here in snow country.

Luckily, because the fungus is so exposed on the leaves, some simple and fairly nontoxic fungicides will provide excellent control. For many years people have used baking soda (sodium bicarbonate) to treat powdery mildew, but more recently research has shown that a similar compound (potassium bicarbonate) is even more effective. Ultrafine horticul-

Leucanthemum × *superbum* 'Alaska' is a mildew-resistant cultivar.

tural oils are also effective, and when combined with the potassium bicarbonate they are even better, as the oil helps the bicarbonate to spread and adhere to foliage. You have to be careful with the oil, though, as it can cause leaf damage with repeated use. Several commercial fungicides (e.g., MilStop) combine potassium bicarbonate with another "spreader-sticker" that is less likely to cause leaf burn. Potassium bicarbonate is also very effective against botrytis and soft-bodied insects such as aphids and mealy bugs.

Downy Mildew
Downy mildews primarily attack the lower surface of leaves and produce brown or black, fuzzy lesions that cause yellow spots on the upper surface of the leaves. Like *Pythium* and *Phytophthora*, downy mildews are not fungi but oomycetes thought to be related to brown algae, so treatment and control are different than for powdery mildew. Downy mildew can

develop only when there is abundant water on leaves and in the air, and it thrives when temperatures are cool. It is usually not a major problem in gardens but can be in nurseries. Perennials susceptible to it include many members of the aster family including aster, coreopsis, sunflower, and coneflower, as well as geranium, *Geum, Lamium*, potentilla, veronica, and violets, but it is rarely enough of a problem to warrant treatment. Copper fungicides sold by organic supply houses are the best control if one is warranted.

Botrytis
Botrytis cinerea, or gray mold, is abundant everywhere, and I am sure you have breathed in a few trillion of its spores over the years. Fortunately it does not harm us, but it is the fungus that causes your overripe fruit to become fuzzy gray. It is a true fungus, but like downy mildew it thrives in cool, humid weather, erupting almost overnight on stems, flowers, and

Monarda disease-resistance trials at the Chicago Botanic Garden. One of the roles of public gardens is to evaluate, promote, and even introduce superior cultivars.

shoot tips with that familiar gray fuzz. As soon as the sun comes out, the fuzz withers and only brown spots or patches on foliage, stems, and flowers remain. We battle this fungus in the nursery, especially in the propagation greenhouse, where tender stems combine with high humidity and close spacing to encourage the disease. It also causes quite a bit of damage to potted perennials overwintered at cool to cold temperatures in a greenhouse or under winter blankets, where very high humidity and very cool temperatures along with quantities of weak or dying older foliage and flowers allow it to run rampant. In fact, I believe that gray mold rather than cold damage is responsible for most winter losses in a typical perennial

nursery. In the garden, however, it is rarely a serious problem because good air circulation and lower humidity keep it in check, though gardeners in the Pacific Northwest and other regions where damp, cool weather persists may find it troublesome. Potassium bicarbonate has proven very effective at controlling it in our nursery.

Gray mold is a generalist that attacks many different plants when the conditions are right, but others are very host specific. *Botrytis paeoniae* (peony blight) afflicts the flower buds of peonies, *B. elliptica* (lily leaf blight) causes watery spots or streaks on the leaves of true lilies and some relatives such as trillium and Solomon's seal, and it can be a serious problem in damp weather. Control is the same as for gray mold.

Rusts

Rust and smut fungi are very interesting organisms, really, though they can be quite a nuisance on particular perennials. Their often extraordinarily complex life cycles appear to have been designed by some obscure mycological bureaucracy. Take aster rust (also known as needle rust, caused by *Coleosporium asterum*), for example. One type of spore blows onto aster or goldenrod leaves in summer, inconspicuously infecting them until fall, when the foliage erupts with small, rusty orange blisters that are composed of millions of another type of spore. These have to then become airborne and land on certain species of pine, infecting the leaf and growing there until summer, when blisters erupt and produce the other type of spore that will infect the next crop of asters. Many rusts rely on two alternating hosts, and many have as many as five different spore stages and several reproductive stages in their complicated life cycle. As I often mutter while waiting in line at the motor vehicles department, "There has got to be a better way!" Rusts are fairly host specific, and there are species that infect ferns, grasses, and flowering perennials as well as woody plants and annuals. Though they do weaken the plant by damaging foliage and stealing sugars and nutrients, at least some rusts have developed mutualistic relationships with their hosts. Some of the rusts that infect grasses manufacture toxins that

OPPOSITE LEFT: Downy mildew on hepatica. Though less obvious than powdery mildew, this disease is often more debilitating.

OPPOSITE RIGHT: *Arisaema* smut. The telltale orange blisters of sporulating *Arisaema* smut on the spathe of *Arisaema triphyllum.* Though the disease is often not fatal, it is incurable; the only remedy is to quickly dispose of the plant.

Systemic Acquired Resistance

A new and fascinating line of pest control I should mention involves the discovery of harpin proteins. These are proteins released by certain disease-causing bacteria like the one that causes fire blight. The protein induces the plant equivalent of an immune response—systemtic acquired resistance—boosting levels of defensive chemicals such as terpenes and phenols to fight the disease. Amazingly, if you spray a plant with these harpin proteins, it causes a general immune response that resists not only bacteria but fungi, viruses, and insects as well. It is like treating the plant with a supervaccine that helps it fight off a host of diseases and pests. Harpin protein is marketed under the brand name Messenger, and though it is certainly not a cure-all, it does represent a new direction in managing plant disease by *preventing* infection rather than treating it. Along the same lines, researchers have discovered that the active ingredient in aspirin, salicylic acid, is the hormone that plant cells use to signal "attack, attack" to the rest of the plant. Basically, when the powdery mildew or aphid stylet penetrates the leaf, the cells start pumping out salicylic acid to produce the immune response. That got me thinking, "Can you just spray aspirin on your plants to keep them healthy?" The answer appears to be yes, you can. Research at the University of Rhode Island using sprays of ground-up aspirin has proven very promising. Simply crush up 1.5 regular-strength, uncoated aspirin tablets

(81 grains) and stir them into 2 gallons of water along with 1 teaspoon or so of mild dish soap to act as a spreader-sticker. Spray the foliage of your perennials every three weeks with the concoction. Though the research was done on vegetables, others swear by aspirin sprays for perennials and roses, too. I will have to try this one out; kind of convenient when you can treat a headache, lower your risk of heart attack, and prevent plant disease and insect attack all with the same little white pill! Actigard is a commercial version of salicylic acid registered for use against downy mildew and several other diseases. Some organic gardeners also swear by compost tea. Foliar sprays of compost tea are said to inhibit bacterial and fungal disease in four possible ways: competition for space from the beneficial organisms, an inhibitory compound (antibiotic or antifungal agent) excreted by the beneficial organisms, parasitism of the disease-causing organism by fungi or bacteria in the tea (similar to treatment with *Trichoderma*), and/or systemic acquired resistance induced by chemicals in the tea. The research on this aspect of compost tea use, as with others, is contradictory, which may be due to the lack of standardization among the various teas themselves. Friends who have used them recommend teas made from leaf and bark compost rather than manure or green plant materials, as these are higher in beneficial fungi.

Arisaema candidissimum. Though *Arisaema* smut is not necessarily fatal to native **jack-in-the-pulpits,** it can devastate exotic species growing nearby like these stunning pink ones. Luckily for gardens afflicted with smut, many *Arisaema* flowers emerge very late, well after the smut has come and gone for the year.

are poisonous to herbivores, so infected plants are not eaten. Other rusts cause what appears to be systemic acquired resistance in their host, resulting in a more vigorous and otherwise disease-free plant.

Smuts differ from rusts in several ways. They typically require only one host, not two, they infect only flowering plants, and they act systemically. You can cure rust infection by treating or pruning out the infected stems or leaves, but once a plant has smut, there is no way to cure it aside from digging up and destroying the whole thing. We associate the name *smut* with lewd or disgusting things, and for good reason, as smut eruptions can be pretty gross. One serious smut (anther smut, caused by *Ustilago violacea*) affects members of the carnation family such as *Dianthus* and *Silene*. Afflicted individuals grow normally and produce flowers, but just as the flowers open, the smut takes over the anthers so that instead of releasing pollen, the plant produces yellow spores that are carried by insects to other healthy plants, deposited on their female stigmas, and thus are allowed entry into a new host. The spores grow inside the flower's ovary along with its seeds and coat them as they fall from the plant, so as soon as the new seedlings germinate, the smut readily infects them. It is the sort of science fiction horror show that leaves little seedlings trembling in their transplant beds; but it's true, seedlings, it's true!

Another serious smut to be concerned with is arisaema smut (*Uromyces ari-triphylli*). This fungus is well established in many wild populations of native jack-in-the-pulpit (*Arisaema triphyllum*), and infected plants are easy to spot in spring when they erupt with rusty orange dots all over the leaves and stem. The smut weakens but often does not kill the plant, so it comes back year after year. There is no cure for the disease, and it is devastating to many of the Asian arisaemas, including the spectacular *Arisaema sikokianum*. The only thing you can do if you find this disease is to dig up and burn or bag all infected plants and keep vigilant every year thereafter. Alternatively, you could focus on some of the late-emerging species such as *Arisaema consanguineum*, which does not rear his head until June—well after the spores have been dispersed. The smut is not transmitted directly to seeds, so you can collect it from infected plants and surface sterilize it for 20 to 30 minutes in 3 percent hydrogen peroxide or 10 percent household bleach solution (1 part bleach to 9 parts water).

There are rusts for just about every plant, and you are probably familiar with carnation rust, hollyhock rust, and daylily rust. Because the plants do not show noticeable symptoms until the spores erupt, rusts have an easy time riding the tide of international commerce to new shores. If you are a rust, it is easy to turn over a new leaf! Daylily rust (*Puccinia hemerocallidis*) is native to Asia (where daylilies—*Hemerocallus* spp.—are native too, of course). It was first discovered at two large wholesale nurseries in Georgia and Florida in 2000—most likely recently arrived on a shipment of infected plants from Costa Rica, where the disease was imported originally from China or Japan. By 2001 it had been found in 24 states, and by 2002 the USDA gave up any hope of containing the disease as nurseries and hobbyists spread it around. Daylily rust uses patrinia (*Patrinia* spp.) as its alternate host for sexual reproduction, though it can produce asexual spores on daylily alone if the alternate host is not present (this adaptive ability is why measures to eliminate rusts from economically important crops by eradicating alternate hosts for the fungus have largely failed). The best way to control the disease is to remove any infected leaves and clean up and discard any dead foliage in autumn. The rust is not completely winter-hardy, and spores appear to die at temperatures below 0 degrees F. Therefore, it is most prevalent in the warmer parts of the United States. There are fungicides labeled for use against rusts, and Messenger, MilStop, and horticultural oil sprays will treat it. Some individual plants are genetically more resistant than others, so it is possible to select highly resistant varieties. For example, among tens of thousands of daylilies, some cultivars appear especially resistant:

RUST-RESISTANT DAYLILY CULTIVARS

Age of Gold	Holy Spirit
All-American Hero	Joie de Vivre
Antique Rose	Jolyene Nichole
Barbara Mitchell	Lavender Bonnet
Butterscotch Ruffles	Lilac Lady
Catherine Neal	Mac the Knife
Creole Blush	Mae West
Dainty Designer	Meadow Sweet
Devonshire Cream	Neon Pink
Ed Brown	Pink Flirt
Fashion Design	Prairie Blue Eyes
Femme Fatale	Raspberry Splash
Gentle Rose	Siloam Bill Monroe
Golden Melody	Siloam Double Classic
Happy Returns	Siloam Ury Winniford
Heartfelt	Yangtze

Smut diseases in perennials are, thankfully, less common than rusts, as control requires the rather draconian total destruction of infected plants. Besides the two already mentioned, white smut affects members of the aster family, and smuts are known on delphiniums, anemones, lobelias, and poppies.

Bacterial Diseases

Bacterial infections are difficult to distinguish from fungal ones, though they are generally less common in perennials. One type that is problematic affects perennials with fleshy corms, bulbs, or rhizomes and causes rapid rotting of the tissues. Several bacteria are responsible for the disease (called bacterial soft rot), but with all of them the effect is the same. Bacterial infections usually smell very foul, for some reason, so that is one way to distinguish them from fungal problems. Cuts or wounds caused by us or animals and insects are primarily responsible for the disease, as the outer skin of the plant usually protects it. When dividing fleshy rhizomes such as those of trillium, iris, and others, it is a good idea to treat wounds with a fungicide or ground charcoal, powdered sulfur, or cinnamon (the nicest option) to help prevent infection.

Viruses

Of all the problems that afflict perennials, virus diseases are to me the most troubling and insidious. Like smuts, virus infections are systemic and incurable without heroic intervention. (It is possible to raise virus-infected plants from tissue cultures on an antiviral medium and isolate uninfected cells that grow back into disease-free plants.) Viruses, as well as the even smaller mycoplasmas and phytoplasmas, are life at its simplest—a vessel containing a bit of RNA and a few receptors. Life cannot get any more basic than that and still be alive, and you could even argue that without its host, a virus is not really alive. This makes viruses extremely difficult to treat, be they HIV in humans or one of the many that infect plants. The disease is transmitted in the sap; typically, plant viruses are spread by sucking insects (see Aphids, p. 139), though we do our fair share with pruners, string trimmers, chain saws, and shears. Viruses usually weaken but do not kill the host under cultivation, and often symptoms are subtle. In the wild, even a slight decrease in vigor can spell the difference between life and death, but in the favored world of the garden, sick plants may live on indefinitely. Thus, viruses are much more common in cultivation than in the wild, a phenomenon exacerbated by horticultural practices. I do not know anyone who walks around the garden with a propane torch or bucket of bleach to sterilize their pruners before moving on to another plant. It is simply not feasible to maintain this level of sanitation outside of a propagation greenhouse. Consequently, we effectively spread viruses around without realizing it. Most viruses are not particularly host specific, though they often bear the name of the plant they were first identified in. Cucumber mosaic virus (CMV) is able to infect plants in about 200 different families and is the most common virus in perennials, but others include tobacco rattle virus (TRV), impatiens necrotic spot virus (INSV), and tomato spotted wilt virus (TSWV). There is even a new hosta virus yet to be identified called hosta virus X. Infected plants may exhibit irregular spots, mosaic patterns, or lines on leaves, stems, or flowers, blackened tissue, and an overall loss of vigor. TRV is very common among garden phloxes—especially named cultivars propagated by cuttings—but it cannot be passed from mother to seed, so seed-grown phlox begins disease free. I had been used to growing *Phlox divaricata* cultivars from cuttings and was amazed when we began propagating a superior seedling I named 'Blue Moon'. Coming from seed, it had no viral load, and we made sure to sterilize our pruners with a propane

TOP LEFT: *Phlox divaricata* 'Blue Moon' with *Tiarella cordifolia* var. *collina.* Usually viruses are not transmitted from the mother plant to the seed. I grew this superior wood phlox from seed, and the difference in vigor between it and the virus-infected cultivars was striking.

TOP RIGHT: *Lilium canadense* with CMV. Though the plant may not be killed outright by this virus, it will be considerably weakened. This lily should be dug up and destroyed.

BOTTOM LEFT: Sterilizing pruners with a 10 percent bleach solution. Ideally they should be soaked in the open position for ten minutes after each use on a plant. In the propagation greenhouse we flame pruners with a propane torch, a much faster method of sterilizing.

Lilium 'Stargazer' with tulip breaking virus (TBV). The mottled, varicolored flowers of this Stargazer lily are interesting, but the coloration is caused by the virus.

Tulip with TBV. The tulips in the background are uninfected, so they don't display the variegated coloration of the sick one in the foreground.

torch before taking cuttings of it. The difference in vigor between this cultivar and older, virused selections was phenomenal. Though the sick ones showed little outward sign of infection other than a bit of irregular variegation in the foliage, 'Blue Moon' grew to maturity from cuttings two to three times more quickly.

One of the most famous stories about plant viruses involved the tulip breaking virus (TBV), responsible for the attractively flamed, broken, or bicolored tulips that helped create tulip fever in seventeenth-century Netherlands. The disease affects pigment production in the bloom, causing attractive feathered patterns of one color against another background shade. Astronomical prices were paid for what we now know to have been simply sick tulips. At the height of the craze, one gentleman paid today's equivalent of three million dollars for one especially fine bulb. You can still buy bicolored 'Rembrandt' tulips today, but the patterning in these plants is a product of genetic mutation, not virus. TBV is still around, especially in lilies, though the effect on the blooms is far less attractive.

In recent years the perennial industry has begun to take notice of viruses, and labs now offer viral assays for the most common types. Tissue culture labs are also "cleaning up" tried and true garden cultivars and offering virus-free plantlets to nurseries. As with most diseases, resistance to viruses varies from one individual to the next, and consciously or unconsciously, breeders are selecting virus-resistant varieties based on vigor and appearance. There is also some evidence that induction of systemic acquired resistance using Messenger or aspirin sprays helps the plant fight viral infection.

CHAPTER 7

THE NAME GAME

Many folks never bother learning the Latin names for the plants they grow, or at least not the *full* Latin names. You can certainly have a long and happy life in horticulture and never bother to learn the scientific species names (I use "Latin" and "scientific" interchangeably), I urge you to try for a couple of reasons. It is cumbersome at first, but once you get the hang of it, the Latin names (or to be technically correct the Latin-Greek names, as many of the word roots are Greek) really help you understand the relationships between different plants, and they are the lingua franca when it comes to talking or writing about them. Common names, while sometimes distinctive and poetic, are often vague and misleading. Names such as wallflower, primrose, and daisy have been applied to too many different species from region to region and country to country to be really useful without adding on a lot of qualifiers like "red-necked black-eyed daisy."

A particular Latin name such as *Stylophorum diphyllum* applies to only one species (celandine poppy), and no matter

ABOVE: *Astilbe chinensis* **'Vision in Red'.** This vibrant astilbe is a cultivar (named clone), as indicated by the English name in single quotes.

Stylophorum diphyllum. **Celandine poppy** is a card-carrying member of the poppy family **(Papaveraceae).** Even if I knew nothing about this particular species, its familial association would provide clues as to its garden-worthiness.

Sanguinaria canadensis. Though the leaves of **blood-root** look very different from celandine's, the sexual parts in the center of each flower are nearly identical in shape and arrangement. To a taxonomist, such similarities signal close evolutionary ties.

if the speaker is from Boston or Beijing, he or she will refer to it that way. Furthermore, if you see a reference to the Chinese species *Stylophorum lasiocarpum* in a seed catalog, you can safely infer quite a bit about it based on your experiences with its sister species from the Appalachians. I find this tremendously helpful when trying to navigate intelligently through catalogs and reference books. Latin family names are helpful, too, for the same reason. I like many of the plants in the Papaveraceae (poppy family), and knowing nothing else about the genus *Stylophorum* than that it is a poppy tells me that it is a plant I might want to know better. In an ideal world, scientific names would remain unchanged through the ages so that you could read a garden book circa 1950 or even 1750 and still recognize all the Latin names. Alas, as we all know this is not the case.

Few groups get gardeners hot under the collar like taxonomists and their incessant renaming and reclassifying. Latin names are troubling enough for folks to remember, so

when they change completely, it causes quite an understandable ruckus. It is much harder for me to make the case for the general use of Latin names if they change as fast as a politician's opinions. Why, then, do scientific names change so often?

A Matter of Perspective

Taxonomists study the genealogy of life. The traditional, albeit flawed, way of determining relationships between species was to study their parts, and if enough parts were similar, then a common ancestor was judged to be involved. You can see the familial resemblance between a house cat and an ocelot, or a frog and a salamander, but a salamander does also look like a lizard even though they are not in fact closely related. Things get even more confused with plants, because their parts are a bit less familiar to us and it is sometimes hard to tell if a certain characteristic indicates a familial relationship or not.

TOP ROW: Based on similarities in flower structure, it has long been thought that trilliums (*Trillium sulcatum*, southern red trillium, left) are closely related to *Medeola virginica* (Indian cucumber root, center); indeed, the flowers are quite similar. However, recent work in molecular genetics has placed trilliums closer to plants in the bunchflower family, like this *Helonias bullata* (swamp pink). On the surface, the two look nothing alike.

BOTTOM ROW: I am a fan of plants in the small and challenging family *Diapensiaceae*, such as *Galax urceolata* (wandflower, right). This has led me to seek out other members of the family, like *Berneuxia thibetica* from the Himalayas.

Certainly many of the most obvious things—flower color or whether a plant is herbaceous or woody, evergreen or deciduous—have no genealogical value. Taxonomists study more obscure characteristics such as the shape of hairs, the number of chambers in a seed capsule, or the pattern of venation in a leaf because these evolve and change more slowly over time. What you are hoping for is that by following certain inherited traits through a group of related species, you can begin to understand who is whose brother, uncle, second cousin, or great-great-great-grandmother, so to speak. Like my example of the salamander and lizard, physical characteristics can be misleading, so it would be far simpler to follow the trail of heredity directly in the genetic code, and this is exactly what the science of DNA analysis has allowed us to do. Now taxonomists can look directly at the DNA of different plants and figure out which ones are closely related, tracing inherited mutations back through time to draw very accurate family trees.

The goal of plant systematics (yes, even taxonomy itself has been renamed!) is to have all the species in one family group relate back to a single ancestral species, like the branches of a tree connecting back to its base. If some of the species cannot trace their lineage back to this common ancestor, they must be put into a new group. In the past this was always a matter of conjecture, but when you examine the DNA along with other clues, for example, the number of chromosomes and traditional features such as the structure of flower parts and leaf venation, the picture becomes much clearer. This is precisely what has happened to the genus *Aster*, a group of some 175 mostly North American daisies. The first *Aster* to be named was the Italian *Aster amellus*, which looks like an aster I might have growing wild in my yard. However, its DNA and chromosomal counts revealed that it does not share an ancestor with any New World asters, so all of these have to be moved to a different group. It is as if a human family that always thought it was descended from George Washington finds after genetic testing that it is not. On even closer scrutiny, many of the North American asters were found not to be closely related, either, so they have been further split into 16 new genera: *Symphyotrichum, Ionactis,*

Sometimes looks can be deceiving. *Coreopsis rosea* (pink tickseed, top), a member of the aster family, is popular for its colorful blooms. Though superficially similar and native to the same Atlantic coastal pond shores, *Sabatia kennedyana* is in the completely unrelated gentian family. It is very possible that the sabatia evolved flowers resembling those of its neighbor to lure away pollinators.

Clematis texensis. Latin names often provide information about a particular plant. In this case the specific epithet *texensis* refers to the Lone Star State, where this lovely **clematis** is found.

Doellingeria, Oclemena, Psilactis, Machaeranthera, Eurybia, Sericocarpus, Eucephalus, Ampelaster, Xylorhiza, Tonestus, Oligoneuron, Chaetopappa, Sericocarpus, and *Almutaster.* Need I say more?

My only gripe is that these names sound like they were hammered out by a monkey on a keyboard. This sort of reclassification is going on among all the plants, with some being lumped together as well as split (*Hepatica* is now *Anemone,* and *Cimicifuga* is now *Actaea*). The big problem—and this is a big problem—is that there is no one place to go for up-to-date Latin names if you are a nursery person, garden writer, or just a gardener trying to stay abreast of things. Primarily this is because even with DNA evidence, plant classification remains partly conjecture, and thus taxonomists often disagree heatedly about name changes. While one camp may support the placement of *Hepatica* in *Anemone,* another may lobby to retain *Hepatica* but to reclassify the species within it. Taxonomists tend to be black-and-white thinkers by nature, so you can imagine how heated these debates over "correct" names often become. All it really takes to rename a plant is to simply publish your argument—often in the form of a monograph—in a scientific journal. It may be a scientific journal read by only 15 people in Uzbekistan, but as long as it is officially published, then other taxonomists need to determine its validity. In the end, name changes are not the clear result of empirical analysis but rather of consensus that develops over time. It may take 10 to 15 years for newly published revisions to be debated and finally accepted by the botanical community and another 10 to 30 years for them to catch on in horticultural publications. During this slow period of transition, certain plants may be written about under two or three different Latin names. In many cases, the plant ends up reverting to its old name after decades of debate. To a horticulturist trying to name plants correctly, this constant back-and-forth is extremely frustrating. So . . . my best advice is to embrace name changes cautiously and not feel like you have to be out in front on every revision that comes down the pike.

The Anatomy of a Plant Name

OK, so you are willing to give Latin names a go. Now what? The key to understanding Latin names is their binomial format, and to understand this, it is important to have some notion about the concepts of species, genus, family, and so on.

A species is technically a group of very similar organisms that freely interbreed to produce fertile offspring and that are genetically very close to each other. The concept of species is easier to understand with examples a little closer to home than the world of plants. Our species is *Homo sapiens,* the only living species in the genus *Homo* (extinct species include *H. erectus* and *H. neanderthalensis*). In theory, at least, if members of *H. neanderthalensis* were alive today, they could not bear fertile children with us. I am tempted to inject some really bad jokes here but will restrain myself. We members of the genus *Homo* are in essence more closely related to each other than we are to other related genera, for example, *Pan*

Camassia leichtlinii ssp. *suksdorfii.* Camas lily is a lovely spring-flowering bulb from northwestern North America. The variety *suksdorfii* has particularly vivid blue blooms.

Asphodelus albus (white asphodel) is an Old-World equivalent to camas lily with a very similar ecology, form, and requirements under cultivation. Like *Camassia,* it blooms in spring and goes dormant in summer.

Silene regia. Taxonomists are not known to gush very often, but occasionally the beauty of a particular flower exerts its influence on the namer. Regal catchfly lives up to its aristocratic billing.

TOP: *Iris* **species (China).** Even today, new plants are being discovered. This iris from China is undescribed, meaning that no taxonomist has given it a Latin name and published its description in a scientific journal.

LEFT: *Saxifraga michauxii.* André Michaux was one of the most prolific and persistent plant explorers working in the southern Appalachians during the second half of the eighteenth century. This saxifrage, which he discovered in North Carolina, was named in his honor by Nathaniel Lord Britton, a taxonomist and the founder of the venerable New York Botanical Garden.

(the chimpanzees) or *Gorilla* (more bad jokes). Thus *Stylophorum diphyllum* (celandine) is more closely related to *S. lasiocarpum* (Chinese wood poppy) than to *Chelidonium majus* (greater celandine) from Europe. Still, *Chelidonium* and *Stylophorum* are distantly related, which is obvious if you see them side by side. Thus they are both placed within the poppy family along with the true poppies (*Papaver*) and bloodroot (*Sanguinaria*) among others. Family names always end in "-aceae" to make it easier on us. Families are gathered into even larger related groups and so on, but for our purpose, that is about as far as we need to go. As I mentioned earlier, certain traits tend to run in families, so if you are drawn to the hellebores, you might also like hepaticas, anemones, and columbines—all members of the Ranunculaceae or buttercup family. Many catalogs list the families in the plant descriptions, which can help you determine if it is one you want to try or to avoid. I tend to shy away from plants in the Polygonaceae and Euphorbiaceae because many of the species are weedy or aggressive. On the other hand, I am drawn to members of the Liliaceae, Ranunculaceae, Primulaceae, Asteraceae, and Orchidaceae, as each contains a plethora of garden-worthy species. Notice that the genus and species names are italicized and the family name capitalized.

Variety, Subspecies, and Cultivar

Obviously, all the plants within a particular species are not exactly alike. Like us, individuals vary in qualities such as height, coloring, and hairiness, just to name a few. Botanists and horticulturists label this variation in three ways: by variety, by subspecies, and by cultivar. Unfortunately these terms have become a bit jumbled in the gardening world, so a little clarification is in order.

Variety

Certain easily recognizable traits—red hair, left-handedness, or green eyes—are uncommon enough in the general human population to be thought of as special. In plant terminology, individuals or populations of a certain species that are a bit different from the norm are given varietal names (variety is abbreviated as either var. or v.). A white-flowered form of a typically colored plant is called var. *alba* or var. *album*. Especially hairy forms might be called var. *pubescens* or var. *tomentosa,* and red-leaved individuals might be labeled as var. *atropurpurea* or var. *purpureum.* Variety names usually either describe the trait that makes the plant different or indicate the place or region the variety is from, as with var. *alabamense.* The word or abbreviation for variety is not italicized, but the varietal name is (this is true of subspecies as well).

Subspecies

A subspecies (abbreviated subsp. or ssp.) can be thought of as a race that has evolved through geographical isolation. Over time, if a population of a particular species is isolated by a mountain range, body of water, or other barrier, it tends to drift genetically from the main population and develop certain unique characteristics that are consistent from one individual to the next but not different enough from the typical form to warrant recognition as a new species. *Lilium pardalinum* subsp. *shastense* is a subspecies of the California leopard lily that grows around Mount Shasta in northern California, where it has become cut off from other populations of the plant. With its many mountain ranges and varied climate, California is rife with subspecies. There are five among *L.*

pardalinum alone. Think of subspecies as in the process of evolving into something new. Because they are not quite the old species and not quite a new species, subspecies are hotly debated among taxonomists. Some scientists might argue that a particular subspecies is not valid, while others feel it is different enough to be recognized as a new species. Partly for this reason and partly because it makes Latin names even more lengthy and cumbersome, many horticultural references ignore subspecies. On the other hand, for students of the wild flora like me, subspecies provide a fascinating window into the machinations of the evolutionary process.

Cultivar

Scientific names have one primary purpose, and that is to categorize life and show how all the different branches of the evolutionary tree fit together. It is a system that downplays individual variation in favor of averages and norms. Even at the level of variety, we are referring to a specific trait, not to an individual plant that might have that trait. However, we gardeners are very focused on individual variation between the plants we grow. If you raise 100 *Primula* × *bullesiana* from seed and one proves to be especially deep red and vigorous, it would naturally draw your attention. You might even dig it out and propagate it to share with a friend. When others visit your friend's garden and remark on what a lovely primrose that is, they might say, yes, that is Sarah's Red,

Heuchera villosa var. *atropurpurea.* The venerable red-leaved variety of hairy coralbells has conferred its unique leaf color on many a coralbells hybrid.

Pronunciation

Some folks get quite bent out of shape if they hear you mispronouncing a Latin name, occasionally launching into some pompous treatise about Latin and Greek. What you need to remember the next time you are lambasted for saying CLEM-at-is instead of clem-AT-is is that botanical Latin *is not* classical Latin and does not really have any rules. It is a scientific language that first developed in Rome in the first centuries after Christ and uses Latin, Greek, and later made-up word roots to describe plants. There is really no right or wrong way of saying things, just convention. The English convention regarding pronunciation of scientific Latin names is as follows: the emphasis is placed on the first syllable in two-syllable names such as AS-ter, but these are rather rare. With three or more syllables, the emphasis is placed on the second-to-last (penultimate) syllable or sometimes on the one before it if the penultimate syllable contains a short vowel. So, in the case of *Clematis*, both pronunciations are technically correct. However the botanical world is riddled with names that do not follow the rules, such as PRIM-ul-a, which should technically be prim-U-la.

You may have wondered why species names have different endings—alba versus album or albus, for instance. Well, Latin nouns can be masculine, feminine, or neuter, and the ending (suffix) of the species name, as well as the ending of the variety or subspecies name, needs to agree in gender with the genus. The suffix *-us* is masculine, while *-e, -a, -is, -es, -ia,* and many others are feminine. The suffix *-um* is neuter. Thus you have *Sisyrinchium album, Dicentra eximia* var. *alba,* and *Helleborus foetidus* var. *albus.* All the suffixes agree in gender. This is also a matter of convention, and many times taxonomists simply ignore the rules when naming a new plant. *Lilium* (gender neuter) has some feminized species within it, such as *Lilium regale.* I have to admit that *regalum* does not sound very aristocratic, and the *e* gives the name a lighter, feminine sound appropriate to a beautiful lily.

Species named after a place end in *-ensis, -(a)nus, -ana,* or *-ianus.* Those named after a person use the following convention: an *-i* is added to a name ending in *-r, -y,* or a vowel other than *-a* (*parryi* or *weberi*); *-ii* (masculine) or *-iae* (feminine) is tacked onto names ending with a consonant other than *-r* (*michauxii*). Names that end in *-a* have an *-e* added to them, so if anyone wants to name a plant after me (please, *oh,* please), it would be *cullinae*—what a nice ring that has . . . Some older names honoring a person end in *-ana* or *-anus,* but these have been discontinued. I wonder why?

and so a cultivar is born. Cultivars are simply individuals that have been picked out of the crowd by a gardener, breeder, or nursery person for some rare or unusual trait that often has little or no value from an evolutionary point of view. Dwarfism, double flowers, and variegation are all things that would likely doom a wild plant, but they are cause for celebration if they appear in your garden. The variegated Jacob's ladder I named 'Stairway to Heaven' (p. 120) survived past infancy only because I dug it out and nurtured it to adulthood in the nursery. With less chlorophyll than its all-green siblings it would otherwise have been shaded out very quickly. Now, thanks to tissue culture, it has been cloned by the hundreds of thousands and grows in gardens from New Mexico to New Zealand. Ironically this odd mutation, which would have doomed it in nature, has made it arguably the most successful single *Polemonium reptans* in the history of the species.

Cultivars are strictly horticultural entities designated with a non-Latin name that is capitalized and put in single quotes. Technically, the cultivar should follow the complete Latin name, as in *Polemonium reptans* 'Stairway to Heaven', but often this is shortened to just *Polemonium* 'Stairway to Heaven' in catalogs and books. Cultivars that date from Victorian times may have latinized names such as *Athyrium filix-femina* 'Frizelliae', but this practice was abandoned to lessen the confusion between scientific names and horticultural names. The important thing to realize about cultivars is that they are *usually* clones, so one *Hemerocallis* 'Happy Returns' is genetically identical to the next. Just to confuse things, though, the international code of botanical nomenclature allows seed strains to be referred to as cultivars. I personally feel this is a silly rule as it muddies the waters around the concept of cultivar. The problem with seed strains is that they tend to drift away from the original plant if nursery workers are not extremely diligent in the way they pollinate and harvest the seed. Remember that cultivars are now often patented with one name and trademarked with another name (see p. 123).

When two species cross-pollinate in the wild and produce offspring, these offspring are considered hybrids. Natural hybrids occur all the time in the wild and help drive evolution forward. They are written with the multiplication symbol, ×, between the genus and species names. *Primula* × *bullesiana* is a natural hybrid of the pink Chinese *P. beesiana* and orange *P. bulleyana* that blooms in shades of orange, red, apricot, yellow, orange, pink, and cerise. Hybrids that are created in the greenhouse or laboratory, not in nature, are supposed to have non-Latin specific epithets, such as *Cypripedium* × Gisela, that are capitalized, nonitalicized, and not in quotes. This refers to a specific hybrid involving two specific parents. However, many complex garden hybrids are just listed as × *hybrida* (*Hemerocallus* × *hybrida*, *Paeonia* × *hybrida*, *Helleborus* × *hybridus*), which really tells us nothing about their parentage other than that they are hybrids.

ABOVE: *Primula* × *bullesiana* 'North Hill Strain'. By selectively collecting seed only from red and pink individuals, Wayne Winterrowd and Joe Eck of North Hill, in Vermont, have created their own unique seed strain of this beautiful primrose hybrid, which now self-sows in damp areas of their garden.

RIGHT: *Hemerocallis* × *hybrida* 'Happy Returns'. Happy Returns daylily is an extremely popular cultivar because of its repeat bloom, bright color, and small size. The species name *hybrida* is applied to many garden hybrids of mixed genetic background.

CHAPTER 8

PERENNIALS BY DESIGN

It is important to know how plants work, but it is also important to know how to work them into your garden. There is certainly a plethora of books on garden design, and I do not feel I have to reinvent the color wheel here, so to speak. However, I think that garden design, like propagation or plant nutrition, can appear much more complicated than it is, so in the spirit of this book I will attempt to make what follows as straightforward and nonintimidating as possible.

Gardens connect us with the extrahuman world and provide a place of retreat and beauty. They teach us respect for plants and nature and relieve stress and anxiety—at least in theory! I find that I fret so much about the health of the plants, the plethora of weeds, lack of rain, impending frosts, Japanese beetles, deer, rabbits, woodchucks, voles, and yet-undiscovered ravages lurking deep underground. Add to this a very busy schedule and the pressures of a young family, and

ABOVE: The Steven M. Still Garden at Ohio State University was designed by Adrian Bloom in honor of Dr. Still, who has done a great deal to popularize perennials over the past thirty years. Massed grasses and perennials are planted in meandering drifts to lead the eye as if following a lazy river upstream.

Countless **daffodils** in overlapping masses coalesce like pixels in a digital image to paint a larger picture at Winterthur Gardens in Delaware.

my garden never receives the attention I would like. Fortunately plants can mostly take care of themselves.

I admire folks who take the time to plan and design new projects in advance, but I also know that most of us have had the following experience: (1) Wake up one fine spring morning and think, "Wow, what a lovely day. I think I'll do some planting." (2) Grab a breakfast bar and coffee, then drive to a favorite local nursery. (3) Purchase an assortment of blooming plants in quantities of ones and twos because larger quantities would be too expensive and the trunk can only hold so much. (4) Come home and spend a half hour trudging around the yard looking for a place to accommodate these new treasures. (5) Dig a new bed because all existing gardens are full. (6) Set out plants in the new bed only to realize that some are for sun and some are for shade: a second bed becomes necessary. (7) Dig second bed. (8) Plant the two beds with what turns out to be a woefully inadequate and mismatched collection and mutter something like, "What was I

thinking?" (9) Fill in the beds over time with more odds and ends purchased on impulse, until the whole has the cobbled-together je ne sais quoi of a junk shop's bargain bin. (10) Swear to do it better next time.

Though I do not always practice what I preach, I do believe it is very valuable to spend some time with tracing paper, a scaled ruler, and colored pencils working out a design before actually buying plants. Designing to scale on paper allows you a certain objectivity to consider things such as

With a few colored pencils, some tracing paper, and templates, you can record your ideas. Here I am creating a planting plan for a new garden at the Coastal Maine Botanical Gardens.

form, texture, circulation, and appropriate quantities of plants for the space at hand. It also results in a more realistic plant list you can take shopping. Even if you cannot afford everything all at once you can phase in sections as money allows. Dreaming up new gardens for the spring is a wonderful way to spend a Sunday morning in January. When I put my mind to it, I find garden design—like any creative endeavor— to be very fun and rewarding.

One of my first surprises when I arrived to study landscape architecture at the University of Connecticut was that we would not actually take planting design until our third year. Being plant obsessed from childhood I naïvely imagined that all of my time in the studio would be spent combining my favorite plants into fantastic gardens on paper. On the contrary, my first two years in school focused first on color theory, designing with three-dimensional forms, painting, creativity training, and eventually designing outdoor spaces with attention to site conditions, circulation, uses, and so forth. Until our final year, plants were merely abstractions that helped define the space. It is difficult for a plant lover like me to see plants as green abstractions, but I think at least initially it is beneficial. Before choosing the plants, take the time to plan out where the paths go, what needs to be screened, views you might like to enhance, natural features such as rock outcrops that could be incorporated, trees that might need to be pruned or removed. Whether you are planting 100 square feet or 100 acres, also consider soil conditions, sunlight, wind, and slope.

It takes practice to learn to design from a two-dimensional, bird's-eye perspective (what designers call the plan view)—especially when working with three-dimensional objects like plants, but it is a helpful exercise when considering the relationships of different areas to the whole, defining beds, and working out paths for pedestrian and vehicular circulation. If you can get a plot plan of your property with topographic information, plan view is also perfect for illuminating patterns of runoff and drainage as well as determining setbacks from wetlands or property lines. When it comes time to add the three-dimensional objects, I like to project pictures of the area on a white wall covered with tracing paper. I can sketch out the forms of plants and structures in a more natural perspective. This technique is also very handy when renovating or tweaking an existing garden. You can go so far as to erase the parts of the garden you do not like with image-editing software on your computer and then play around with forms and colors to fill

Rudbeckia fulgida with *Physostegia virginica, Perovskia,* and *Agastache.* Digital image processing can reveal patterns of color, form, and texture that are less obvious in the unretouched slide. I used Adobe Photoshop to filter this image and make it look like a dry-brush painting. The uniform texture and dominance of yellow suggest that some bold-leaved and purple-flowered plants would make the planting more interesting.

the blank spaces. The better software allows you to filter the image to make it more abstract—sometimes a useful exercise when attempting to diagnose problems in an existing design. I find it very helpful to photograph problem areas during the growing season and store the images in a file on my computer. That way I can go back to them during the winter when I have the time and inclination to tweak and redesign them. Try not to jump to any plant conclusions at this stage, focusing instead on forms and colors in the abstract. After I have worked out the outlines of beds and paths and determined roughly the heights, forms, colors, and textures of plants I need, I sit down and make a list of all the possibly appropriate varieties I can think of. It is helpful to page through reference books, peruse photos, and search for relevant on-line lists (perennials for dry soils, deer-resistant perennials, etc.) to jog your memory. Write down more than you will need because it

is helpful to have some choices. Start by going through the list and picking your absolute favorites, and then pencil a few of these into the proper locations. At this stage it becomes easier to work in plan view to determine quantities and spacing, using the perspective sketches as a guide. I have two circle templates I picked up at a local artists' supply store, filled with circles of different sizes. If I know that a particular perennial has a mature width of two feet, I can choose the circle that corresponds to this size in the scale I am working in. As I add plants into the plan, this insures proper spacing and quantities. Detailed plan drawings are scaled down to between one-twelfth and one-four-hundred-and-eightieth of life size. The smaller the scale, the easier it is to see fine details, but a scale of one inch to one foot requires a *big* sheet of paper for all but the smallest spaces. I find that a scale of one inch to eight feet is about right for planting design. This way you can use a reg-ular ruler and not have to buy a specially scaled engineer's ruler like the ones designers use (one foot will correspond to the eighth-inch tick mark on the ruler, four feet to the half-inch mark). Once you get your first plant placed, you can work out from there, choosing others from the list that complement the first and more to complement those until the bed is full. I have a set of colored pencils that I use to shade in different plants as I add them so they read more easily. If there are just a few in the plan I try to color-code them based on flower or leaf color, but in more complex designs there are not enough colors to remain true to life and I simply make a mark next to the appropriate variety on my plant list with the corresponding colored pencil.

One of the valuable things about designing on paper is that you will tend to use larger masses of plants. It is much, much easier to design a garden using drifts or masses of 12 or 24 than to compose one out of ones and twos. Drifts and masses give the finished garden an uncluttered look and reflect what we see in nature. Acquiring the discipline to plant in groups of six or more is not easy for two reasons. First, if you buy plants at retail prices, it gets very expensive very quickly, and second, it goes against out basic human desire for novelty and collection. The best way to counter the first problem is

Dianthus planted in drifts. Because of the small scale, when I design on paper I invariably paint with larger drifts of each plant than I do when I design on the ground.

Eutrochium purpureus and *E. perfoliatum.* Though designed by bovines rather than humans, this cow pasture in western Massachusetts has a gardenesque feel to it. The simple color palette and uniform texture and form make the whole work as a composition rather than just a collection of plants.

to learn how to propagate your own plants. As I can attest, there is no easy cure for the second, though heading to the nursery with a shopping list derived from a plan will help. As far as quantities go, I have found that it takes at least twenty-four of the same kind of plant to make a satisfying visual mass, using average-size perennials in a large space. Six or twelve might also accomplish this if the plant in question is unusually large or the space very small.

The Time Warp

True gardens exist in four dimensions, not two or even three, and this is perhaps the most difficult thing about garden design. A building or a painting may look different in the morning or afternoon light, but in the scheme of things each is relatively static over time. A garden, however, begins to change the moment it is planted, as the seasons march on and the plants grow, bloom, and die. Temporally sensitive design that celebrates change is difficult to accomplish in plan view, even for experienced designers, and nearly impossible until you begin to know the plants personally and can picture their seasonal dance as you put pencil to paper. I think this is why so many commercial landscapes look static and boring: the plants were sized and engineered like the drainage pipe under-

neath to do a job consistently and unwaveringly until instructed otherwise. A true garden, though, is a dynamic place where change is welcomed, be it the quality of light over the course of the day or the way the crackled silhouettes of dried grasses

Uvularia grandiflora in the fog. What could be more transitory than fog coalescing on the leaves of great merry-bells?

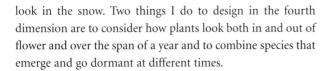
Dryopteris erythrosora with **narcissus**. Late-emerging fronds of autumn fern begin to hide aging leaves of the daffodils planted among them.

A random arrangement of different forms lends this garden a certain spontaneity verging on chaos.

look in the snow. Two things I do to design in the fourth dimension are to consider how plants look both in and out of flower and over the span of a year and to combine species that emerge and go dormant at different times.

Personality Theory

You may have heard it said that the three elements of design are form, texture, and color. They are bandied about in horticultural writing so frequently that I imagine few of us give them real consideration from day to day. However, the interplay of these three elements and how we perceive them, along with nonliving features such as structures or water, is what gives a garden its personality, moods, and charisma. Perhaps it is appropriate to consider the following discussion as a sort of horticultural psychology theory, because what we are really talking about is how the plants, paths, and structures in a garden affect us.

We are naturally attracted to color, and certainly, colorful flowers are the primary reason we plant perennials, but from a design perspective color is probably the least important element precisely because it is so fleeting. Most perennials are in flower for merely a week or two, so for the other 50 weeks of the year it is the form and texture that must be considered first.

FORM

Perennials have four basic forms: tall and narrow, rounded, carpeting, and what I call explosive in that they grow every which way like curly hair in an electrical storm. Perennial planting beds are either geometrical with strong lines and corners or organic with curving lines. The use of only one basic form of plant gives uniformity even when flower colors are varied (imagine a large bed of variously colored daylilies), while a combination of forms gives variety and a feeling of spontaneity (think of a cottage garden). Geometrical beds are considered formal and organic ones informal, but you can soften sharp geometries by utilizing all four plant forms and likewise formalize highly curvilinear beds by massing similar forms together. Personally I like curvilinear beds over square ones, and to complement this I tend to plant in masses to give the finished design a slightly stylized but still naturalistic form.

RIGHT: Drifts of *Anemone blanda* surround pillarlike **European beeches** in the famous March Bank at Winterthur. I call the combination of strong verticals emerging from sweeps of lower plants the "islands in the sea" motif.

BELOW: A classic tiered English border utilizing annuals and perennials at Cornell Plantations in Ithaca, New York.

TOP LEFT: *Deschampsia flexuosa.* **Tufted hairgrass** blazes amid swaths of wild blueberries on a coastal Maine blueberry farm.

TOP RIGHT: *Miscanthus* **'Morning Light'** with *Sedum* **'Autumn Joy'.** A similar effect is achieved in the garden using variegated **maiden grass** and **sedum.**

OPPOSITE: *Coreopsis* **'Moonbeam'** with *Liatris spicata.* A classic combination of two different forms.

Tallest Kids in the Back

Classic Victorian perennial borders are long and narrow with tall stuff in the back (against a wall or fence, if you have one) and progressively shorter plants toward the front. This mimics on a smaller scale what you see all the time in a successional plant community, where first mosses and other low plants, then taller perennials and shrubs, then finally trees come in so that the whole slopes down from high to low. As one mass, this high to low approach is visually boring, so instead I have

adopted what you might call an "islands in the sea" motif where shorter plants meander and swirl around taller ones much as they would in a prairie. The rivers of lower plants add visual movement and interest to what would otherwise be basically flowering bleachers. Other motifs include randomly scattered taller plants amid lower ones, and masses of similar forms but various textures or colors that flow in waves, spirals, or serpentine lines through the bed. In all cases, the fewer varieties you use, the more stylized the design becomes. When you set your pots out to plant, try to avoid placing them in rows or lines. Instead, stagger your plants so that the finished garden will appear less geometrical. I find it helpful to set out pots in triangles, with each pot forming a new triangle with its two nearest neighbors.

TEXTURE

If form is simply the shape of objects in the garden, texture is meant to describe how they "feel," both tactilely and emotionally, to the eye. Small or narrow leaves, stems, and flowers have blurry edges when they mass together so they appear soft and impressionistic. This effect is even more pronounced from a distance or when backlit by the sun. I think fine-textured

The scattered pattern of *Hudsonia ericoides* along the Wonderland Trail in Acadia National Park (right) is similar in effect to a planting of crested iris, Labrador violet *(Viola labradorica),* sedum, and foamflower at Bartram's Garden in Philadelphia (left).

Mertensia virginica in southern Pennsylvania. Masses of wild Virginia bluebells spilling down the banks of this woodland (left) are truly inspiring. The same effect can be achieved in the garden by letting the plants self-sow, as here at Garden in the Woods.

TOP LEFT: *Amsonia ciliata* var. *tenuifolia.* Some **bluestars** have wonderfully fine-textured foliage that softens any planting.

TOP CENTER: Similar forms but different textures and colors make **crested iris** and *Hosta* 'Francee' a winning combination.

TOP RIGHT: *Hosta* 'Krossa Regal' with *Astilbe chinensis.* When fine and bold textures combine with different forms, the effect is visually complex.

LEFT CENTER: *Diphylleia cymosa.* **Umbrella leaf** is one of my favorite shade perennials. Its 16-inch leaves create a striking textural statement.

BOTTOM LEFT: *Eutrochium maculatum* with *Perovskia atriplicifolia.* Similar colors but strongly contrasting forms and textures also make an extremely effective combination.

plants lend the garden an ethereal, transcendent quality. Large leaves and flowers have strong edges and "feel" coarse. Like bikers at a tea party, they foster an aggressive, exaggerated mood so are often called bold textured. In between fine and coarse are leaves and flowers of average size that you might say have a medium texture. The vast majority of perennials fall into this category, and as such, medium texture is a sort of visual average that is neither ethereal nor exaggerated. Designs that use only medium-textured plants look rather mediocre and visually uninspired unless color and form are exaggerated instead. Texture works the same way as form in that you can create more stylized plantings by using only fine- or coarse-textured plants, or conversely create amazing visual energy by combining fine- and coarse-leaved plants. Structural elements such as rocks, path surfaces, arbors, and sculpture function

similarly. A coarse, blocky stone sculpture will look very different in a bed of fine ferns than in a sea of large-leaved hostas.

Color

I think most of us got into flower gardening because it is so colorful. I have never read anything to substantiate it, but I really believe that intense colors shoot right through our eyes to the pleasure center of our brain, and consequently the lack of bright colors in winter is one of the reasons the cold months are so hard on us folks in northern climes. By February I am nearly screaming for my color fix, and I am easy prey for glossy nursery catalogs that arrive proffering untold floral delights in shades of crimson, apricot, and aquamarine. Do not be surprised if you roll up my driveway in April only

Mind-blowing color with a pleasing rhythm at the Cox Arboretum in Ohio. With consistent forms and textures, this hot color palette is attention-getting but not overwhelming.

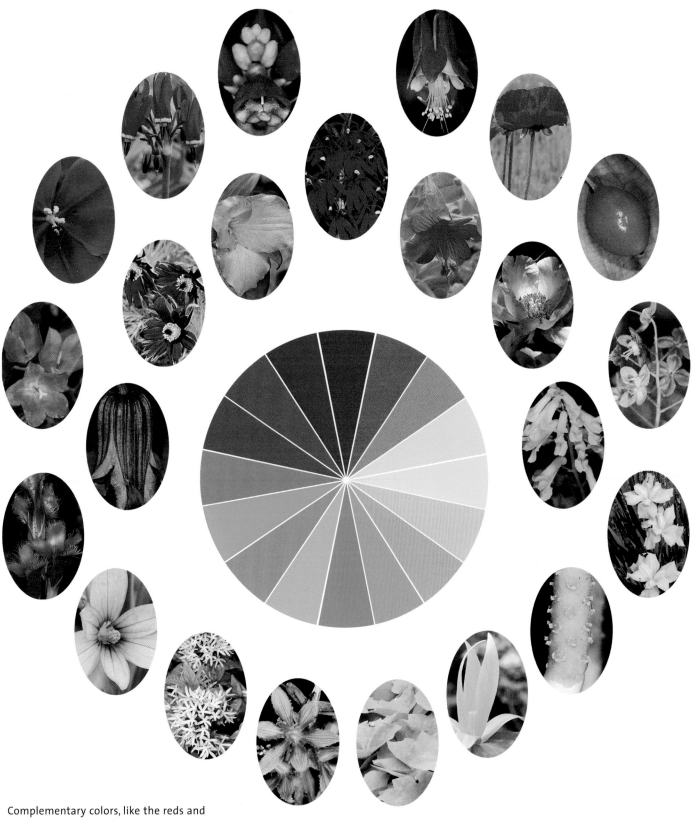

Complementary colors, like the reds and
yellows of the tulips (opposite), are those near
each other on the color wheel. Contrasting colors, like
blue and orange, which are far apart on the wheel, are
more difficult to combine effectively.

TOP: The contrasting colors and textures of *Heuchera* 'Obsidian' and *Lamium maculatum* 'Purple Dragon' (dead nettle) are more distracting than the simpler combination below.

BOTTOM: *Rudbeckia maxima* with *Colocasia esculenta* 'Black Magic'. Similar forms and textures allow the color contrast between purple taro and cabbage-leaf coneflower to really stand out.

to find me stooped down and enraptured by the first pale violet hepatica blooms or rolling around like a pig in mud at the sight of the first daffodils poking up through snow-trodden leaves.

Much has been written about designing with color, and for good reason. Flowers of complementary colors blooming side by side are the visual equivalent of musical harmony: pleasing alone but transcendent when brought together. It may sound a bit trite, but I do believe that a garden full of complementary colors flows and blends like a symphony for the eye, while a planting full of clashing hues is the visual equivalent of heavy metal played backward through a broken speaker. Generally, blue complements purple, green, yellow, and pink, and red works with orange and yellow, but so much depends on the hue and intensity of the colors that simple rules such as this are full of exceptions. Orange clashes with pink and purple, and red with blue, but white and even yellow tend to soften and blend strongly contrasting colors and tone them down in the same way that adding white paint to a strong color makes it less intense. As I mentioned earlier, similar textures or forms benefit from more outlandish color combinations to lift them from mediocrity.

You Should Have Seen It Yesterday!

One of the sad realities about color in the garden is its transitoriness. Through the magic of film and digital imagery we can capture the garden at the peak of its brain-wiggling psychedelia that may in reality last merely a day or a week. It would be great if perennials bloomed for months, as annuals do, but the need to survive from one year to the next means they cannot squander their reserves on endless flowering. Certainly you can plant a succession of species and varieties that will open a few at a time over the entire growing season, but alas, most of us do our shopping in spring and come home with trunkfuls of plants in bloom. Summer- and fall-blooming flowers stand neglected on the springtime sales benches, and thus we end up with gardens that look marvelous in May but muted come August. So, my first bit of advice the next time you go plant shopping is to pass by some of those blooming spring lovelies for a few vernally unimpressive but autumnally magnificent late bloomers that will end the gardening season on a high note.

Since color is transitory I also choose plants that have other visual interest, be it the way they emerge, their form, their texture, or the patterns of their leaves. Ephemera such as tulips, oriental poppies, bluebells, and crocus are useful because they can come and go like an opening act that clears the stage for others that bloom later on their same square of earth.

Patience

Gardens are never finished, and there are always opportunities for improvement. Realize, though, that it takes three years on average for perennial gardens to mature, and they really shine at five years, then often begin to need some rehabilitation after 7 to 10 summers. If properly spaced, the plants will look a bit sparse the first year or two, but gradually the mulch will disappear under a canopy of leaves and flowers. The old saying "the first year it sleeps, the second it creeps, and the third it leaps" is really true, so do not be too hard on yourself or the plants until a few seasons have gone by. I find it much easier to tweak and edit an existing garden bed than to design one from scratch because it is easier to visualize one or two new things amid plants already present and accounted for. So do not be paralyzed by the fear of failure. Make some sketches, plant some gardens, and improve them as you go. While you are at it, stick that little critic on your shoulder deep in the compost pile where his or her pointless negativity belongs, and have some fun!

Echinacea purpurea with *Rudbeckia fulgida* var. *sullivantii*. **Coneflowers** and **black-eyed Susans** display contrasting colors but similar forms and textures.

CHAPTER 9

CULTIVATION WITH AN ECOLOGICAL EYE

They Are My Babies!

There is a crucial difference between true gardeners and nature lovers who revel in the diversity of life or well-meaning homeowners who like the hedges shaped and the lawn trimmed: we gardeners feel genuinely parental toward our plants. If you are not a gardener, this will likely strike you as completely pathetic, just as the excesses of show-dog owners seem to me. If you are one of us, let's face it, in a weird sort of way, your plants are your babies. Haven't you ever bundled tender new leaves up against an impending frost, spent inordinate amounts of money on organic plant food instead of those cheap chemical brands, fretted when seedlings were sick, or found yourself filled with an unshakable and slightly unsettling bloodlust when they were bullied by an obese, unsavory woodchuck? Granted, I would not throw myself in front of an oncoming truck to save the peony that just rolled off my wagon, but there is no question that gardening is a type of

ABOVE: *Shortia galacifolia.* Oconee bells is a rare, slow-growing wildflower from the southern Appalachians. Finding a prize garden patch denuded by deer fills me with blood lust.

parenting. I had never shot an animal in my life, but the relentless munching of a burgeoning deer population spurred me to dispatch my first buck with the old .22 rifle I got as a teenager. My lucky shot became legend at work, where I became Bill the Great White Hunter who could slay a deer with a popgun. I hated to kill a beautiful animal like a white-tailed deer, but after seeing my beloved trilliums decapitated and my rhododendrons stripped, I was filled with a righteous anger that surprised even me. In many ways, gardening is as maddening and confusing as parenthood.

Many of us are not lucky enough to have learned gardening from a parent or grandparent and must hone our skills though trial and error, always wondering if our garden is as neat, well-behaved, and attractive as the ones we see on TV or in the magazines. My aim in writing this book was to create an owners manual of sorts, but you might say it is also a guide to plant parenthood. The first four chapters explain how the root bone is connected to the stem bone, the fifth is a primer on sex education, the sixth is about health and wellness, the seventh genealogy and heredity, the eighth socialization and creativity, and this ninth one details what you can do to insure they grow up right (upright?). What I hope is that after reading all the previous chapters, what follows will prove to be both a review and a synthesis that will make your job rearing a fine garden of perennials all the easier and more enjoyable.

Why Do the Most Expensive Plants Die the Fastest?

As I get older, I am more reluctant to adopt every new, expensive, and marginally hardy treasure that peers out at me with flowers open wide from the pages of my favorite mail order catalog. Tales of its discovery in some remote corner of China accessible only by yak, its celebrated birth from seeds brought hopefully back to the States, and its remarkable, magnificent, sublime, redolent, unmatched beauty fill me not with lust but with anxiety. I think back on other such treasures I have ordered with frenzied excitement and set lovingly into the choicest earth only to fret for the next three years every time the thermometer dipped below zero, the rains failed to come, or the heat of summer raged unrelenting. I imagine you have problem children like this in your garden as well. Perhaps they are better off living in China than dying in Connecticut.

When I got my first job in a nursery I wanted to save every sick little plant that came my way, despite the admonitions of the manager to "compost it!" After years of growing

and unavoidably killing plants, my heart has hardened to the point that I find myself now admonishing my own staff to do what I once could not. I think every gardener has to come to terms with the fact that plants die—sometimes from our mistakes and sometimes because of things like hurricanes, floods, and insect invasions that are beyond our control. Much about gardening is beyond our control, and some is within it. Cultivation, then, is learning to accept the things we cannot change, having the tools to change the things we can, and the experience (or reference book) to know the difference. Wait a minute—haven't I seen that on a bumper sticker?

Agastache 'Black Adder' (hyssop) with *Stenanthium gramineum* var. *robustum* (featherfleece) and *Vernonia noveboracensis* (New York ironweed).

TOP LEFT: *Viola lanceolata* grows with wild abandon in my back woods.

TOP RIGHT: *Eschscholzia californica* (California poppy). In its native haunts, this beautiful wildflower is an easy, drought-tolerant perennial. However, in the northeastern United States it is best treated as an annual.

BOTTOM RIGHT: *Polygonatum cirrhifolium,* a tall, vining Solomon's seal from China, has never thrived in my garden, even after ten years.

Lessons from Ecology

The Chinese rarity I mentioned above and the little violet out in my woods in Connecticut grow in their particular places for the simple reason that they can survive there better than other plants can. Nature looks peaceful, but as we know, it is a ruthless and unforgiving place where only the strongest and most fit survive. Despite what some politicians say, resources are not limitless, and no matter where you look, something is in short supply. Plants need light, water, nutrients, and temperatures within a certain range to survive. Alaska may generally have plenty of water, acceptable levels of nutrients, and lots of light (in the summer), but it lacks the warmth perennials from warmer climes require. Arizona has too much warmth and not much water, while a spot deep within the Black Forest of Germany is critically short of sunlight above all else. From an ecological perspective, resources in short supply within a given habitat limit the number of plants and animals that can survive there. Extreme environments limit many of the resources critical for plant growth and thus can support relatively fewer species. Diversity is further impacted by unstable environmental conditions, which further explains why you find more species in the tropics than on the tundra. Gardens are not unlike wild places in that each is blessed or cursed with a set of constraints that limits the choices we can make as gardeners. You may curse your clay soil or winter cold, but really, you have only two choices: choose from a more limited suite of plants that can handle your conditions, or "improve" the site to make it amenable to a larger group.

I Want Them All

We have inherited much of our gardening tradition from Victorian England, where gardens were awash in fabulous new plants from every corner of the empire. The name of this gardening game was to assemble and grow as many different plants as you could, regardless of their origin. Plants from Chile and California mingled with others from Crete and the

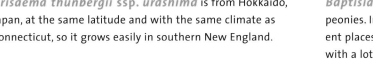

Arisaema thunbergii ssp. *urashima* is from Hokkaido, Japan, at the same latitude and with the same climate as Connecticut, so it grows easily in southern New England.

Baptisia sphaerocarpa (yellow false indigo) with peonies. In the garden we bring together plants from different places and very different habitats. This is possible only with a lot of horticultural artifice.

Caucasus in a horticultural smorgasbord unimaginable a generation earlier: it is a style of gardening that is very much alive and well today. In order to grow a collection of plants from many different regions and habitats in one small garden one must basically make limited resources limitlessly available. The gardening tradition we have inherited requires us to build superrich soils; apply ample water and fertilizer; construct greenhouses, cold frames, cloches, and burlap body wraps; reduce competition from indigenous plants (aka weeds); spray fungicides, herbicides, and insecticides; and prune, stake, and pamper, all to keep this multinational conglomeration alive and tolerably well. It is certainly not a very environmentally sustainable approach, and it is a heck of a lot of work. I get tired just thinking about it (remember that the folks who invented this style had gardeners to do the work for them).

A Lighter Shade of Green

There are some easy and obvious ways to garden more responsibly, and others that require more resolve and restraint. Gardening, by definition, requires us to tinker and modify things a bit in order to grow certain plants at their best, so a cynic might say if you want to be truly "green," leave mother nature alone and give up horticulture entirely. However, I firmly believe that we can have beautiful gardens and leave things in better shape than when we found them.

Natural systems have very little waste, and over time natural habitats generally become better and better places to live for an ever-widening variety of life. Thus, the best guide to gardening more sustainably is nature itself. The most obvious lesson is the one I discussed at the beginning of this section: the species that are best adapted for the particular environmental constraints of a given place will be the ones most likely to thrive. Look at your property with a critical eye. Where is the shade heaviest? Where is the soil leanest? Where does the winter wind blow hardest? Before doing extensive modifications to improve these marginal sites, think about what plants might be able to grow there as is. The best place to find these plants is in analogous natural areas nearby. In general, the indigenous species are best adapted to the vagaries of climate, geology, and soils that define your region. You can look for

Polystichum acrostichoides (Christmas fern) tolerates dry soils and shade better than most perennials.

TOP LEFT: Gardening is about more than just the plants. *Liatris ligulistylis* (meadow blazing star) draws in monarch butterflies better than any other plant. It is thrilling to see dozens of these charismatic butterflies enjoying the flowers I planted.

TOP RIGHT: *Uvularia grandiflora* (great merry-bells) self-sows lightly in the woodland garden. When a plant begins to seed in on its own, it is proof positive that it is well adapted to your garden.

BOTTOM RIGHT: *Tulipa marjoletti.* Species tulips are often tougher and better adapted than hybrids bred for color and size. This lovely species, native to the Savoy Alps of France, is thought to descend from cultivated tulips brought there in the seventeenth century. Not only is it perennial, it actually self-sows in the garden.

Woodland garden at Garden in the Woods. Though absolutely charming in the spring, this garden does need regular irrigation during the summer because it was built on glacial till that is unsuitable for plants from a rich woodland habitat.

ecological appropriateness resulted in a garden that requires constant irrigation even during the spring to keep it alive and thriving. I can only imagine the millions of gallons of well water and countless hours of staff time wasted lugging hoses and sprinklers around the place for the past 80 years to sustain this artifice. Do not make the same mistake.

Recycled

The second thing I have learned from nature is that nothing is wasted. When plants or plant parts die, most of the nutrients they contain, along with all of the stored energy they once garnered from the sun, are fed back in to the system through decomposition. With the exception of some steep slopes or windy, exposed sites prone to water or wind erosion, all soils become gradually more fertile over time. It is a slow process, but over decades and centuries, nutrient levels rise and soil depth increases until some catastrophic event—flood, fire, or ice age—strips it down to bedrock again. We humans do a pretty good job of erosion ourselves, and in most parts of the United States and southern Canada the soils today are substantially thinner and less fertile than they were 400 or even 200 years ago. Consequently, many gardeners find they have to build back topsoil before beginning to garden. In nature, soils build up when more organic and mineral particles accumulate than are lost to erosion and weathering. In temperate climates, topsoil builds up at a rate of one to two inches per century on average, but we can speed things up exponentially with just a modicum of effort. I will get to this in a bit, but first I need to touch on the nature of soil.

What Is Soil?

Soil is primarily composed of bits of rock along with some bits of organic debris. As rock weathers over time, it is eroded, cracked, pulverized, and broken down into smaller and smaller particles. The largest particles that are considered to be soil

plants from similar habitats far away, and these may prove suitable as well, but be cautious, as sometimes they can be too well suited and become invasive pests. If you have a site that is, say, both dry and heavily shady, there are very few potential choices as not much can survive under such extreme conditions. In this case some modification of the existing conditions may be called for. Pick the easiest and least intrusive first. It is far easier to limb up a few trees or cut back some of the understory than to set up irrigation systems. Besides, a number of plants will grow in dry, bright shade. If the site is sunny and dry, there are even more options. One of the ironies about the woodland garden at Garden in the Woods is that the original designers and owners wished to have a magnificent display of water-hungry woodland wildflowers and shrubs up on the dry, gravelly glacial moraine near their house rather than on the more suitable areas of rich soils along the brook that dissects the property. This simple choice of aesthetics over

particles are sand. (Larger rocks and gravel are not technically soil, and if you have ever tried to garden in gravel I am sure you will agree.) Sands range in size from 0.0025 to 0.039 inches in diameter, and as such they are relatively heavy and not easily eroded by wind or water. There are large spaces or pores in between the grains, which allow for rapid movement of water and air. Silt particles are much finer, ranging in size from 0.00015 to 0.0025 inches (0.0025 inches is just less than the width of an average human hair). Clay particles are even smaller, from 0.000039 to 0.00015 inches wide. It is hard for me to fathom something less than one-twenty-thousandth of an inch wide. These tiny particles can stay suspended in water for a long time and are too small to feel individually with your fingers, so wet clay rubbed between thumb and forefinger is smooth and slippery whereas sand is rough and gritty. You find silt and clay soils at the base of mountain ranges, in ancient lake beds, and in other low areas where running water slows sufficiently for the suspended particles to gradually settle out. The famous red clays of the Southeast are all that is left of massive ancient mountain ranges that were eroded down over time (the second of these ranges—the Appalachians—was once as tall as the Himalayas are today).

A ROOM FULL OF TOASTERS

Imagine a 10 by 10 by 10 foot room stuffed to the ceiling with upholstered furniture. Because all those sofas, ottomans, recliners, and loveseats are big and angular, there is quite a bit of free space in and around each unit no matter how carefully you pack them. In fact, a small child could probably squeeze through the spaces to get from one side to the other if a candy reward were involved. Now picture the room filled with toaster ovens of various makes. Because the ovens are smaller and all roughly the same size, the spaces between them are smaller

and impossible for a person to navigate, though a spider or maybe even a mouse could do it. Finally, fill the room with stack upon stack of computer paper. Now, there is very little wasted space in what is quite nearly a solid 1,000 cubic feet of paper. Sand, silt, and clay particles behave much the same way in the soil. Sand particles are large and irregular enough that the large pore spaces between them coalesce into channels that allow water to percolate through very quickly (as you are clearly aware if you have ever poured water onto a sandy beach). The large pores are difficult for water to fill even temporarily, so the soil does not hold much moisture but instead facilitates rapid gas exchange, bringing in the oxygen roots need and allowing out the carbon dioxide before they suffocate. Silt particles, like the room full of toasters, have smaller channels so they drain more slowly, holding much more water and less air. Still, the gaps between them are such that some air can move in and out, except when the soil is completely saturated with water after rain, snowmelt, or flood. Clay particles stack up like sheets of paper, so the pore space is very limited and the pores that are present are tiny.

Water percolates very slowly through clay but eventually finds its way between the layers, just as it does between the pages of a heavy book dunked into the water. Also much like a book dropped in a sink, the clay layers expand and hold a great deal of water after rains but then shrink back markedly and crack visibly when dry. Clay can hold so much water not just because the tiny pores and layered arrangement of the particles trap it. Clay particles are also electrically charged so they attract and hold ionically charged water molecules like flypaper does flies. The same goes for the various nutrient ions floating around in the water. Clay particles—especially the smallest, termed clay colloids—hold soluble nutrients that would otherwise be leached by rainwater. Thus clay soils are poorly drained and low in oxygen when wet but often are fairly nutrient rich when compared to sands and even silts.

The ideal topsoil is a combination of breathable sand, water-holding silt, and nutrient-rich clay in roughly a proportion of 2:2:1. This is called loam, the holy grail of most gardeners and the best and most productive agricultural soil on earth. The sand component lets water percolate and oxygen infiltrate, while the silt and clay hold water and nutrients. I have never gardened in true loam. The glaciers scrubbed away most of the clay and silt in New England, so what we have are mostly younger, less-weathered, sandier soils. In North Carolina I gardened on red clay—perhaps the most unforgiving stuff you could try to cultivate. Fortunately there is a fairly easy way to bring both sandy and clayey soils closer to loamy nirvana, and that is to add organic matter.

ORGANIC MATTERS

Organic matter—the partially decomposed remains of plants and animals—is much less abundant in soils compared to mineral (inorganic) particles, but it is of equal if not greater importance to the health of the earth beneath our feet. A fertile, friable soil contains 3 to 5 percent organic matter by weight. When you send your soil off to be tested by the lab, they will give you a percentage of organic matter arrived at by drying, weighing, burning, and then reweighing the sample. The weight after burning divided by the weight before gives the percentage of organic matter in the soil. Since organics tend to be lighter in weight than inorganics, the organic matter makes up a larger *volume* of the soil than these figures might suggest. In any case, organic particles function much like mineral ones. As tree trunks, roots, leaves, excrement, dead animals, and so forth are consumed by decomposing microorganisms, the bits and pieces are broken up into smaller and smaller particles. The largest ones function like sand, opening up and aerating heavier soil. Finer particles hold water, while the finest—tiny, decay-resistant bits called humic substances—are the organic equivalent of clay colloids, attracting and holding water and soluble nutrients that would otherwise quickly leach from the soil. While coarser organic matter breaks down within a week, a month, or a year, humic substances can remain in the soil for as long as 10,000 years. Humic substances stain the soil brown or black, which is why we equate darkness with fertility. They can be found in organic fertilizers and compost teas, as well as in more traditional composts—an added benefit from using these products. In addition to binding up electrically charged nutrient ions, they also bind together tiny soil particles to make bigger ones—a process called flocculation. In this way, organics help "open

My Father's Day present: a 15-yard pile of composted cow manure for the garden. Properly composted cow manure is one of the best possible soil amendments, and I don't mind the slight sharp smell as I spread it around.

Epimedium leptorrhizum. Soils amended with liberal amounts of compost allow slow-growing shade plants such as this yellow epimedium to establish themselves far more quickly than they would otherwise. New plants in enriched soil also require less watering and will bloom more prolifically.

the friability of heavy clay soils while raising the fertility, bolstering beneficial microorganism populations, protecting finer soil particles from erosion, and keeping soil temperatures more moderate.

ON THE HORIZONS

Topsoil is basically the upper layer (horizon) of soil where mineral particles mix with organic ones. This is often called the A horizon by soil scientists, and it is the layer of soil where you will find most of the roots and microbes. Below this is a layer of mineral soil with very little organic matter, called the subsoil or B horizon, and below this is the bedrock, the C horizon. Some highly acidic forest soils in which the acidity slows decomposition have a well-defined layer of nearly pure organic matter composed of partially decomposed leaves and woody debris that is called duff (F horizon). Species native to such soils often require a highly organic layer like this to thrive (p. 209), but in general, perennials relish deep topsoil that combines mineral and organic particles into a fertile, friable black or brown loam. In other words, the deeper your topsoil, the better your perennials will grow.

up" heavy clay soils. Because these bundled particles are held only by electrical forces, they are relatively fragile and can be disintegrated by such things as rototillers, feet, and tires.

It is important to remember that as organic matter decomposes, nutrients and other beneficial organic compounds locked up in the large carbon molecules that are the building blocks of wood, flesh, blood, leaves, and bone become available to plants. Decomposition is a nearly perfect closed loop where essential nutrients are recycled and recycled so that over time, fertility slowly builds up if any additional nutrients are added. By adding organic matter to the soil in the form of composts and mulches, you can improve the moisture- and nutrient-holding capacity of sandy soils and

The famous topsoils of Iowa—some of the richest farmland on earth—have developed fairly recently and provide a good model for us here. During the last ice age, glaciers coming down through the Rockies carved away and pulverized the mountain rock and carried it along in the ice. As the ice melted, huge piles of glacial till—the jumbled bits of rock, gravel, sand, silt, and clay contained in the ice—were exposed and set upon by winds blowing eastward across the plains. The finer particles of silt and clay traveled farthest, piling up eventually into huge dunes in the Midwest. The soil of these silt and clay dunes is known as loess. As prairie grasses and wildflowers colonized the loess, bringing up nutrients and building up organic matter as roots and tops died, the soil became

gradually darker and more fertile, so that by the time the sod-busters found it, it was deep, rich, and nearly black. Digging prairie dogs, worms, and roots carried organic materials deep in the loess deposits to create a layer of topsoil sometimes as much as 6 to 10 feet deep. It is almost unimaginable to a New Englander. Here, we are happy to have just six inches of the stuff. One problem with loess is that just as it blew in, it can blow out. Once the protective blanket of plants was removed by the plow, the soil began to blow and wash away, so that now—150 years later—much has been lost into the Gulf of Mexico.

SCRAPED CLEAN

In contrast to the mythical prairie soils of the Midwest, the dirt underneath a typical suburban lawn is close to being subsoil devoid of organic matter and life. Several factors are responsible for this. Some unscrupulous builders scrape off the topsoil and sell it for a profit, leaving the happy homeowner with a thin A horizon or none at all. Even well-meaning contractors tend to mix the topsoil in with the subsoil in the process of removing it with heavy equipment, stockpiling it and then spreading it back out. This is further compounded by the actions of the homeowner him- or herself. Instead of building up organic matter in the soil, the vacuuming or raking off of grass clippings and leaves further depletes the soil of its stores. Chemical fertilizers may encourage more leaf

ABOVE: A highly acidic woodland soil in Connecticut develops a matted, peatlike "duff" layer of partially decomposed leaves and wood debris in which most of the roots and soil microbes live. There is a thin band of topsoil between the duff and the pale orange subsoil (B horizon) beneath. It is a starkly different soil from the one pictured on page 191, and it supports a very different plant community. Species like gaywings (*Polygala paucifolia,* left) thrive in it, but the epimedium pictured previously would struggle.

growth, which is in turn removed, but they do not add soil-building humic substances as their organic equivalents would. Close-cropping the green carpet keeps grass roots short so they do not penetrate down and build topsoil in that way. Fungicides, herbicides, and insecticides along with excessive fertilization severely impact microorganisms that are needed to decompose what little is left. The weed-free, chemical lawn sits atop a virtual biological desert. You can tell much about the health of your soil by the way the existing plants are growing and by the color of the stuff itself. Remember that as a rule, red, pale brown, gray, or tan color indicates a lack of fertility, while dark brown or gray black indicates health.

LEFT: Perennials can grow quickly in good soil. I rototilled this 200-foot by 12-foot strip of good topsoil at the nursery after spreading 20 yards of manure from the farm next door. We planted hundreds of perennials the next day.

BELOW: Fourteen months later the results speak for themselves.

Cultivation with an Ecological Eye   195

The effect of organic matter on postconstruction fill is dramatic. The fill on the left received no amendments and looks as pale and sterile as the day it was spread four years earlier. The clump in the middle was mulched with bark and composted manure, creating a black upper horizon and flocculated lower horizon. On the right is the same fill soil, into which I tilled a six-inch layer of compost two years earlier. Incorporating the compost has produced a deep, rich topsoil from depauperate fill in only two growing seasons.

The first order of business when beginning a new woodland garden is to thin out some of the trees. Here I have cut about half of the trees, focusing primarily on weak or rotten ones. I also favored oaks and pines over maples because maple roots are very shallow and aggressive.

OPPOSITE: With some of the trees gone and leaf compost dug in, wildflowers like this **wood phlox** simply thrive.

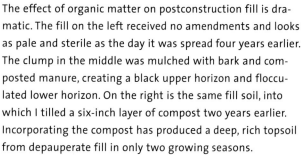

However, you can quickly bring back even degraded soil by digging in an ample supply of well-rotted compost. So, if you have inherited such a yard and now want to garden in it, remember that the deeper you dig and the more you dig in, the faster the ground will heal. Try to dig and turn in compost to a depth of at least six inches (and up to 12 inches or more if you can). When planting into areas covered in turf or coarse grasses, I like to kill the existing vegetation by laying down 10 sheets of overlapping newspaper covered with four to six inches of compost. After a month or two the ground should be ready to work. In a pinch I will use a rototiller or mattock to slice up the turf thoroughly and incorporate it before digging deeper with a spade or digging fork. In this case you will have to be diligent about pulling out the bits of grass and weeds that start to sprout up again after a week or two. After initially digging up and turning over degraded soil, I work in six inches of compost by turning it and stirring it with a digging fork. Even larger rototillers go only six inches deep or less, so hand mixing is more thorough. If you are very ambitious, you can double-dig the bed by starting a trench wide enough to work in and digging it a second time to a total depth of 16 to 20 inches. You will have to add about twice the compost, but man will those perennials thrive. Digging up and then adding

compost to the soil will fluff it up temporarily, so the finished bed will be slightly mounded. Additionally I mulch the bed after planting (see p. 201).

Life under Trees

Cultivating perennials under trees can be challenging, as the tree roots are very aggressive and scavenge up most of the available nutrients and water, while their leaves cast a heavy shade. The first order of business when considering a new garden under trees is the type and density of the tree species present. Evergreen trees create a very different woodland environment than deciduous species do, primarily because they cast shade all year long. This is a disadvantage if you want to cultivate many spring-blooming flowers, as they really require the month or so of sun that they normally receive before deciduous trees leaf out. However, evergreen trees are often better for evergreen perennials, as the shade these trees cast in winter prevents winter burn. The soil under evergreen conifers is generally cooler and more acidic than under broadleaf evergreens such as oaks and deciduous maples, oaks, ash, beech, aspen, and tulip poplar. My first task is usually to cut out some of the weaker trees to open gaps in the canopy. As a rule of

Pictured here is a newly planted bed in the cleared area shown on page 196. I prefer to create scattered beds like this because it is easier on both the trees and my back. I have mulched this planting with chopped leaves.

Helleborus orientalis. Hellebores thrive in a woodland garden bed enriched with leaf compost.

thumb in young, second-growth forest, I cut out about half of the existing trunks and limb up the remaining trees to a height of 15 to 20 feet with a pole saw. More mature forests will likely need less cutting and more limbing up, as the trees are larger and more widely spaced. Though it may seem like a hard job, limbing up the trees makes a huge difference in the amount of light coming in. It also opens up the forest visually and gives even young stands a feeling of greater age. Existing understory trees and shrubs can add form and interest to the woodland garden, but you need to plan how you will work your planting areas around these, as they will cast even more shade. I know that many people resist cutting trees, but remember that by taking some trees out you are allowing those that remain to become healthier while also creating more diversity in the understory. Many of the trees in a typical forest are weak and likely on their way out already. I leave as many of the stumps and fallen logs as I can to create habitat for insects and salamanders, recycle nutrients, provide material for fungi, and add a more natural look to the forest. There is some risk—especially when dealing with tall, thin

evergreens such as spruce—that opening up the woods may expose the remaining trees to wind and cause them to blow down. Trees that have been growing in a dense stand need some time to reinforce their trunks once things are opened up, but it is a small risk I am willing to take.

WOODLAND SOIL AMENDMENT

It is usually necessary to create amended areas with higher fertility to allow herbaceous plants to thrive under trees. It may be tempting to just dig up little areas for individual perennials, but unless the soil there is fairly rich, the plants will rarely thrive like they do when you create a larger root run. Even if you are lucky enough to have a good layer of dark topsoil already, digging in some additional compost will both loosen the soil and trim back some tree roots temporarily to let the perennials become established. If you have the sort of thick, acidic duff layer underlain by mineral soil I find in my woods and you wish to grow acid-loving species, then little is required other than perhaps a dusting with organic fertilizer, but most woodland plants, from ferns to hostas, hellebores, trilliums, epimediums, and jack-in-the-pulpits, need a richer soil. I dig in three to six inches of compost to a depth of four to eight inches to create an excellent root run for the perennials. Some folks prefer to just pile on a few loads of topsoil atop the existing soil, which is certainly easier than digging in among tree roots and is especially productive if you have heavy clay. In this case I recommend what is called composted loam—basically stumps, roots, and other debris that have been ground up in something called a tub grinder, then composted. It is a manufactured product that is usually fairly free of weeds, and you can rest assured that it does not come off your poor neighbor's new house lot. I have built small beds (less than 200 square feet) up over tree roots to a depth of 12 inches without any damage to the trees as long as the soil is not piled up against their trunks. Every subsequent fall or early spring I apply a topdressing of about one inch of compost to the bed to keep building the soil up and adding fertility. I also let the fallen leaves remain on the bed either as is, or I rake and shred them with a mower or gas-powered leaf shredder and reapply. The combination of an inch of yearly compost plus the leaves builds up topsoil about 10 times faster than would the leaves alone.

How Good Is Your Compost?

All composts are not created equal, and it is useful to understand a few things about the different types. Compost, by definition, is partially decomposed organic matter that has been manipulated so that the natural processes of decay have been greatly sped up. The advantage of compost is mainly that it has been predigested so that some of the nutrients in the material have been liberated by decomposition. It is also far less bulky than the raw materials and, if made correctly, free of weeds and pathogens. In order to kill weed seeds and disease spores the compost needs to heat up to around 150 to 160 degrees F. The heat comes from the respiration of trillions of microorganisms growing and digesting the organic wastes. If the pile is large enough to insulate and contain the heat, the materials are damp but not sodden, and there is plenty of easily digested material such as leaves, stems, fruits, and animal manure, the pile will heat up to the target temperature even if the air temperatures dip down near freezing. The process works most quickly and successfully if plenty of air is available for the decomposers. The pile should be restacked (or turned) at least once or twice a year, though you can turn it much more frequently to speed up the process (commercial compost facilities turn their piles daily or weekly). It usually takes four or five turnings to "finish" the compost process. If the material looks like dark soil and does not give off heat after it is turned, then the compost is finished. Traditionally, garden compost was made from animal manure mixed with straw animal bedding, plant debris, and kitchen scraps. The high

TOP: **Partially composted manure.** This pile is still fresh and smells like it! Turning and stirring the pile to aerate it will speed decomposition and let the pile heat up sufficiently to kill weed seeds and disease spores.

BOTTOM: **Leaf compost.** Leaves break down into an excellent black compost. To heat up sufficiently for proper composting, leaf piles need to be large and the leaves themselves should be damp. Shredding the leaves with a mower or leaf shredder prior to piling speeds the process. This pile is 6 feet high and 15 feet in circumference.

Lilium 'Casa Blanca'.

fully composted, the material is still full of recognizable bits of wood and corn silage that settle out when it is used as mulch. The danger when using it as a soil amendment is that all this wood will tie up nutrients as it continues to break down. Ideally, I use what is called finished compost for incorporation into new beds. This has an earthy smell and resembles black topsoil. You may see a few recognizable pieces of organic debris, but it is primarily a granular material due to the flocculating effects of all the humic substances in the mix. If the compost has a foul ammonia or sulfurous smell it means that is was not properly aerated, and there is some research to show that anaerobic compost like this can be harmful to certain plants due to the high levels of ammonia. Anaerobic compost also does not heat up very well, so this type is usually full of weeds, and it is nasty to work with. Fortunately, if you turn an anaerobic pile a few times and let it compost aerobically, you can reverse some of the problems.

Now that many landfills are full to capacity, municipalities are beginning to compost yard wastes and make them available for free or at low cost to residents. In my area, the raw materials are mostly leaves, sticks, and grass clippings raked and vacuumed off area lawns. Because of the tannins and other compounds in many tree leaves, this compost is jet black and quite good if made properly, though it varies from town to town and year to year. If not piled and turned correctly, you can end up with lots of weeds in your garden (along with the inevitable bits of plastic, aluminum beer cans, lost toys, etc.). In general, leaf composts are lower in nitrogen than manure-based composts, so I actually prefer them in the woodland garden, where many species are sensitive to high levels of (ammonium) nitrogen. Tree leaves and woody debris are also the preferred diet for many of the mycorrhizal fungi that inhabit the woods, so leaf-based compost is their preferred food.

You can make your own leaf compost, but you need to

nitrogen and generally good nutrient content of the manure and urine-soaked bedding composts very quickly and yields a "hot" or nutrient-rich material that is great for most perennials. In our area, farmers have switched from straw bedding to sawdust, which I imagine is cheaper to obtain in an area that boasts far more forest than wheat fields. Wood is far harder to break down than straw, so the compost is almost better used as mulch than soil amendment. Even after the manure has wait until the leaves have been well moistened with rain before gathering them. Make very large piles (at least six feet high and wide) to insure adequate heating. Leaves piled and turned three times the following year will be ready for use in 18 months from the time they were gathered. As with manure compost, more frequent turning speeds up the process, as does a larger pile, which contains more heat during the winter. Even if you do not let them finish composting, partially decomposed leaves from your own property do make a fine, dark mulch. Though it is counterintuitive, the pH of acidic leaves and needles tends to increase as they compost aerobically. In fact most composts are only slightly acidic to near neutral in pH even without the addition of wood ashes or lime.

Types of Mulch

Unlike compost, which resembles soil, organic mulches contain mostly easily recognizable organic materials that have yet to decompose fully. Finished compost does not make a good mulch because it washes away easily and provides a wonderful seed bed for weeds to germinate in. Partially decomposed materials such as straw, wood bark, leaves, cocoa hulls, and pine needles do make excellent mulches because they weave together like a blanket to protect the soil, and because they are not fully composted they make a less-suitable place for weeds. A proper layer of mulch is essential for both the health of the soil and your back. Mulch cools the ground in summer and keeps it warmer in winter, reduces evaporation, helps increase organic matter content and build topsoil, adds nutrients to feed plants and microorganisms, and reduces weed problems by hindering seed germination. Personally I prefer organic mulches over stone except in certain rock or desert garden settings, where gravel looks more appropriate and improves drainage around the plants. Plastic mulches and weed blankets are an abomination, and I strongly discourage their use. The ideal organic mulch should be attractive, easy to spread, inexpensive, last at least one year, and be suitable for the plants

being grown under it. The most common mulches for perennial gardens are tree bark or wood-based products, pine needles (pine straw), various hay and straw materials derived from grasses, chopped or shredded leaves, and partially finished compost. You can also buy buckwheat, cocoa, and peanut hulls, which are very easy to spread but a bit unnatural looking for my taste. What type you use is mostly a matter of preference and availability, though be aware that any raw (undecomposed) mulch will pull nitrogen out of the soil. It is

TOP: **Pine needles (pine straw)** make attractive mulch, though they do acidify the soil. Because they stay dry and fluffy, pine needles may also serve as a winter blanket to protect tender plants or young transplants, like the fall-planted delphinium pictured here.

BOTTOM: *Amsonia hubrichtii* under **hardwood chips**. After composting for a year, hardwood as well as **softwood chips** make an inexpensive mulch, though nutrient and pH problems are an issue.

phenols (not to mention the dye!) and tie up the nitrogen they need to grow. Ironically, dyed mulch is considered a premium product that costs more than the real thing!

Genuine shredded bark mulches are a product of the lumber industry. As softwoods such as pine, hemlock, fir, and cedar are debarked prior to sawing, the shaved-off bark is then run through a grinder and piled to partially compost. While the uncomposted products may look attractive, I prefer the dark brown, composted types because they still function well as mulch without affecting the nutrient balance of the soil adversely. One to two inches will suffice, though because it mats down as it dries, try to avoid piling it directly on the crowns of emerging perennials. Bark nuggets differ from shredded bark in that they are chipped rather than ground, and they are sold fresh, not composted. For this reason the nuggets are more like wood chips in their effects, so I do not like to use them.

Pine needle straw is popular in the Southeast, but it is harvested from forests in a way that to me seems unsustainable. It is also highly acidic and not suitable for any but acid-loving perennials. Grass-based straw (wheat straw, oat straw, or barley straw) looks very natural under meadow-type perennials and it is nice to kneel on and fairly easy to spread. The main drawback is that it is often full of both weed and grass seeds that sprout after it is spread. To combat this, I stack the bales up, wet them down thoroughly and let them sit for a few weeks in spring. The seeds mostly germinate and are then killed as I open up and spread the straw. It is certainly harder and clumpier to work with in the short term but saves weeding in the long term. Dry straw should be spread about four inches thick, as it settles quite a bit. I put down about half that thickness if the straw is wet. Straw is basically what is left after the cereal grains have been harvested, so it is mostly dried grass stems. It is nutritionally poor for livestock and intended mostly for bedding. Hay is harvested from noncereal pasture grasses when they are still green and growing, so it is much more nutritious for horses and cattle and intended for feed. Hay is often a mix of grasses and forbs, but it is harvested before most of the plants have flowered and set seed, so is

not the material itself but the microorganisms that need nitrogen to set to work breaking down the new source of food you provide. Wood chips and sawdust are the worst in this regard, and I recommend piling them for two years before using them. This also allows potentially toxic tannins and phenolics in the wood to break down or leach out. I generally try to avoid using even aged wood chips on all but acid-loving perennials because the chips tend to bring the pH down. In the past few years colored or dyed bark mulches have become common. These are made from ground up pallets and other hardwood wastes dyed red to resemble either premium softwood bark such as cypress or cedar, or dyed brown or black to simulate naturally composted bark. In my opinion these dyed mulches are the biggest scam to hit the landscaping industry in recent years. Not only is the color unnatural, the mulch itself is basically fresh hardwood chips disguised as bark or composted bark. Putting this stuff on your plants will release

often lower in weed content than straw harvested late in the season. Because it is younger, greener material, it breaks down more quickly than straw. Feed hay can be very expensive, but often farmers will sell "mulch" hay that is basically low-quality material cut late in the season or from marginal lands. Mulch hay usually has a higher weed seed count but is substantially cheaper.

As I mentioned earlier, animal manures mixed with wood bedding make excellent mulches that are easy to spread, brown or black in color, and much higher in nutrients than other mulches (so you do not have to fertilize). I get mine right from the farmer, though sometimes you can get them through landscape suppliers. Mushroom mulch is basically the same thing, though it has gone through a pasteurization process prior to inoculation at the mushroom farm.

At the Garden in the Woods, all the gardens are mulched with chopped leaves that have been collected and run through a shredder to reduce them to dime- to quarter-sized pieces. Small five-horsepower home shredders work well for this, though I find running over the pile several times with a lawnmower finishes small batches more quickly. We shred and pile the leaves in autumn, then apply the mulch in the spring.

If the chopped leaves are damp, they will not blow away very easily, but if they are dry or it is especially windy, water them after spreading to mat them down. Shredded leaves are wonderful in the woodland garden, but they work well in any situation, really.

DEPTH AND TIMING

Too much mulch can smother your plants, while too little will not work effectively. I use a two-inch layer over bare soil and half that if some old mulch is already in place. You can adjust this depending on the particular product. I will often first sprinkle around some compost (half an inch or so) before applying the mulch if I am really trying to build up the soil in a particular area. As I mentioned above, in woodland gardens I apply an inch of mulch, then put the leaves (chopped or unchopped) back on top of it, since tree roots deplete the soil more quickly than would be the case out in the open. Chopped leaves, hay, and straw are looser than wood mulches and so can be put on about twice as deep. Stringy mulches such as pine bark or partially decomposed animal bedding will lock together into a solid cover that may become impermeable when it dries, so use this type a bit more sparingly (one inch or so). I prefer to mulch in early spring either before the plants are up or just after they break ground. In this way I can do all my fall and winter cleanup and cutting back, and the garden looks fresh and neat as the growing season begins. This is also a good time to fertilize or lime if necessary, which I will discuss next. For tender plants or those planted late in the season, I sometimes add a cover of a loose, eight-inch layer of straw or pine needle insulation to soften winter's blow; remove some or all of this in spring. The main dan-

Clematis glaucophylla.

ger with fall mulching with fluffy material is that it encourages the rodents to come in and feast, which is another reason I prefer to mulch in spring if winter-hardiness is not an issue.

Fertilize It

If you take the time to prepare the soil before planting and topdress with a thin layer of compost annually, you should not need to add much in the way of fertilizers—at least not after the first few seasons. Unlike garden vegetables and other annuals, perennials store some nutrients from one year to the next, so their needs are proportionally lower. If you are used to socking it to tomatoes, corn, or petunias, realize that perennials will need only about one-half to one-fourth this amount once established. New beds and newly transplanted perennials will often benefit from an additional fertilizer application at planting to get things going. Sprinkle one-fourth of a cup or so of granular organic fertilizer around the base of the plant,

or even better stir it into the planting hole before setting the roots into it. Incorporating fertilizer into the top few inches of the soil is more effective than simply broadcasting it on the surface. If I do not have the time to spread compost before I mulch in spring, I put down some organic fertilizer instead to counter the nitrogen-robbing effect of the mulch itself. Fertilize existing perennials as they begin growing in spring, taking care not to get fertilizer down inside leaves and crowns. Use organic fertilizers, which are more expensive than inorganic (chemical) fertilizers but will give you many of the same benefits as compost albeit in smaller doses. Organics are lower in soluble nutrients and salts, so they are less likely to burn roots, and they contribute organic matter and humic compounds as well. Chemical fertilizers may be cheap (although as oil goes up so do they), but they add little to the soil, and the mostly soluble nutrients they contain are prone to leaching into groundwater and streams. I like to fill a four- to six-inch clay pot with my granular organic fertilizer of choice for

The application of organic fertilizer doesn't have to be complicated.

Stenanthium gramineum forma *robustum* with *Osmunda cinnamomea* (cinnamon fern).

An outcrop of Conestoga limestone. Powdered or pelletized limestone is simply pulverized limestone rock.

centrations of nitrogen, phosphorus, potassium, and other nutrients, plus the percentage organic matter. It will suggest amounts of lime or sulfur to apply to correct pH, and recommend fertilizers to correct deficiencies. Typically, since nitrogen is the most commonly deficient nutrient (nitrogen is highly soluble and leaches very quickly from the soil), the test will give you a recommended amount to apply in pounds per acre. Since organic fertilizers come blended together, it is difficult to follow these fertilizer recommendations exactly. It is possible to buy dried blood or something similar if only the nitrogen is low, or greensand if the test confirms a potassium deficiency, but these are costly and often difficult to find. Instead I use the test to adjust my application of a balanced organic fertilizer, using the recommended nitrogen as a guide. To calculate the rate you need for 100 square feet, use the following formula: (recommended pounds per acre N) ÷ 435 ÷ (percentage of N in your fertilizer). As you probably know, fertilizer bags must list the percentage of nitrogen, phosphorus, and potassium (N, P, and K) they contain by weight. A 6-5-4 fertilizer contains 6 percent nitrogen by weight. So, using this fertilizer as an example, say my test comes back indicating I need 110 pounds per acre N: 110 ÷ 435 ÷ 0.06 = 4.2 pounds of fertilizer per 100 square feet. This means a 50-pound bag would cover about 1,000 square feet or a bed 10 feet wide and 100 feet long.

Generally, I use fertilizers with relatively similar amounts of the three major nutrients, and unless your test comes back indicating that your phosphorus or potassium is very high, these should be fine. A good organic fertilizer blended from manures, animal and vegetable meals, and minerals will also supply trace or minor nutrients such as boron and zinc. Thus, if your soil test comes back indicating a boron deficiency, it should be corrected if you use the recommended rate of fertilizer to correct nitrogen deficiency. Remember, if you have a highly organic soil, soil tests tend to underestimate the nutrient levels because much is locked up in the bodies of living things.

applying to existing beds. I can regulate flow with a finger over the drain hole and refill it from a larger bucket nearby. If I keep the pot moving I can put down a precise amount of fertilizer very rapidly. I find this works better than a fertilizer spreader with organics, because some of the ingredients are very fine and dusty, ending up in the air and in your lungs rather than the soil.

SEND YOUR SOIL TO COLLEGE

It is very helpful to have a soil test done every few years. It is not very expensive (some state soil-testing labs will do it for free) and can be very illuminating. Contact your state agricultural extension office or university for instructions and fees. Usually the form has a check box for flower beds or landscape plants, so the lab can adjust its recommendations accordingly. It is very important that you follow to the letter the instructions on collecting and packaging your soil sample, as improper collection and handling risk drastically skewing the results. The test report will give you the pH and relative con-

DEFICIENCY SYMPTOMS

Often you can get a sense that perennials are nutrient deficient even without a soil test. The following table lists the function of all the plant nutrients and the most common signs of deficiency. In my experience, though, the two that you are most likely to encounter are nitrogen and iron deficiency. Minor nutrient deficiencies can occur in pots—especially if you are growing your plants in the type of organic peat and bark-

TOP LEFT: *Mitella diphylla* (miterwort) with a nitrogen deficiency; notice the generally pale color of the foliage, which is most severe in the older leaves.

TOP RIGHT: *Clematis addisonii* with an iron deficiency. The younger leaves of this **Addison's leather flower** display the interveinal chlorosis characteristic of iron deficiency.

BOTTOM LEFT: Magnesium deficiency resembles iron deficiency but is concentrated in the older leaves.

based media common today because they are obtained mostly from the minerals in soil. If raising plants in containers, you should make sure you fertilize with a "complete" fertilizer—one containing all the nutrients listed in the table that follows. The label on the fertilizer will indicate if this is so. Blending a small amount (10 percent) good topsoil into your potting soil will also alleviate some minor nutrient deficiencies, but you will need to pasteurize it first. I pasteurize small amounts in a metal can or bucket. Fill with soil, water well, and put it on a gas grill or over an outdoor fire until it is really steaming for 20 minutes.

pH

I have touched on the importance of pH in controlling certain diseases (p. 149) and alluded to the effect that pH has on nutrient availability, but a more detailed discussion is called for here. The term pH refers to the relative concentration of hydrogen ions (H^+) in the soil solution expressed on a scale of 1 to 14, with 7 considered neutral. Soils rarely fall below 4 or above 9. A pH of 4 is extremely acidic, whereas a pH of 9 is highly alkaline. It is important to understand that the pH scale is logarithmic, so it rises and falls exponentially. For every full one unit rise in pH (say from 4.5 to 5.5) the acidity is 10 times lower. An increase of two units means the pH is 100 times less acidic. This becomes a practical issue when you attempt to raise or lower the pH due to the sheer quantity of the proper amendment needed to make major adjustments.

Calcium and magnesium are what are called strong bases, and it is these two elements that make the soil alkaline when they are abundant and acidic when they are scarce. Though common, they are very readily leached out of the soil

Soil Deficiency Symptoms

THE MAJOR NUTRIENTS	USES	DEFICIENCY SYMPTOMS
Nitrogen (N)	Nitrogen is necessary for the synthesis of amino acids (the building blocks of proteins). It is easily leached from soil in rainwater or lost as ammonia gas, so nitrogen is usually in short supply.	The most common symptom is stunted growth and pale green or yellow leaves. Nitrogen can be moved from older leaves to young ones, causing the older leaves to yellow and fall first. Anthocyanin pigments do not need nitrogen, whereas chlorophyll does, so certain plants will develop a reddish cast in leaves, stems, and petioles as a result.
Phosphorus (P)	Phosphorus is a component of cell membranes and in the machinery of photosynthesis. It is also necessary to make DNA and RNA.	Phosphorus deficiency manifests as dark green, stunted growth often with a reddish or maroon cast. It is the dark green as opposed to yellow green color of the stunted plant that differentiates this problem from nitrogen deficiency.
Potassium (K)	Potassium is integral for the proper function of the osmotic pumps used to create osmotic pressure, which moves liquids around the plant.	Potassium deficiency manifests as yellow patches or margins on the leaves. Leaf tips and edges may also die or curl. Potassium is mobile in the plant, so these problems are first obvious on older foliage. This deficiency is easily confused with fungal disease or pest problems.

THE MINOR NUTRIENTS		
Calcium (Ca)	Calcium is used in cell wall construction and is necessary for cell division and likely acts as a messenger within the plant, similar to some hormones in effect.	Calcium is not mobile in the plant, so symptoms are most obvious in the growing tips. These may turn yellow or brown, while young leaves curl downward. Because calcium availability is closely tied with pH, deficiency is linked to a low pH and is easily corrected with the application of limestone.
Sulfur (S)	Sulfur performs many of the functions that nitrogen does as regards protein synthesis.	Sulfur deficiency resembles nitrogen deficiency except that—because it is not mobile in the plant—it is the young leaves not the oldest ones that yellow first.
Magnesium (Mg)	Magnesium is important in the photo-synthetic process and is needed to make chlorophyll.	Magnesium deficiency manifests as interveinal (between the veins) yellowing of the older leaves because chlorophyll in the leaf blade is more susceptible than its counterpart in the veins. To prevent magnesium deficiency, always use dolomitic lime as opposed to calcic lime when correcting for low pH. Dolomite contains magnesium while calcite does not.
Iron (Fe)	Iron is needed to make certain enzymes required for metabolism.	Iron deficiency is just like magnesium deficiency except that the problem is concentrated in the youngest leaves because iron is not mobile in the plant. In extreme cases, shoot tips and young leaves may turn completely white. Iron is abundant in most soils but becomes markedly less soluble at higher pH. Plants adapted for growth in acidic soils often exhibit iron deficiency when grown at a higher pH.
Copper (Fu)	Copper plays a similar role to iron in metabolism.	Though rare, copper deficiency results in dark green leaves (but not stunted growth as with phosphorus). The leaves may develop brown spots or leaf tips.
Boron (B)	Boron is implicated in the synthesis of DNA and in the proper functioning of plant hormones.	Like most other minor nutrients, boron deficiency is rare, especially when the soil has been amended with compost and a balanced organic fertilizer. Deficiency symptoms include death of stem tips, flower buds, and fruits, black spotting of young leaves where they meet the petiole, and excessively bushy or branched growth.
Zinc (Zn)	Zinc is needed for enzyme synthesis and possibly chlorophyll production.	Zinc deficiency, while also rare in gardens, manifests as stunted stems and distorted leaves similar in some respects to herbicide damage.
Manganese (Mn)	Manganese is necessary for enzyme synthesis and the stage of photo-synthesis where water molecules are cleaved into oxygen and hydrogen.	Symptoms of manganese deficiency are interveinal yellowing (chlorosis) of both young and old leaves.
Molybdenum (Mo)	Molybdenum is needed for the uptake of nitrogen by cells.	Molybdenum deficiency is much like magnesium deficiency but much less common.
Chlorine (Cl)	Like manganese, chlorine is needed to help split water molecules during photosynthesis.	Early deficiency symptoms include wilting and yellowing of stem tips followed by a bronzing of the foliage.

manganese, copper, and cobalt are most available below that number. A slightly acidic pH of about 6.5 allows all of these nutrients to be at least somewhat soluble, and thus it is the preferred range for many plant species. The exception is plants that evolved in highly acidic soils, where most nutrients are scarce but iron, aluminum, and the others listed above are abundant. These species can suffer deficiencies—especially iron deficiencies—when grown at a higher pH. I imagine that acid-loving plants have just become lazy when it comes to taking up iron because they are spoiled by its abundance. As it becomes less soluble, they simply cannot absorb it fast enough. They may also be harmed by an overabundance of other nutrients such as nitrogen and phosphorus that they are used to having to really work for.

Gardeners often raise the pH of acidic soils in order to cultivate a wider variety of plants. This is easily done with pulverized or pelletized limestone (crushed limestone rock). Dolomitic limestone has high levels of calcium and magnesium, so it raises the pH slowly over the course of several years as it weathers. Since a pH of 4 is 100 times more acidic than a pH of 6, the lower the pH, the more lime will need to be applied per square foot.

Pounds of dolomitic limestone needed per 100 sq ft to raise the pH to 6.5

PH	Sandy	Loam	Clay
4.5	12	15	22
5.0	8	10	15
5.5	6	8	10
6.0	3	4	6

Hydrastis canadensis. Goldenseal prefers soils with a pH above 6.0. I sprinkle limestone around it every other year because my soil is naturally too acidic for it.

when it rains, so in areas with high rainfall, the soils are generally acidic unless derived from calcium- or magnesium-bearing rock such as limestone, serpentine, or basalt.

Plants can absorb nutrients only when those nutrients are dissolved in soil water; when the pH is low (acidic), many of the nutrients needed by plants are simply insoluble. A soil may have plenty of phosphorus in it, but at the very acidic pH of 4.3, none will be available to the plants without the aid of mycorrhizal fungi (fungi are adept at scavenging nutrients that are unavailable to the plants themselves). The same thing happens at a high pH. Nitrogen, phosphorus, potassium, magnesium, calcium, molybdenum, aluminum, and boron are most readily dissolved above a pH of 5.5, while iron, zinc,

Notice in the table that sandy soils need far less lime relative to loam or clay. This is due to the colloidal properties of the clay. The colloidal layers can hold far more hydrogen ions than an equal amount of sandy soil, so much more lime is needed to displace all that extra acid. Lime can take two or three years to be completely effective, so when I am putting in a new bed I dig in wood ashes from our stove. Wood ash is a type of burned lime that begins acting immediately when applied, so it can raise the pH almost instantly. It also contains significant amounts of phosphorus and potassium, which are often deficient in acidic soils. Though it varies depending on the species burned and amount of charcoal remaining in the ash, this material is about half as strong as limestone. When creating new beds I use a mixture of 1:1 ash to lime at the recommended rate for lime alone. Wood ashes are too strong to put directly on growing plants (they can burn the roots), but I will sometimes spread ashes atop the snow so the nutrients percolate down as it melts. Wood ash is most effective when the pH is below 5.5. Above this it can quickly make the soil too alkaline. As a case in point, I once rented a place from people who boarded horses. I was happy to have a ready supply of manure compost that I mixed into various garden beds with impunity, only to get a soil test back showing I had achieved a pH of 8.1! This is alarmingly high in the high-rainfall, acidic Northeast. I discovered that the landlords mixed their stove ashes into the manure, and I had unwittingly been adding large quantities to my compost.

Now you might feel that manipulating the pH to grow a larger assortment of plants is a questionable practice from an ecological point of view. Granted, it would be most sustainable to stick to those species appropriate for the pH conditions of your site rather than trying to manipulate things. We gardeners are curious by nature, though, and in reality it is pretty easy to fall off the ecology wagon and bring in some not completely suitable treasures. I myself love trilliums and lady's slipper orchids, and most of these require a higher pH than is present on my property. So I lime them. Liming species that need it often boosts their resistance to disease—both because they are healthier when receiving proper nutrition and because the higher pH suppresses certain diseases that otherwise afflict them while bolstering the microorganism population overall. If done in moderation, raising or lowering the pH should not have negative impacts on other plants nearby, but I do try to group calciphiles (plants that like limestone) and calciphobes (those that prefer low pH) separately. Furthermore, a pH hovering around 5.8 to 6.0 will allow both types to grow in relative harmony.

In parts of the western United States where rainfall is not sufficient to leach calcium and magnesium from the soil, the soil may be too alkaline for many plants, and farmers and gardeners apply powdered sulfur to bring the pH down.

Polypodium appalachianum. **Appalachian polypody fern** grows best on acidic rocks, as here in West Virginia.

Pounds of sulfur per 100 sq ft needed to lower pH to the desired level in a loamy soil. If your soil is sandy, multiply these amounts by 0.66, and if your soil is clayey, multiply by 2.

pH	DESIRED pH				
	6.5	6.0	5.5	5.0	4.5
8.0	3	4	5	6	7
7.5	2	3	4	5	6
7.0	1	2	3	4	5
6.5		1	2	3	4
6.0			1	2	3

CHAPTER 10

PROPAGATION

We live in a world of convenience where everything is done for us, and in this culture of expediency, raising plants from seed or cuttings has become as rare as baking a cake from scratch or sewing one's own clothes. I have worked professionally as a propagator for many years, but even before that I was propagating perennials in my garden, on my windowsill, and under lights. I also build my own furniture and buildings, make my own pottery, brew my own beer, and grow my own vegetables, so I have wondered why I spend so much time "doing it myself." I think it stems in part from a desire for self-sufficiency, a need to save money, and a curiosity about how things are made, but more importantly I believe that immersing myself in the process from beginning to end fosters both a deep connection to the product and a richer understanding of everything that is connected to it. As Barbara Kingsolver writes in *Animal, Vegetable, Miracle,*

ABOVE: *Chamaelirium luteum* division. Sometimes propagation is just like surgery. The only easy way to divide devil's bit is with a knife. The key is to cut carefully between the painted buds, severing only the short rhizomes in between them.

A lot of human hobbies, from knitting sweaters to building model airplanes, are probably rooted in the same human desire to control an entire process of manufacture. Karl Marx called it the antidote to alienation. Modern business psychologists generally agree, noting that workers will build a better car when they participate in the whole assembly rather than just slapping on one bolt, over and over, all the tedious livelong day. In the case of modern food, our single-bolt job has become the boring act of poking the thing in our mouths, with no feeling for any other stage in the process. It's a pretty obvious consequence that one should care little about the product.

I have read some of Marx's writings, and I know he tried to relate *everything* in life to his economic model. However, there is some truth in the notion that if you are part of the process from beginning to end, you will make a better product. As I tell my students, the finest gardeners are also propagators, because the best way to really get to know the wants and needs of your plants is to raise them up from seeds or cuttings. Growing your own plants also gives you access to a host of material that you cannot find at your local nursery or big-box store. With some basic skills you can raise rare and choice plants from seed, create your own hybrids, or multiply a pricy but minuscule specimen you purchased though the mail. Good propagators always have extra plants to share and trade, and there is no better way to foster lasting horticultural friendships than by sharing plants.

In my native plant series, I included lengthy propagation sections with very specific directions for different plants. In the spirit of this book, I want to go about it a bit differently and present propagation in a less technical way that I hope will be approachable and understandable to even the most propagation averse.

Division

If you have ever divided an overgrown perennial, then you have done some propagation. Dividing perennials is the most straightforward way to multiply them, and fortunately, many types are easy to propagate in this way. Any perennial that grows from bulbs, corms, tubers, or interconnect-

ed rhizomes can be dug and split apart, and the best time to do this is in either the spring before growth begins or after it has gone dormant again in summer or fall. This is when most of the plant's energy reserves are still in the roots and also when the air temperature is lower and soil moisture higher, limiting stress. Since many species disappear completely belowground during dormancy, be sure to label their location so you can find them again. Garden forks or pitch forks are perfect tools for dividing, as they allow you to extract the rhizomes and roots largely intact and with a reduced amount of soil attached. It is easy to accidentally cut into buried bulbs or rhizomes with a shovel, but a shovel may be necessary if you are removing only part of the clump and wish to leave the rest undisturbed. A flat-tipped digging spade is better than a round-pointed shovel for this, as it is easier to control and mechanically stronger. In most cases I prefer to dig the whole

Phytolacca americana (pokeweed) seedlings.

TOP LEFT: *Eutrochium fistulosum* division sequence. Dividing large perennials like this joe-pye weed is best accomplished in early spring when the plants are still dormant. Using a digging spade, I have dug in a circle around the stems and am levering out the clump.

TOP RIGHT: Next I insert two digging forks perpendicularly into the center of the root ball and pry the handles apart. This damages fewer roots and buds than slicing the clump in half with the spade would.

BOTTOM LEFT: One of the two halves after division. Because the roots are exposed and in danger of drying out, get the division back into the ground as fast as you can. Cover it with wet burlap or soil if it will sit out for more than 10 minutes or so.

BOTTOM RIGHT: Finally I set the division into a hole as deep as the one from which it was removed and pack loose soil around the roots with my fingers. A good soaking with the hose will further settle the soil and ensure that the proper root/soil contact has been restored.

clump out to divide it and then replant the sections again after digging in some compost to freshen the soil, though sometimes, if I just need one division I can leave most of the clump in place and simply excise the one section, with obvious benefits to the plant.

I find it helpful to shake or wash off some of the soil from around roots and rhizomes and trim off dead leaves and stems before dividing. It really helps me to see where the best place to cut, pull, or pry may be, and it will not do the plant too much harm to be exposed for a short while. If you dig a number of plants at once, protect the roots with soil, compost, or wet burlap until you can get to them. You can dig up and leave *dormant* perennials out of the ground for several weeks if you protect the roots in this way. Typically I have to do this when redesigning or renewing a garden area.

Some perennials divide very easily into separate clumps, each clump with its own leaves, buds, roots, and rhizomes. Others require cutting or sawing to separate, while

TOP LEFT: *Dicentra eximia* var. *alba* division sequence. If you want to simply double a plant by division, it is often easiest to use a fork to split and pry off one half while leaving the other half in place.

TOP RIGHT: I gingerly insert the forks through the center to try to minimize damage to the swollen buds.

BOTTOM LEFT: I have put the smaller division into the new hole in the foreground, while the larger part remains in its original spot with at least half of its roots undisturbed. For species like bleeding hearts, which are a bit resentful of root disturbance, this method hedges your bets.

BOTTOM RIGHT: The same two divisions eight weeks later.

TOP LEFT: *Actaea racemosa* division sequence. **Black cohosh** grows from an almost woody crown or rhizome hidden by many roots. To make the job of division easier, I have washed off most of the soil with a hose.

MIDDLE LEFT: Using the blade of my pruners like a spear, I jab into the center of the crown, trying to avoid any of the white buds in the process.

BOTTOM LEFT: With one third cut away, I repeat the process, but this time it is a little easier to see what I am doing.

MIDDLE RIGHT: After severing the rhizome, I tease the sections apart by gingerly rocking them back and forth.

BOTTOM RIGHT: The finished product: three nice divisions ready for replanting.

Hemerocallis fields at Klehm's Song Sparrow Perennial Farm in Wisconsin. Traditionally, many perennials were grown in the field, then divided for sale. Tissue culture has begun to supersede this space-intensive method.

Agapanthus (blue lily) is easy to divide, but don't do so when it is in full flower.

EASY TO DIVIDE

Achillea (yarrow)
Agapanthus (blue lily)
Ajuga (bugleweed)
Allium (onion)
Aster (aster)
Astrantia (masterwort)
Bergenia (bergenia)
Camassia (camas lily)
Chrysanthemum (garden mum)
Convallaria (lily of the valley)
Coreopsis (tickseed)

Crocus (crocus)
Dianthus (pinks)
Helianthus (sunflower)
Hemerocallus (daylily)
Hosta (plantain lily)
Iberis (rock cress)
Iris (iris)
Maianthemum (false Solomon's seal)
Narcissus (daffodil)
Mentha (mint)
Monarda (bee balm)
Pachysandra (spurge)
Phlox (phlox)

Podophyllum (May apple)
Polygonatum (Solomon's seal)
Primula (primrose)
Rudbeckia (black-eyed Susan)
Sanguinaria (bloodroot)
Scilla (scilla)
Sedum (sedum)
Solidago (goldenrod)
Stachys (lamb's ears)
Uvularia (merry-bells)
Most ferns
Most grasses and sedges

DIFFICULT, BUT RARELY NEED DIVIDING

Aconitum (monkshood)
Amsonia (bluestar)
Aquilegia (columbine)
Asclepias (milkweed)
Baptisia (false indigo)
Dictamnus (gas plant)
Diphylleia (umbrella leaf)
Echinacea (coneflower)
Euphorbia (spurge)
Gentiana (gentian)
Glaucidium (Japanese wood poppy)
Gypsophila (baby's breath)
Hexastylis (ginger)
Lavendula (lavender)
Lupinus (lupine)
Paeonia (peony)
Papaver (poppy)
Porteranthus (wild ipecac)
Spigelia (Indian pink)

TOP: *Ionactis (Aster) linariifolius.* Like all of its clan, prickly aster is fairly easy to divide.

BOTTOM: *Phlox maculata.* After being in the garden for at least three years, meadow phlox grows large enough to be easily divided in the spring or fall.

others are just about impossible to divide because they spring from a central taproot or woody crown of buds.

I end up doing a lot of division with my fingers and a pair of old pruners that I don't mind using in the soil. Pruners, a knife, or even a pruning saw are all helpful for severing rhizomes or tangled roots with surgical precision, though for larger clumps or especially tough plants such as grasses, two digging forks for prying or a sharp spade for slicing are very helpful. Often I will use a spade or set of forks to make initial divisions and then come in with a knife or pruners to make finer divisions.

HOW MUCH AND HOW OFTEN?

As a rule, I find that I can expect to divide a plant once for every year it is in the garden. Therefore a four-year-old clump will on average yield four divisions, and a seven-year-old one can be easily split seven ways without compromising the health of the pieces. This is because healthy perennials usually double in size every year until they reach a point of stasis that varies from species to species. Very few perennials require division more than every three to five years, and many species (including the ones listed as difficult to divide, above) really never need division. If you are trying to multiply your plants through division, I would wait at least three years before lifting and dividing even the easiest types, because perennials really do follow the timeline spelled out in the old adage about gardens: first year sleep, second year creep, third year leap. The

OPPOSITE: *Astrantia major* (masterwort) is a very unusual flower; cultivars are available in white as well as pink and plum. The clumps send out smaller clumps just a hair removed from the rest, and these can easily be severed with a trowel or spade.

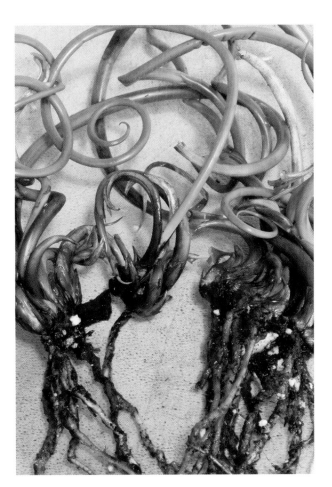

Juncus effusus 'Unicorn'. Unusual cultivars such as this corkscrew rush must be propagated asexually to ensure that the progeny will be just like the original. Rushes grow from a creeping rhizome closely set with vertical stems.

Using my fingers and a thin knife, I have severed the rhizome in two places to yield three actively growing divisions. The one in the center has but a single root, so it will have to be pampered for a few weeks until other roots form.

first year, a newly planted or divided perennial puts most of its resources into building a root system and recovering carbohydrate reserves, and it is only in the third year that all but the most aggressive species really come into their own. After several more years—it could be 2 years or 10—many perennials either die out in the middle as the rhizomes creep slowly outward, or they begin to loose vigor as the roots and rhizomes become entangled with each other. I am sure you have noticed this and have a sense for the point at which favorite perennials need some scheduled maintenance.

OPPOSITE: Peonies grow from a dense woody root that is not easy to divide, though you can do it if you follow the procedure outlined for black cohosh on page 214. The plant pictured here, however, is a tree peony, which is more shrub than herbaceous perennial. Tree peonies are usually grafted onto seedling rootstocks.

I am often asked whether it is worth treating wounded rhizomes to prevent infection. If the rhizome is less than a fourth of an inch in diameter I do not feel it is necessary to treat wounds unless the plant is particularly valuable or difficult to grow. For larger rhizomes, it is helpful to treat cuts with some sort of disinfectant, and I use either ground charcoal (from fireplace ashes, not charcoal briquettes) or ground cinnamon (either true cinnamon or culinary cinnamon). Both are nontoxic and just as effective as fungicides.

In the spring before growth starts in earnest, even moderate divisions will often take root and grow as long as they have a few active leads showing buds or emerging leaves along with some healthy roots. If in the process of dividing you have shaken or washed off all the soil so that your divisions are bare-root, you may want to dip the roots into a slurry of sodium polyacrylate (see p. 30).

Very small divisions with just a small bit of rhizome, roots, and leaves should be treated like stem cuttings and kept

in a humid, sheltered environment until new leaves begin to grow (signaling that roots have also become reestablished). Small irises, grasses, members of the lily family, and others that do not root from stem cuttings can be propagated from small rhizome cuttings in this way.

Stem Cuttings

Dividing perennials is so natural that I suspect you may not have even considered it propagation, and sowing seed or transplanting seedling volunteers is also a fairly natural and straightforward procedure. Making new plants from stem cuttings is something else entirely—a conscious manipulation of nature that requires more sophisticated technique and practice to get right. This fact scares away many budding propagators, but I really encourage you to give it a try with some of the easier species, if for no other reason than to witness the small miracle of roots appearing out of bits of stem. Stem cuttings are more challenging than divisions, but many perennials do root very easily from stem cuttings, and it is a great way to make a lot of copies of a particular favorite. When you take a stem cutting at the appropriate time from suitable species and keep the cutting in a sheltered, humid environment, roots grow from the stem at or near the cut end, while dormant axillary buds along the lower part of the stem transform into rhizomes. It is amazing that many perennials can regenerate their complete anatomy from a small stem tip like this.

TIMING AND SELECTION

With a few exceptions, the time to take perennial cuttings is in late spring when stems are growing vigorously. These are what are termed softwood cuttings because the stems should still be green and somewhat flexible. If you can bend the stem slowly into a

Polygonatum verticillatum. Some plants look as if they would root from stem cuttings but will not. Whorled Solomon's seal is a member of the lily family and will root only from rhizome cuttings.

Pycnanthemum clinopodioides. Basil mountain mint, on the other hand, is very easy to root from stem cuttings when not in flower. Rooted cuttings mature much faster than seedlings, which are rare anyway in this natural hybrid.

semicircle, it should still be soft enough to root. Some perennials (e.g., most of the mints) root very easily from softwood cuttings, while other groups are either very difficult or impossible to root.

Though many do not even have aboveground stems, do not bother to try stem cuttings of ferns, clubmosses, or horsetails, or of flowering plants in the following families (many of these can be propagated easily by rhizome division, however):

Arum	(*Araceae*)
Barberry	(*Berberidaceae*)
Borage	(*Boraginaceae*)
Buttercup	(*Ranunculaceae*)
Canna	(*Cannaceae*)
Carrot	(*Apiaceae*)
Ginger	(*Zingiberaceae*)
Ginseng	(*Araliaceae*)
Grass	(*Poaceae*)
Iris	(*Iridaceae*)
Lily	(*Liliaceae*)
Milkweed	(*Asclepiadaceae*)
Mustard	(*Brassicaceae*)
Orchid	(*Orchidaceae*)
Peony	(*Paeoniaceae*)
Pitcher plant	(*Sarraceniaceae*)
Poppy	(*Papaveraceae*)
Primrose	(*Primulaceae*)
Saxifrage	(*Saxifragaceae*)
Sedge	(*Cyperaceae*)
Spurge	(*Euphorbiaceae*)
Violet	(*Violaceae*)
Wood sorrel	(*Oxalidaceae*)

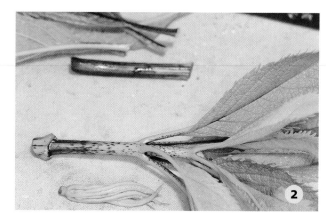

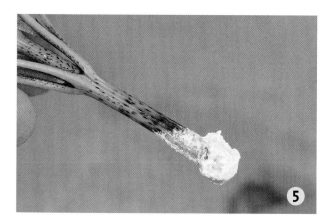

TOP LEFT: *Eutrochium purpureus* stem-cutting sequence. I have snipped off the tip of a **purple joe-pye weed** stem in very late spring, when it is still soft and nowhere near flowering.

TOP RIGHT: Next I trim both the youngest part of the shoot and the whorl of leaves around the lower node. Excess stem below the lower node has also been trimmed.

MIDDLE LEFT: Because the leaves are so large, I snip off the tips to reduce transpiration and make the propagation tray less crowded.

MIDDLE RIGHT: The cut end and lower node are dipped in rooting hormone powder.

BOTTOM LEFT: The talcum powder in the preparation causes it to stick to the areas that are damp from exposed sap.

BOTTOM RIGHT: The finished cutting is stuck into a very loose, light potting mix, about two-fifths perlite, two-fifths pine bark, and one-fifth peat moss. It will now go into a plastic bag on the windowsill until it is firmly rooted (about two to three weeks).

Most members of the following families will usually root from stem cuttings:

Aster	(*Asteraceae*)
Begonia	(*Begoniaceae*)
Bellflower	(*Campanulaceae*)
Buckwheat	(*Polygonaceae*)
Cactus	(*Cactaceae*)
Gentian	(*Gentianaceae*)
Geranium	(*Geraniaceae*)
Honeysuckle	(*Caprifoliaceae*)
Madder	(*Rubiaceae*)
Mallow	(*Malvaceae*)
Mint	(*Lamiaceae*)
Pea	(*Fabiaceae*)
Phlox	(*Polemoniaceae*)
Pink	(*Caryophyllaceae*)
Pinkroot	(*Loganiaceae*)
Potato	(*Solanaceae*)
Purslane	(*Portulacaceae*)
Rose	(*Rosaceae*)
Spiderwort	(*Commelinaceae*)
Valerian	(*Valerianaceae*)
Verbena	(*Verbenaceae*)

Take stem cuttings from healthy, actively growing stems that show no evidence of flowers or flower buds. Use only the top three to eight inches of stem, pinching off the very tender tip. You want to snip the stem an eighth of an inch below a leaf node or set of leaf nodes, as the small, dormant axillary buds in the node(s) will become the new rhizome or crown for the cutting. Dip the cut end about a half inch into rooting powder (see p. 97), and then poke the cutting into a mix of 1 part sand or perlite and 1 part potting soil. For most perennials, powder containing 0.1 percent active ingredient (the hormone IBA) will suffice. More recalcitrant species could require 0.3 percent IBA for maximum rooting. Place the cuttings in a clear plastic bag or a covered fish tank and keep them on a sunny windowsill or under fluorescent grow lights. (Large plastic storage tubs work well, especially if you find ones with clear lids). After two to four weeks, tug gently, and if you feel resistance then the roots have begun to grow. You can remove the cut-

LEFT: Roots are only half the story when it comes to stem cuttings and perennials. Pictured are two *Helianthus resinosus* (resin-dot sunflower) cuttings that have been overwintered from the previous year.

CENTER: The knobby callus at the base of this healthy stem has given rise to some nice roots, and because the cutting was taken just below a node, a vigorous white shoot has formed from the dormant axillary bud in the node. This new shoot has begun to develop a rhizome that will ensure the cutting's future.

RIGHT: This second cutting was taken above a node, so even though roots formed the previous summer, no axillary bud was available to become the new root and rhizome. Despite good rooting during the summer, this cutting was doomed from the start.

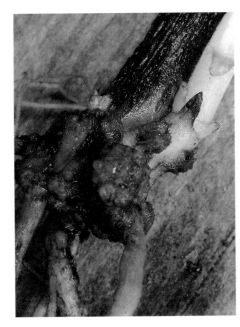

TOP LEFT: *Vernonia lettermannii,* rooted cutting. After three weeks under mist in the propagation house, the lower stem of this Letterman's ironweed cutting has erupted in thick white roots. This will be potted and grown in the nursery for the rest of the season so it can mature the crown buds it will need to become perennial.

BOTTOM LEFT: *Arisaema triphyllum* (jack-in-the-pulpit), mature fruits.

BOTTOM RIGHT: *Thalictrum thalictroides* (rue anemone) seedlings emerging after a winter chilling.

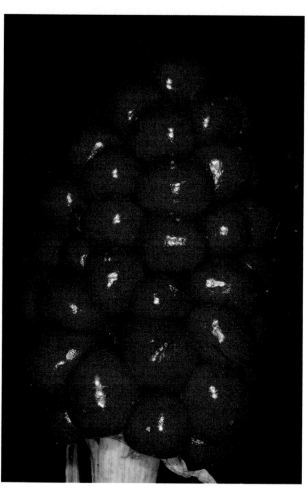

tings from the container once roots are over an inch long and pot the cuttings up separately. Stem cuttings taken in late spring and potted up to gain size will be ready for the garden by fall, or you can overwinter them in pots protected in a cold frame for spring planting.

Raising Perennials from Seed

Seed propagation has several advantages over vegetative propagation (division or cuttings). Seeds are inexpensive, easy to store, and a snap to send through the mail, so you can obtain an amazing variety of plants from mail-order nurseries, various plant societies, friends, and other enthusiasts you meet via the Internet. Seeds offer genetic diversity that clonal propagation does not, and by the very process of growing up a pot of seedlings and weeding out the stragglers you are performing a sort of horticultural selection that leaves you with the seedlings that are a bit better adapted to your specific conditions. Seedlings are generally free of diseases such as viruses that might have plagued their parents. You never know; you may find that million-dollar mutant in your seed pots as well.

If you are interested in native plants and want to grow local genotypes, collecting and germinating seeds you collect from your own neighborhood is the best way to do it. Sometimes these advantages are also disadvantages if you seek the uniformity of clonal plants or you want to multiply a special selection. Generally, seedlings require more time to reach maturity than equivalent plants from division or cuttings.

COLLECTING SEED

There are plenty of exceptions, but as a very general rule for seed collecting, look for ripe seeds about four to eight weeks after flowers wither. Several clues help me determine if seeds are ripe. If they are enclosed in a fleshy berry, then collect them when the berry begins to turn its ripe color (you do not have to wait until the fruit is completely ripe, which makes it more tempting to birds and mammals). If seeds are contained in some sort of capsule or pod, wait until it begins to die and dry out, turning brown, yellow, or tan. Seeds that have some sort of fluffy appendage for wind dispersal (many grasses and aster relatives, for example) will be ripe when the fluff begins

LEFT: *Trillium cuneatum* cross-pollination. For heavy seed set, I sometimes hand-pollinate certain plants that are not always effectively pollinated by insects. This whippoorwill trillium is shedding golden pollen that I can sweep up with a small paintbrush.

CENTER: I swished the pollen-laden brush around the sexual parts of this second flower, and the whitish, three-horned stigma (inside the anthers) is now heavily dusted with pollen.

RIGHT: This third whippoorwill trillium flower is not yet mature. The anthers have not begun to shed pollen, and the sticky white surfaces of the stigma are still enclosed in the red exterior. I will check this one again in a few days.

Genotype and Provenance

After many generations, a population of wild plants becomes finely tuned to its particular environment. Through natural selection, those individuals most able to grow in a certain area's soils, deal most effectively with its weather patterns, and attract the highest number of available pollinators will survive and pass their genes most effectively on to the next generation. Over time, members of a species growing in one area will begin to drift toward this localized fitness and away from their kin growing in other regions where conditions differ. The *Muhlenbergia capillaris* I mention on p. 93 is a good example of local adaptation. Whereas southeastern U.S. seed sources (southeastern genotypes or seeds with a southeastern provenance) do not overwinter here in Connecticut, our local genotype does fine because over the millennia the most winter-hardy individuals in the population did better than others and so passed on their hardiness genes. At the other extreme, I have had poor luck cultivating the lovely blue bead lily (*Clintonia borealis*) in Connecticut when I have raised it from seed collected at our family camp in northern Maine. (This might be described as having a northern Maine provenance. The words *genotype* and *provenance* mean slightly different things, but they are used interchangeably.) The seedlings would simply melt away during our summer heat. When I discovered a small local population near my house and grew up some seeds from it, the plants thrived and multiplied into beautiful clumps. In this case it is heat tolerance rather than cold tolerance that has been selected for over time. Local populations have many other ways of fine-tuning themselves, such as adapting to available mycorrhizae or soil pH, or by calibrating their seasonal clocks to time emergence, flowering, and dormancy to come at the best time in the proper season. If growing native species, it definitely pays to seek out local sources, but the same is true if you are interested in plants from more exotic locales. A Chinese perennial that grows over a wide range will have similar local strains adapted to different conditions, but often only one plant or one population will be available commercially here in the West. In many cases, a particular plant long thought to be marginally winter-hardy because the first collection came from a warm locale has proven to be quite tough once additional material from farther north or higher elevation becomes available.

In much the same way as wild populations are shaped by local forces, garden plants are shaped by human forces. Though not a perennial, our lovely native shrub mountain laurel (*Kalmia latifolia*) provides an interesting example of this. I have grown a number of the selected forms of mountain laurel in the nursery over the years—plants with richly colored flowers and compact form that are the result of much breeding work and nursery selection. These grow very well in pots in the nursery forming good, bushy specimens with attractive leaves and blooms, and they also grow handsomely when planted in the garden. However, when I plant them among wild laurels on my property, they are noticeably less vigorous, grow more slowly, and suffer more noticeably from winter burn and drought. On the other hand, when I raise seedlings from my own wild plants in the

Hepatica nobilis var. *acuta.* Collections of seed from different areas yield variety in the garden. These sharp-lobed specimens from New Hampshire have lovely variegation.

nursery they grow poorly in the pots. It takes them twice as long to reach salable size, and they suffer more from root rot and nutrient problems and are more sensitive to chemical fertilizers. If I plant these languishing seedlings out in my woods they immediately begin to thrive and grow like their parents. Obviously the breeders who developed the fancy-colored laurels were also selecting—whether consciously or not—for adaptability in cultivation, not adaptability in the wild. Some "difficult" perennials such as the Himalayan blue poppies (*Meconopsis* spp.) and lewisia (*Lewisia cotyledon*) are available from seed as named strains that are markedly more amenable to cultivation than their wild cousins. I suspect these cultivated strains would die as fast as a city mouse in the jungle if returned to their native haunts, but they are a boon to gardeners.

One of the unfortunate results of the consolidation of the nursery business in recent years and the loss of many small nurseries is that a vast amount of horticultural germplasm has been lost. Like the loss of heritage breeds of cattle or heirloom vegetables, obscure plants or locally adapted garden strains are kept alive by small backyard nurseries; giant multinational nurseries and the big-box stores have little use for them. As is the case if you want to eat heirloom tomatoes or feast on heirloom turkey, if you want to grow interesting but obscure garden strains you have little choice but to raise them up from seed obtained through specialty houses, seed exchanges, or your own collections.

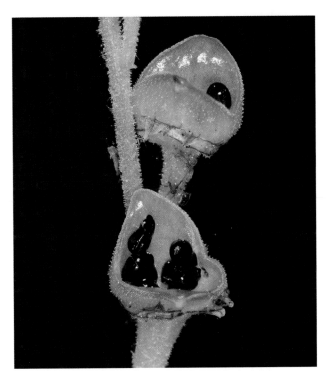

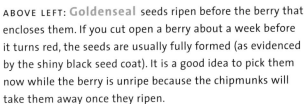

ABOVE LEFT: Goldenseal seeds ripen before the berry that encloses them. If you cut open a berry about a week before it turns red, the seeds are usually fully formed (as evidenced by the shiny black seed coat). It is a good idea to pick them now while the berry is unripe because the chipmunks will take them away once they ripen.

BELOW LEFT: Miterwort seeds are also shiny black when mature. They splash out of these chalices when it rains or are shaken out when the wind blows.

ABOVE RIGHT: *Viola pubescens* (downy yellow violet) seeds do not all ripen at the same time. When collected and cleaned, a percentage are white and immature, while the rest are darker and further along. Some of the white seeds will not sprout, but there are enough good ones here to suit my purposes.

BELOW RIGHT: *Chelone glabra* (white turtlehead) seeds spill from a hard capsule that cracks open when they are ripe. The papery ring around each dark, teardrop-shaped seed functions as a sail to aid in wind dispersal.

A brass screen such as this is great for seed cleaning, but an inexpensive kitchen sieve works just as well.

to puff. It is also helpful to examine the seed coat (the protective outer shell of the seed itself). Immature seeds have soft green or white seed coats, whereas mature ones are typically black, brown, tan, or gray (the better to blend in with soil and debris). You should bring along a small 10× hand lens to get a look at small seeds. Because the seed coat needs to stretch as the small embryo grows, it does not begin to harden up and darken until the baby seedling is fully mature and has stopped growing. Thus seed coat color is a good indicator of embryo maturity and seed ripeness.

With the exception of recalcitrant or hydrophyllic seeds, which I discuss next, perennial seed should be collected, cleaned, dried, placed in a paper envelope, and stored in a refrigerator until used. Wash off pulpy fruits in a sieve or strainer, and let capsules and pods dry until the seeds can be shaken or scraped out. Then let the seeds air-dry for a day or two before placing them into a paper envelope in the refrigerator. Junk mail return address envelopes are perfect for this use. Both the drying and cold help retain good viability, and

seeds processed promptly and stored like this will last for several years or more.

HYDROPHYLLIC OR RECALCITRANT SEEDS

Some perennials have seeds that are intolerant of dry storage:

Bleeding heart	(*Dicentra*)
Bloodroot	(*Sanguinaria*)
Blue cohosh	(*Caulophyllum*)
Clematis	(*Clematis*)
Corydalis	(*Corydalis*)
Hellebore	(*Helleborus*)
Hepatica	(*Hepatica* or *Anemone*)
May apple	(*Podophyllum*)
Merry-bells	(*Uvularia*)
Oconee bells	(*Shortia*)
Solomon's seal	(*Polygonatum*)
Spurge	(*Pachysandra*)

TOP: *Stylophorum diphyllum* (celandine poppy) seeds need to be sown immediately.

BOTTOM: *Penstemon arkansanus* seedlings. After all your hard work, it is extremely gratifying to see healthy young seedlings emerge from the soil and begin to grow.

Trillium	(*Trillium*)
Twinleaf	(*Jeffersonia*)
Umbrella leaf	(*Diphylleia*)
Violet	(*Viola*)

In general, seeds that are large or very oily do not store very well because the process of drying and rehydration causes irreparable cell damage. Most of the perennials with this sort of seed are woodland species from the temperate forests of Eurasia and North America that ripen in the summer. The best way to handle such seed is to simply plant it immediately upon collection, either near the base of the parent plant or in another area in the garden. In the nursery, we collect, clean, and sow trillium and similar seeds in flats that we leave outdoors until the seedlings germinate. You can store hydrophyllic seeds in a sealed plastic bag in your refrigerator for a month or more, still in the berry or capsule or after you have cleaned them. This is useful if you want to share them with a friend or are unable to sow them right away. If in doubt, it is usually safe to store any cleaned seed for a few months in a plastic bag, provided you have toweled it dry first.

SOWING SEED

It would be nice if all seed sprouted right after planting, the way garden vegetables do. Unfortunately, the vast majority of perennials need a period of chilling after sowing to overcome dormancy brought on by high levels of the hormone abscisic acid (see p. 87). The length of time needed varies from as little as 10 to as long as 100 days at temperatures below 45

degrees F. As a rule, seeds originating from low elevations or warmer latitudes need substantially less chilling than those from high elevations and more northern latitudes, simply because here the winters are shorter. The easiest way to satisfy the chilling requirement is to plant the seeds outdoors in the fall and let them come up in the spring; but if you want to speed the process up you can place potted and watered seeds in the refrigerator for 10 weeks or so, which is usually enough time for most perennial seeds. It will not hurt seeds that need less to spend a bit more time in the cold. Even seeds that do not require any chilling will not be harmed by it, so when in doubt I chill seeds after sowing.

Alternatively, you can sow the seeds and keep them at room temperature to see what happens. If no plants are evident after 21 days, place the pot in the refrigerator for a cold treatment then bring them back into the warmth. If space is a problem, wrap the seeds in a damp paper towel and then put this in a sealed plastic bag. You can fit quite a few of these in even a small refrigerator. If you are really impatient, try soaking the seeds in gibberellic acid (see p. 99). Understand that the seeds have to take up water first in order for the chilling to have any effect. Seeds that have been kept dry in the refrigerator will still need to be planted, watered, and chilled for the requisite time.

Warm before Cold or Cold before Warm?

Some perennials—especially many of the recalcitrant types or those that ripen early in the growing season—require a 4- to 16-week warm period before chilling so that they can germinate successfully (this is often called a period of after-ripening). Seeds of this type have embryos that do not fully mature on the mother plant and need to spend additional time growing bigger once in the ground by utilizing the stored resources within the seed. If you chill such seeds too early they will not come up when brought into warm conditions. Still other species require some combination of warm and cold periods stretching out over several years to germinate, but thankfully, such extreme reticence is rare. In my propagation books I go into much greater detail about the

Transplanting *Trillium cuneatum* seedlings. Transplanting seedlings into larger pots or to a place of their own in the garden is best done when they are small, for the roots are less numerous and easier to untangle.

native species with protracted germination, and information on similar species from other parts of the world is also available on the Internet and in print. One of my favorites is Norman C. Deno's *Seed Germination: Theory and Practice*, which you can order directly from him at the address in the bibliography.

Whether you plant them in pots or in the ground, be sure not to bury your seeds too deeply. As you may remember from my discussion of the pigment phytochrome (p. 100), small seeds often will not germinate unless exposed to light for a sufficient time. My rule of thumb is to sow seeds smaller than a grain of salt on the surface of the soil and then either lightly scratch them in or cover them with a light sprinkling of sand if I am sowing in pots or flats. Seeds bigger than an eighteenth of an inch can be planted up to an inch deep, while those in between these two extremes should be lightly covered with soil or potting mix.

It is vital that you water your seeds regularly once planted, as once sown, most seed will die if it dries out again. If you plant the seeds in the ground during the autumn, water them after sowing and again if there is no rain for a few weeks. In pots, water as soon as the surface of the soil begins to dry. Assuming you start with fresh, viable seeds, the most common reasons for failure are burying seed too deeply, letting them dry out, or giving them an inadequate chilling and/or warm period.

HANDLING SEEDLINGS

Whether you are transplanting seedlings that have sown themselves in your garden or ones that you have carefully tended in a pot, the ideal time to move them is just after the seed leaves (cotyledons) have reached their full size. At this stage the seedling root system is still small, and the tiny plants are remarkably resilient if you handle them gingerly. I will continue to add images of young seedlings to my Web site to make it easier for you to distinguish the good from the bad at this early age. Very tiny seedlings can wait until they are big enough to see. Make a mental note of how deep the seedlings are in the earth before you dig so that you can set them to the same depth in their new location. Stems that are buried too deep are prone to rot and those set too high may get sunburned because the blanched area lacks the pigments to protect tissues against the sun. Though there are plenty of exceptions, especially among the shade-loving species that naturally grow more slowly because they must compete with the trees, perennials will flower in one to two years from seed.

Pulmonaria saccharata. Like many perennials, lungwort will self-sow if the gardener allows.

GLOSSARY

ABSCISSION LAYER A zone of specialized tissue where two plant parts, such as leaf and stem, separate.

ACIDIC Having a pH under 7.0, as related to soils, generally found in high-rainfall regions without limestone-derived soils.

ALKALINE Having a pH over 7.0, as related to soils, generally found in low-rainfall and/or limestone regions.

ALKALOID A large group of nitrogen-based compounds produced by plants, many poisonous or otherwise pharmacologically active.

ALPINE Technically, any plants growing above the tree line in the mountains, but horticulturally used more broadly to refer generally to mountain plants with low, cushion-forming, or otherwise compact habits that are useful for the rock garden.

ALTERNATE Having flowers and leaves attached one per node; not paired.

ANNUAL A plant that lives for less than one year.

ANTHER The pollen-bearing tip of the male part of the flower (stamen).

APOMECTIC Capable of setting seed without fertilization.

ARIAL Above the ground.

ASEPTIC Sterile (without symbiotic organisms or diseases).

AWN A slender bristlelike tip found on the bracts surrounding the flower and seed of some grasses.

AXIL The point or angle where the stem connects to the leaf.

AXILLARY Arising from an axil.

BASAL Coming from the base of the plant, not on an aerial stem.

BIENNIAL Living only two seasons and typically forming a low rosette of leaves the first year and a tall flowering stem the next.

BOLT The flowering pattern seen commonly in biennials but not limited to them, where a rapidly elongating flower stem emerges from a clump of leaves.

BOREAL Northern; typically referring to the cold temperate, coniferous forests of northern North America and Eurasia.

BRACT A modified leaf associated with but not part of a flower or inflorescence, often brightly colored and acting in lieu of petals to attract pollinators. In grasses and sedges bracts act to shield the sexual parts of the flower and developing seeds.

BULBLET A small bulb or bulblike growth arising at the base of the leaf axil.

CAESPITOSE Densely tufted or tightly clumped.

CALCAREOUS Soil or rock with a high concentration of calcium.

CALLUS Thickened tissue, often associated with wound healing.

CALYX The sepals of a flower, taken as a group.

CARPEL The modified, fertile leaf that surrounds the seeds.

CAUDEX A swollen, perennial, woody stem or base at or below ground level.

CAULINE Leaves attached to an aboveground stem, not the base of the plant.

CIRCUMBOREAL Literally "around the north," meaning a distribution in both northern North America and Eurasia.

CLEISTOGAMOUS A flower that is self-pollinating and never opens.

CLUMPING A habit of growth characterized by tightly spaced stems and/or rhizomes or bulbs.

COLD STRATIFICATION A period of time (typically one to three months) in which a plant or seed is exposed to temperatures consistently below 45 degrees F; important for overcoming dormancy in many temperate species.

COLONY Spreading patches or loose clumps of plants, connected by underground rhizomes or roots.

COMPOUND A leaf composed of two or more leaflets.

CONNATE Grown together or fused.

COROLLA The petals of a flower, taken as a group.

COTYLEDON The first or embryonic leaf (or leaves) of a seedling.

CRESTED A mutation giving rise to multiple meristems (growing tips) that cause leaf or stem tissue to grow in a knotted, fanlike, or ruffled manner. Many fern species produce occasional crested individuals. In the case of ferns, the mutation can often be passed on to the next generation, meaning crested forms can be readily raised from spore.

CROSS Shorthand for a hybrid between two species or the act of creating such a hybrid with controlled pollination; represented in the Latin name as "×."

CROWN The typically enlarged junction of the stem and roots, and important in herbaceous plants as the source of new stem buds.

CULM An individual stem of a grass or grasslike plant.

CUSHION-FORMING Having a tight bun- or pillow-shaped habit.

CYME A flat-topped flower cluster with flowers opening in the center first.

DECIDUOUS Typically, a plant that loses its leaves at the end of the growing season.

DICOT Short for *dicotyledon*, the class of angiosperms characterized as having two cotyledons, net-veined leaves, and flower parts typically in fours and fives.

DIMORPHIC Bearing two different types. In ferns this refers to species whose fertile fronds are noticeably different from the sterile ones.

DIOECIOUS A species that bears male and female flowers on separate individuals.

DIPLOID Bearing a normal double set of chromosomes per cell.

DISJUNCT Occurring far outside the primary natural range of the species.

DRYLAND Plants originating from or adapted to environments receiving an average of 10 or less inches of rain yearly.

ECOTYPE A geographically limited population of a species adapted to a specific set of environmental conditions.

ENDEMIC Having a small native range encompassing a particular geographical area or region.

ENDOSPERM Tissues surrounding the seedling embryo designed for food storage.

FERTILE FROND A fern leaf that produces spores.

FILTER SAND A coarse washed sand that is sold for swimming pool filters and good as a cover for small seeds after sowing.

FRASS The fecal remains of insects.

FRUIT A ripened ovary and any affiliated tissue, containing seeds; in popular usage, a berry.

GA3 Gibberellic acid. An important plant growth hormone that induces stem elongation, flowering, and seed germination. It is used to overcome dormancy in seeds requiring a period of cold stratification.

GAMETOPHYTE The life stage of ferns and fern allies that produces sperm and eggs for sexual reproduction. In mosses,

this is the main, visible part of the moss plant, whereas in ferns and other fern allies, it is small and ephemeral.

GENERA Plural of *genus*.

GENUS A group of closely related plants; the first (capitalized) word of the binomial Latin name.

GLABROUS Smooth, hairless.

GLAUCOUS A waxy bloom that covers leaves or stems and imparts a bluish cast.

GYNODIOECIOUS A species in which some individuals have female flowers and others have perfect flowers.

HAPLOID Having only one complete set of chromosomes, usually referring to reproductive cells.

HEAD A dense cluster of flowers.

HERBACEOUS Lacking woody stems, usually indicating the plant dies back to the ground in the dormant season.

HIRSUTE Covered in coarse, stiff hairs.

HUMUSY Soil with a high (more than 5 percent) organic content composed of partially decomposed leaves, dead roots, and woody debris.

HYBRID A plant with parents that are different species or even different genera.

HYDROPHILIC Water-loving, referring to seeds that are intolerant of dry storage.

HYPOGEAL Germination in which the cotyledons remain underground and the first true leaf or leaves emerge (opposite of epigeal). Many hypogeal germinators are also two-stage germinators, requiring more than one season to emerge aboveground.

INDETERMINATE Growth that is not terminated, in contrast to determinate growth, which stops once a genetically predetermined structure (leaf, stem, or flower) has completely formed. Indeterminate plants can continue to grow through the season provided conditions are favorable, whereas determinate species cannot.

INDUSIUM The cover that protects the developing sporangia of many ferns.

INFLORESCENCE A cluster of flowers.

LANCEOLATE Lance-shaped; long and narrow, widest below the middle.

LEMMA The larger of two fertile bracts that surround each grass flower and seed.

LOBED Leaf margins that are deeply indented but not divided into separate leaflets.

LODGE To fall over.

MAFIC Rock containing relatively high concentrations of iron, magnesium, and also calcium. Mafic rocks create soils that have a high pH.

MALLET CUTTING A softwood cutting with an attached heal of older wood or rhizome. Most grass cuttings are mallet cuttings.

MONOCARPIC Flowering once then dying. Many monocarpic

plants are annual or biennial, but some, for example, bamboos, live for many years before finally flowering.

MONOCOT Short for *monocotyledon*, the class of angiosperms characterized as having a single cotyledon, parallel venation, and flower parts typically in threes.

MONOECIOUS A species that bears both male and female flowers, or perfect flowers, on the same plant.

MORPHOLOGICAL Regarding form and structure.

MOSS Nonvascular plants with rootlike rhizoids.

MYCORRHIZAE Plural of *mycorrhiza*, a symbiotic association between certain fungi and the roots of higher plants.

MYCORRHIZAL Modified roots containing mycorrhizal fungi.

NITROGEN-FIXING Organisms (typically bacteria in the genera *Rhizobium* and *Bradyrhizobium*) capable of converting gaseous nitrogen into the fixed or reduced form (ammonium) that can be used in biological processes.

NODE Place on a stem where a leaf or leaves attach.

OPEN-POLLINATED Opposite of hand-pollinated; when the pollen that fertilizes the ovary is free to come from any available source. In gardens, open pollination can lead to hybridization between related species typically separated in the wild.

OPPOSITE Having two flowers or leaves attached at the same node; paired.

ORTHODOX Seed that is tolerant of dry storage.

OVARY The structure that contains the ovules/seeds.

OVIPOSITOR An extension of the abdomen of certain female insects through which eggs are deposited.

PALEA The smaller of two bracts that surround grass flowers and seeds.

PANICLE A branched inflorescence.

PEDICEL The stalk of a single flower in a flower cluster.

PEDUNCLE The primary stalk attaching a flower or inflorescence to the stem.

PEDUNCULATE Borne on a peduncle.

PERENNIAL Any plant with a life span of two years or more.

PERFECT FLOWER A flower that has functional male and female parts.

PERIANTH The sepals and petals, collectively.

PERIGYNIUM A papery sack that surrounds the seed in sedges (plural: perigynia).

PETAL A modified leaf surrounding the sexual parts of the flower variously colored, shaped, and patterned to attract pollinators.

PETIOLE The stalk of the leaf below the blade.

PILOSE Covered with sparse, long, and straight hairs.

PINNA A single leaflet of a pinnate leaf (plural: pinnae).

PINNATIFID Leaves that are not quite twice divided. In ferns, the leaflets are lobed but the sinus or space between each lobe does not extend completely to the midrib of the leaflet.

PINNULE The smallest part of a bipinnate leaf; in ferns, the leaflet of the leaflet, so to speak.

PISTIL The female part of the flower, that is, the stigma, style, and ovary as a unit.

POLLEN The male gametophytes or haploid cells that fertilize the female ovule.

POLYPLOID Aberrant cells (or organisms) having more than the standard two sets of chromosomes.

PROSTRATE Growing low or flat on the ground.

PTERIDOPHYTE Ferns and fern allies.

PUBESCENT Hairy.

RACEME An unbranched inflorescence of pedunculate flowers that is typically long and thin.

RACHIS The central stalk, typically of a pinnately compound leaf.

RECALCITRANT Seed that cannot tolerate dry storage (see hydrophyllic).

REFLEXED Abruptly bent backward (more extreme than recurved).

RHIZOME An underground stem, typically prostrate and producing roots below and shoots or leaves above.

ROSETTE A flattened, circular cluster of leaves, usually arising directly from the crown.

SCANDENT Climbing, vining.

SCAPE A leafless flower stem growing directly from the crown.

SCREE Substrate composed of various sizes of rock and grit with very little fine material or organic matter, found in rockfall areas of mountain slopes. Scree soils in the garden can be blended using 1 part topsoil, 2 parts leaf compost, and 8 parts grit and pea gravel.

SEGMENT A part of a leaf or stem; in ferns, often referring to a pinna.

SEPAL One of a set of modified, outermost floral leaves, typically green in color but, as in many lilies, colored similarly to the petals and nearly indistinguishable from them.

SERPENTINE ROCK Serpentine (also called *ultramafic rock*) is a mineral low in key plant nutrients such as calcium, nitrogen, phosphorus, and potassium and high to very high in magnesium. The high levels of magnesium in the soil block most plants' abilities to take up other nutrients, especially calcium. Nickel and/or chromium can also be present at toxic levels. Thus, soils derived from serpentines are toxic to most plants and tend to develop unique plant communities tolerant of them.

SERRATE Sharply toothed along the margin.

SESSILE Lacking a peduncle or petiole; attached directly to the base without a stalk.

SEXUAL REPRODUCTION The production of new individuals through sexual recombination of genes.

Softwood In the context of this book, plant or stem tissue that has not fully matured or hardened.

Spike The entire inflorescence (flower cluster) on one stem of a grasslike plant.

Spikelet One branch of a flower spike.

Spore A haploid reproductive unit consisting of one or several cells enclosed in a hard outer wall that is capable of long-distance dispersal.

Sporophyte The spore-producing generation of ferns and fern allies. In ferns, horsetails, and clubmosses, this is the visible green part of the plant. In mosses, it is merely the sporangium and its stalk and base.

Stamen The male portion of a flower, consisting of the anther and filament (stalk).

Sterile frond A frond that does not bear spores.

Stigma The section of the pistil (typically the tip) that is receptive to pollen.

Stipe The stem (petiole) of a fern frond.

Stolon A long, creeping, aboveground stem; sometimes also used to describe slender rhizomes that grow near the surface.

Stoloniferous Producing stolons.

Style The stalk that connects the stigma to the ovary.

Subalpine Below alpine; plants that grow in the zone just below the tree line in the mountains.

Symbiosis Two organisms that form a close and mutually beneficial association.

Sympatric Occupying the same place; growing together.

Temperate A climate with a distinct warm and cold season, or species adapted to life in such a climate.

Tepal Sepals and petals that are indistinguishable from each other.

Tetraploid Having four sets of chromosomes per cell, or a plant with four sets of chromosomes.

Tiller A single stem (with attached leaves and flowers/seeds) of a grasslike plant.

Tomentose Covered in a dense, woolly hair.

Tribe A taxonomic grouping one level above genus.

Tripartite A union of three elements.

Triploid Having three versus the normal two sets of chromosomes. Triploid individuals are usually sterile.

Tuber A thickened rhizome used for food storage. Tubers can also form on roots (tuberous roots).

Tufa A porous, lightweight limestone rock formed as calcium carbonate precipitated out of mineral-rich water.

Vascular A plant that has specialized tubes to conduct water and other fluids rapidly from one part of the plant to another.

Vegetative reproduction Producing new plants that are genetically identical to the parent. Plants that spread by rhizomes, or in the case of some mosses though the regrowth of small sections of stem, are reproducing vegetatively. Also used with regard to stem or rhizome cuttings.

Whorled Having flowers or leaves attached three or more per node.

Xeric Dry.

Xeriscaping Landscaping with drought-tolerant plants for water conservation.

GLOSSARY OF LEAF SHAPES

ACICULAR Slender, needlelike.

ACUMINATE Tapering to a long point.

ARISTATE Ending in a bristlelike point.

BIPINNATE The leaflets of a pinnate leaf also pinnate.

CORDATE Heart shaped.

CUNEATE Triangular.

DELTOID Triangular with petiole attached to the side.

DIGITATE Divided into fingerlike lobes.

ELLIPTIC Oval, with a short or no point.

FALCATE Sickle shaped.

FLABELLATE Fanlike.

HASTATE Shaped like a spear point, with flaring pointed lobes at the base.

LANCEOLATE Long, widest in the middle.

LINEAR Long and very narrow.

LOBED With several points.

OBLANCEOLATE Top wider than bottom.

OBLONG Elongated with slightly parallel sides.

OBOVATE Teardrop shaped.

OBTUSE Oval but with a blunt tip.

ORBICULAR Circular.

OVATE Oval, egg-shaped, with a tapering point.

PALMATE Lobed like the fingers of a hand.

PEDATE Like the foot of a bird.

PELTATE Rounded, petiole attaches in the center underneath.

PERFOLIATE Stem pierces through the leaves.

PINNATE Two rows of leaflets.

RENIFORM Kidney shaped.

RHOMBOID Diamond shaped.

ROUND Circular.

SAGITTATE Arrowhead shaped.

SPATULATE Spoon shaped.

SUBULATE Awl shaped with a tapering point.

TRIFOLIATE OR TERNATE Divided into three leaflets.

TRIPINNATE Pinnately compound in which each leaflet is itself bipinnate.

TRUNCATE With a squared-off end.

PHOTO CREDITS

All photographs were taken by the author and are © William Cullina, with the following exceptions:

Page 111: *Potentilla anserina* visible light and *Potentilla anserina* UV light, by © Bjørn Rørslett.

Page 60: *Helianthus* leaf under scanning electron microscope, by Dartmouth SEM Lab.

Page 118: Pollen under scanning electron microscope, by Dartmouth SEM Lab.

Page 131: *Vanessa virginiensis* butterfly on sedum. by © Carolyn Hietala,

Back flap photograph of the author by Melissa Cullina.

For most of the close-up photography in this book I used a Nikon D200 or D300 digital SLR with a 105-mm micro Nikkor lens fitted with a Sigma model EM-140 DG ring flash. I purposely included many close-up images because they capture the amazing world of plants in ways the naked eye cannot. I have also focused on species—and particularly North American species—as subjects because these are simply my favorite plants and those to which I have the most ready access. I am grateful to all the gardens and gardeners as well as the wild places that have allowed me to photograph their plants for this book.

BIBLIOGRAPHY

Agrios, G. N. *Plant Physiology.* 4th ed. New York: Academic Press. 1997.

Davies, M. J., Hipps, N. A., and Kingswell, G. The effects of indole-3-butyric acid root dips on the root development and shoot growth of transplanted *Fagus sylvatica* L. and *Quercus robur* L. seedlings. *Journal of Horticultural Science and Biotechnology* 77, no. 2 (2002): 209–216.

Deno, N. C. *Seed Germination: Theory and Practice,* with Supplements 1 and 2. State College, PA: Norman C. Deno. 2004. (Available from Norman C. Deno, 139 Lenor Drive, State College, PA 16801.)

Dharmasiri, N., Dharmasiri, S., and Estelle, M. The F-box Protein TIR1 is an Auxin Receptor. *Nature* 435, no. 7041 (2005): 441–445.

Esau, K. *Anatomy of Seed Plants.* 2nd ed. New York: John Wiley and Sons. 1977.

Givnish, T. J. Leaf Mottling: Relation to Growth Form and Leaf Phenology and Possible Role as Camouflage. *Functional Ecology* 4, no. 4 (1990): 463–474.

Gleason, H. A., and Cronquist, A. *Manual of Vascular Plants of the Northeastern United States and Adjacent Canada.* 2nd ed. New York: New York Botanical Garden. 1991.

Harper, J. L. *Population Biology of Plants.* London: Academic Press. 1977.

Jarosz, A. M., and Davelos, A. L. Effects of Disease in Wild Plant Populations and the Evolution of Pathogen Aggressiveness. *New Phytologist* 129, no. 3 (1995): 371–387.

Kozlowski, T., Kramer, P. J., and Pallardy, S. G. *The Physiological Ecology of Woody Plants.* New York: Academic Press. 1991.

McFadden, C. H., and Keeton, W. T. *Biology, an Exploration of Life.* New York: W. W. Norton and Company. 1995.

Mozafar, A. Enrichment of Some B-Vitamins in Plants with Application of Organic Fertilizers. *Plant and Soil* 167, no. 2 (1994): 305–311.

Niemela, P., and Tuomi, J. Does the Leaf Morphology of Some Plants Mimic Caterpillar Damage? *Oikos* 50, no. 2 (1987): 256–257.

Raven, P. H., Evert, R. F., and Eichhorn, S. E. *Biology of Plants.* 5th ed. New York: Worth Publishers. 1992.

Sage, R. F. The Evolution of C4 Photosynthesis. *New Phytologist* 161, no. 2 (2004): 341–370.

Spaethe, J., Tautz, J., and Chittka, L. Visual Constraints in Foraging Bumblebees: Flower Size and Color Affect Search Time and Flight Behavior. *Proceedings of the National Academy of Sciences USA* 98, no. 7 (2001): 3898–3903.

Taiz, L., and Zeiger, E. *Plant Physiology.* Redwood City, CA: Benjamin/Cummings Publishing Company. 1991.

Telewski, F. W., and Zeevaart, J. A. D. The 120-yr Period for Dr. Beal's Seed Viability Experiment. *American Journal of Botany* 89 (2002): 1285–1288.

Turgeon, D. D., et al. *Common and Scientific Names of Aquatic Invertebrates from the United States and Canada: Mollusks.* 2nd ed. Bethesda, MD: American Fisheries Society. 1998.

William Cullina is curator of plants and gardens for Coastal Maine Botanical Gardens in Boothbay, Maine, and formerly the director of horticultural research for the New England Wild Flower Society in Framingham, Massachusetts. A renowned speaker and educator, he lectures frequently throughout the United States and Canada and writes for popular and professional magazines and journals. In addition to gardening and writing, Bill enjoys furniture making and homebuilding, working with stone, photography, pottery, canoeing, and hiking. He lives with his wife, Melissa, and their three children, Liam, Ronan, and Maeve, on the foggy coast of Maine. For comments and questions, please contact him at info@williamcullina.com, and for more information about his lecture schedule, writing, photography, and more visit www.williamcullina.com.

INDEX

Page references in italics refer to text graphics.

leaves (*cont.*)
    size, 49, *50*, 52, 57
    sun vs. shade leaves, 54, 57–58, *58*
    variegation, 72, *73*, 74
    veins, 49, *50*, 51, 52
    water removal, 53, *61*, 62
    wilting mechanism, 49, 52
Leucanthemum × *superbum* 'Alaska', *151*
Lewisia
    cotyledon, 226
    'Little Plum', *34*
    tweedyi, 32, *34*
Liatris
    ligulistylis (meadow blazing star), *189*
    spicata, *176*
    squarrosa 'Ivory Towers', *73*, 74
lignin, 51, 62, 64
Lilioceris lilii (Asian lily leaf beetle), *134*, 135
Lilium
    canadense, 99, 156
    canadense 'Apple Red', *17*
    'Casa Blanca', *200*
    pardalinum (leopard lily) roots, *40*
    pyrophilum (sandhill lily), *115*
    'Stargazer', *157*
    superbum bulb, *15*
limestone/lime, 205, *205*, 208–9, *208*
Liriope muscari 'Okina', *70*
loam, 192, 208
Lobelia siphilitica (blue lobelia) inheritance, 121–22, *121*
loess, 193–94
lungwort. See *Pulmonaria*
Lychnis
    alpina, *133*
    viscaria, *5*
Lysichiton camtschaticum (white skunk cabbage), *40*
Lythrum salicaria (purple loosestrife), 129, *130*, 131, 134

Macleaya cordata (plume poppy), 127
Maianthemum hybridum (broad-leaved bunchflower) roots, *30*
Mantis religiosa (European mantis), *129*
manure/bark mulch, *202*, 203
Marx, Karl, 211
Matteuccia struthiopteris (ostrich fern), *29*
Meconopsis
    spp. cultivation adaptability, 226
    × *sheldonii* (poppies), 149, *149*
Medeola virginica (Indian cucumber root), *160*
Mendel, Gregor, 120, 121

menthol, 63
meristematic cells, 13, 20, 72, 74, 76
Mertensia virginica (Virginia bluebells), *178*
mesophyll, 57
Metriorhynchomiris dislocatus (red-bordered black plant bug), 134
Michaux, André, *164*
milkweed. See *Asclepias*
milky spore, 136
Mimulus cardinalis (Scarlet monkey flower), *13*
Miscanthus
    'Morning Light', *177*
    sinensis (maiden grass), 22, *177*
Mitella diphylla (miterwort), *206*, *227*
moles, 146
Monarda
    bradburiana (Bradbury's bee balm), *83*
    didyma 'Jacob Cline' (red bee balm), *110*
    disease-resistance trials, *152*
    russeliana (wild bergamot) rhizomes, *21*
Monotropa hypopithys (Indian pipe), 46
moths. See butterflies/moths
Muhlenbergia capillaris (hair-awn muhly grass), 7, *92*, 93, 226
mulch
    depth, 202, 203
    problems with, 201–2, *201*, 203
    timing, 203–4
    types, 200, 201–3, *201–2*
    weeds, 202–3
mycorrhizal relationships
    AM (arbuscular mycorrhizal fungi), 45, *46*, 47
    EM (ectomycorrhizal fungi), 45, *46*, 47
    garden inoculations, 47
    overview, 45–47, *45*, *46*
    plants without, 45–46

names of plants
    components of, 162, 164–65, 167–68
    cultivar, 158, 165, 167
    DNA evidence, 161, 162
    hybrids, 168, *168*
    information in, 158–59, 162, *162*, 164–65
    naming after person, *164*, 167
    pronunciation, 167
    relationships, 159, *159*, 160, 161, *161*, 162, 164–65
    renaming/reclassifying, 159, 161, 162, *164*

subspecies, 165
suffixes, 167
varieties, 165, *165*
Narcissus (daffodils), *8*, *15*, *170*, *174*
nectaries, 115
nematodes, *135*, 136, *142*
nitrogen fixing
    gardening, 44–45
    overview, 43–45, *43*, *44*, *45*
    See also mycorrhizal relationships
Nostoc bacteria, 44, *44*
nutrients
    microorganisms, 40–41, *41*, 62
    roots/exudation, 40–41, *41*
    See also mycorrhizal relationships; nitrogen fixing

oldest organism on earth, 13
oomycetes, 149, 150, 151
Opuntia polyacantha (prickly pear cacti), *92*
Orontium aquaticum (golden club), *44*
osmosis, 35–36, 81
Osmunda
    cinnamomea (cinnamon fern), *204*
    claytoniana (primitive interrupted fern), *50*
ovary of flower, 105, *106*, 119

Pachysandra terminalis (Japanese pachysandra), 95
Packera
    antennariifolia (shale barren groundsel), 60
    aurea (golden groundsel), 60
Paeonia, 75, 89, 218
    suffruticosa (tree peony), 89
    'Yellow Emperor' (peony), *107*
palmate/palmately compound leaves, 53, *53*
pansies, *2*
Papaver orientale (Oriental poppy), *220*
Paris quadrifolia, *6*
pathogenic organisms, definition, 41. See also specific types
Penstemon
    arkansanus seedlings, *229*
    australis (Eustis Lake beardtongue), *76*
    hirsutus (hairy beardtongue), *36*
    serrulatus (cascade beardtongue), *55*
    smallii (beardtongue), *94*
peony. See *Paeonia*
PEP carboxylase, 59
perennials
    annuals vs., 10–11, *12*
    definition/description, 10
    renewal/immortality of, 12–14